T0338406

Untidy Gender

Domestic Service in Turkey

In the series

WOMEN IN THE POLITICAL ECONOMY
edited by Ronnie J. Steinberg

Untidy Gender

Domestic Service in Turkey

Gul Ozyegin

TEMPLE UNIVERSITY PRESS
Philadelphia

Temple University Press, Philadelphia 19122

∞ The paper used in this publication meets the requirements of the
American National Standard for Information Sciences—Permanence
of Paper for Printed Library Materials, ANSI Z39.48-1984

Library of Congress Cataloging-in-Publication Data
Ozyegin, Gul, 1955–
  Untidy gender : domestic service in Turkey / Gul Ozyegin.
    p. cm — (Women in the political economy)
  Includes bibliographical references and index.
  ISBN 1-56639-807-X (cloth : alk. paper) — ISBN 1-56639-808-8 (pbk. : alk. paper)
    1. Domestics—Turkey—Ankara. 2. Women—Employment—Turkey—Ankara.
  3. Social classes—Turkey—Ankara. I. Title. II. Series.

  HD8039. D52 T926   2000
  331.4'8164046'09563—dc21
                                                              00-036423

To my girlhood friend
whose shamed masquerade I revealed

Contents

Photographs follow page 88

Acknowledgments

THIS BOOK, from its inception as a dissertation project to the current state, took a decade to complete, and over these years I have received support and encouragement from many individuals as well as financial support from several institutions.

My research and writing were funded by grants from Temple University, the Margaret McNamara Foundation, the Meawards of the Population Council, and the Institute of Turkish Studies. The Sociology Department at the College of William and Mary also gave financial support for the completion of this book. I am grateful to all these institutions and organizations for their generous support.

My professors at Temple University, where this project first took shape, made distinctive contributions to the research and analysis I present in this book. I thank Julia and Gene Ericksen for restoring my faith in empirical research by demonstrating that empirically grounded work would strengthen and enrich theory. They were also instrumental in making my research doable. Magali Sarfatti-Larson has had a profound influence on my approach to the questions addressed in this book. With her flamboyant brilliance and animated style, she taught me the power of well-crafted small-scale work in illuminating larger sociological issues. I am grateful to Howard Winant for his early passionate support and his urging me to seek greater theoretical challenges. I would like to extend my appreciation to Judy Goode for her critical feedback and offering of her anthropological sensibilities.

I would like to express my deepest gratitude to Sherri Grasmuck, my lifelong mentor, for her great confidence in and nurturance of my abilities. She proved to be an endless source of intellectual inspiration and encouragement. Sherri provided me with the intellectual legitimacy I needed to pursue the study of domestic workers. She gave generous amounts of time and energy in reading various drafts of the book and helped me to clarify my often confused thoughts with her incredible analytical powers. Without her gentle support, force of intellect, and warm friendship, I would have had a much harder time. I am immensely grateful to her.

My family and friends in Turkey made the research process easier and a worthwhile endeavor. I am especially indebted to Nükhet Sirman and Ayşe Saktanber, my loyal friends and colleagues, for their suggestions and support at important junctures during the research in Ankara. Their sensitive insights into the troubling relationship between domestic workers and their employers made me rethink theoretical and working assumptions about the contradictory ways in which women of different classes relate to each other. Ayşe 's poetic sensibility and sharp wit never failed to boost my spirit when I had a "bad" fieldwork day. She continued to give her support and encouragement electronically after I came back to the United States. Nejat Ozyegin contributed to this project in myriad ways. I thank him for offering his intellectual labor and technical support generously. I owe thanks to Sencer Ayata, Nur Koyuncu, and Seçil Büker for their practical and conceptual assistance. My warm thanks to the members of the research team who helped me to conduct the survey: Şermin Elmas, Neşe Öztimur, and Meltem Sancak. I am grateful to them for their willingness to labor for such low wages and for doing an excellent job.

I am very appreciative of the emotional and practical support I received from my friends and colleagues at the Department of Sociology and Women's Studies Program at William and Mary. In particular, I would like to thank Leisa Meyer and Nancy Gray for providing me with an anchor, and to Darlene O'Dell for helping me in reducing the number of tables. Kate Slevin, who plays multiple roles in my life—friend, colleague, chair, and fellow cultural insider/outsider—provided much-needed persistent pressure and inspiration to move forward. Kate's intellectual companionship and good food helped me through the difficult periods of making William and Mary a home for me while writing this book. I have shared so much of the pleasures and frustrations of this project with my close friend Carla Freeman, who engaged in similar research and writing processes during the same time period. Throughout all these years, she provided an invaluable exchange of ideas and honest commentary and never failed to offer her counsel. Thank you, Carla, for inspiring me with the example of your own work.

I am indebted to Ronnie Steinberg, the series editor, for her sustained involvement in the development of the book from its earliest stages. She has been a thoughtful critic, reading early versions of the book with care and precision and providing valuable comments. My warmest thanks to Michael Ames for his unwavering support and continued patience at Temple University Press through so many missed deadlines. I owe a particular debt of thanks to David Bass, an outsider to the discipline of sociology, who made this a better book by helping me to simplify and condense my prose.

This research took me to my mother's home after so many years and allowed me once more to become my mother's daughter. My mother, Suat Bozdemir, provided me with "a room of my own" in her small apartment, looked after me, and kept the volume on the TV low. I will always be deeply grateful to her and my sisters, Oya Ozdağ, Yasemin Erbil, and Fatoş Mersin and my brother, Murat Bozdemir, for their abundant nurturance and their pride in my work. My nephews, Paydaş, Mert, and Ender have given much with their love. My warmest gratitude to my brothers-in-law, Celal Erbil and Selahattin Mersin, for being wonderful brothers to me. I salute them for being excellent role models for the younger generation of Turkish men. My deep appreciation goes to John Weber, who came to my life at later stages of this book but occupied a special place, for illuminating my life with his adventurous spirit and gentle soul.

I am also grateful to eighteen employer women, whose names must remain anonymous, for their participation in focus group interviews and generous sharing of their experiences and perspectives with me.

My most profound debt is to the domestic workers who are the subjects of this book and whose names have been altered in the following pages. They welcomed me into their homes and communities and shared the experiences of their work and private lives generously with me. This book could not have been written without them.

1   The View from Downstairs

EARLY ON a weekday morning in Ankara, people hurry to work as the usual urban scene repeats itself. A middle-class professional woman scurries about her fifth-floor apartment in one of Ankara's elite neighborhoods. She is rushing to prepare her children for school and get herself and her husband ready for the workday ahead. She helps her husband find his blue-and-yellow striped tie while waiting for her crimson nail polish to dry so she can comb her daughter's hair. At the same time, in the basement of the apartment building, another woman also prepares for the day ahead. With work-worn hands, the woman of the basement gently wakes her daughter and reminds her husband that he should not let the child go to school with uncombed hair. This woman does not dress for the chilly morning outside, because she will not join her upstairs neighbors at the crowded bus stops and taxi stands. Instead she takes the stairs to the fifth-floor apartment now vacated by the elegantly attired woman with the crimson nail polish. Here, the woman of the basement will spend her day cleaning and ordering the domestic sphere of the upstairs woman.

In a squatter settlement, on the margin of the city, another woman traverses the sociogeographic boundaries of her neighborhood for work in the homes of upstairs women. She waits at the bus stop with other women from her neighborhood who, like her, are on their way to the middle-class homes of Ankara. At the bus stops linking Ankara's middle-class neighborhoods with its numerous squatter communities, domestic workers stand apart from the women whose homes they clean. Women of squatter settlements appear neither wholly urban nor wholly rural but instead combine elements of both cultures that mark them unmistakably as domestic workers. Ill-fitting outfits of once-fashionable designer skirts and cheap polyester blouses compose the hand-me-down uniform of the commuting domestic worker. Rough, chapped hands clutch plastic bags stuffed with şalvar (the traditional work clothes that speak of peasant backgrounds), which remain hidden until the

1

commute's end when, in isolation from one another, these women prepare to labor in the upstairs apartments of Ankara.

Women of the basement and women of the squatter settlements are the subjects of this book. These rural migrant women, like those in other industrializing countries, comprise an extensive and proliferating informal urban labor sector. They work in private homes, where the terms and conditions of their labor are neither officially determined nor regulated. In fact, neither worker nor employer exists in any legal capacity. Nonetheless, both groups of women significantly shape gender and class dynamics in Turkey—a large, increasingly modern and industrialized nation with a population exceeding 60 million.

Despite their sociodemographic similarities, women of the squatter settlements and women of the basement represent two different modes of entry into the modern world corresponding to their different sociogeographic positions within Ankara's urban landscape. The question of location is central to our understanding of the life conditions and experiences of rural migrant women and the internal transformations wrought by domestic service, as well as of the structure and organization of waged domestic labor in Turkey. The two groups are distinguished by the proximity of their homes to their workplaces. Women of the basement seldom leave their apartment houses and are accompanied by their husbands on the rare occasions when they do leave the vicinity. Squatter women, however, are accustomed to long daily commutes across subcultural and geographic boundaries. The two groups thus experience urban space in quite different ways. While squatter women negotiate the diverse contexts and dynamic pace of urban life and the domestic labor market, women of the basement remain firmly attached to their apartment houses. Indeed, the latter embody the constraints placed on female spatial mobility in Turkey. Location serves as a starting point from which we can conceptualize differences among rural migrant women, who, in most social-scientific accounts, are treated as a homogeneous unit. Moreover, considerations of location allow us to explore important distinctions in the range of experiences that inform migrant women's lives and their encounters with middle-class women. By providing different kinds of opportunities and constraints, location-determined social practices shape these women's lives in ways that inflect their experiences of work, class, gender, community, patriarchy, and day-to-day social relations.[1]

It is impossible to neatly summarize the varied ways in which the lives of these three groups of women interact as basement and squatter women labor for the middle-class women and the middle-class women employ the basement and squatter women as waged domestic workers to substitute for their own unpaid labor. Tracing the incorporation of rural migrant women into the domestic spheres of middle-class women and mapping the economic and social practices that connect these women requires us to look beyond the privatized labor relations that have been the focus of most studies of such informal labor in developing countries. It is also necessary to examine the social and economic practices of rural migrant communities in the city and the gendered division of labor and authority in both middle- and working-class families.

Studies conducted in other developing countries generally assume that employers define both the identity of the domestic worker and the structure of domestic service. I prefer, however, to go beyond the threshold of the workplace to attempt to understand how family and community relations affect the inner workings of domestic service and, in turn, how employment in domestic service shapes family and community relations. In this book I examine the connections between gender relations within the family and the internal workings of the informal labor market by studying the earnings, work schedules, employment and recruitment patterns, and internal transformations required of domestic workers in the renegotiation of patriarchal gender relations. My aim is to locate the interaction between these two spheres and to determine how experiences in one modify and transform those in the other. I also explore the centrality of male power and traditional notions of patriarchy to the configuration of gender and class dynamics, particularly in the ordering of relationships between middle-class women and domestic workers. More specifically, I demonstrate that patriarchal control over migrant women's labor makes their labor expensive and scarce. Thus, traditional patriarchal prerogative limits middle-class women's access to cheap, readily available domestic wage labor. I go on to illustrate how both groups of women strategically use their understandings of domination and patriarchal construction of women's identity in the management of their relationships with one another. By documenting the agency of rural migrant men and women in their relations with middle-class employers, I demonstrate the power of structurally weak actors in cross-class relations in domestic service in Turkey.

This study departs methodologically from other studies of third world domestic workers in that it is based on a representative sample of a group of domestic workers—the women of the basement—thereby permitting generalizations applicable in comparative, cross-cultural studies. While almost all other studies of domestic workers use purposive sampling methods because they lack a sampling frame, my work in Turkey provided the rare opportunity of taking a representative sample of domestic workers. I selected 103 domestic workers in the basement group by using a mixed sampling strategy (systematic and random) within a frame derived from a complete list of buildings prepared by the Construction and Housing (İmar ve İskan) division of the Ankara Municipality. The sampling frame entailed a list of dwellings of which half were located in middle-class residential districts and half in middle-class and upper-middle-class districts in Ankara. I used residential districts as a class indicator because in Turkey residential areas are relatively homogenous and distinguished by social class. In addition, I interviewed 59 domestic workers from four different squatter settlement neighborhoods. Of these, 57 are included in this book. Because of the lack of an adequate sampling frame, though, a representative sampling procedure for this group was not possible. Instead, this group was chosen by a snowball, or convenience, method. My contact with this group was facilitated by employers who introduced me to two domestic workers who further introduced me to their neighborhoods and, thus, initiated my contact with others in the community. The close proximity of domestic workers, enhanced by kinship and ethnic ties, expanded my network and eased entry into these communities. In one case, for example, I interviewed four domestic workers from the same family: my original informant introduced me to her older sister and then three of her sisters-in-law. Two of the communities—Oran and Nato Yolu—are located on the outskirts of the city; domestic workers from these neighborhoods spend considerable time commuting to and from work. The other two—Dikmen and Zafertepe—are located within Ankara's middle- and upper-middle-class neighborhoods and thus are physically integrated with the city.

SITUATING TWO STUDY GROUPS IN URBAN SPACE

Outsiders Within: Women of the Basement

Located in the heartland of Anatolia, Ankara has had only a brief history as an urban center, despite its rich past dating to the Hittite period. Ankara, a provincial town of twenty thousand inhabitants, was designated the capital of the Turkish Republic in 1923 by Kemal Atatürk in the hope of modernizing Turkey's less developed regions and decentralizing its İstanbul-focused economy. The government initiated extensive programs to create a capital city that would symbolize the modernization of Turkey with parks, opera houses, planned housing, large boulevards, cultural centers, and public service facilities (Bozdoğan 1997; Tekeli 1984). Dubbed the country's most planned city, Ankara has grown faster than any other major city in Turkey, housing almost 4 million people as of 1997. Ankara experienced one of the highest rates of urban population growth in Turkey between 1950 and 1970 with an influx of migrants from the country's rural areas. As a result, Ankara now has a higher percentage of squatter settlements than does any other Turkish urban center. The proportion of squatter settlement dwellers to total city population was 60.0 in 1995 (Keleş 2000:387), a slight decrease from an astonishing 72.4 percent in 1980 (Keleş and Daniels 1985:165). Sharp socioeconomic hierarchies are clearly reflected in the city's geography; the lowest income groups are concentrated in the belts of squatter settlements surrounding the city's planned core, modern Ankara. Here, in Ankara's modern core, the more affluent sectors of the population reside in the very same apartment buildings that house, though floors below, the women of the basement.[2]

"Women of the basement" are the wives of the doorkeepers of middle- and upper-middle-class apartment buildings. Unlike the majority of rural migrants, doorkeeper (*kapıcı*) families live and work in middle- and upper-middle-class areas where husbands are employed as doorkeepers[3] and wives as domestic workers, whose entry into the domestic work force is mediated and governed by their husbands. The doorkeeper lives in the basement of the building where his services are required. His main duties include providing building security, operating the central-heating system, taking out the residents' trash, buying and distributing fresh bread[4] twice a day, shopping for groceries for the residents, collecting monthly maintenance fees from tenants,[5] and performing general maintenance duties, such as disposing of refuse from coal-burning furnaces. Other duties may include walking tenants' dogs, tending gardens, or taking tenants' children to school. The doorkeeper deals with strangers (such as salespeople and beggars) and protects the building and the tenants from potentially disturbing and threatening elements. In short, his job is to provide order by policing the door and insuring its sanctity. Wives of doorkeepers constitute a prime pool from which middle-class tenants recruit waged domestic labor. In this way, women of the basement rarely navigate the domestic labor market but hold a virtual monopoly over domestic service.

The rise of the doorkeeper and his family as a significant figure in the Turkish urban landscape occurred during the early 1960s with the passing of a law that encouraged replacement of single-family homes with apartment buildings in order to house a growing middle-class population.[6] This new collective housing created an occupational niche that initially was filled by migrant men and subsequently nurtured as a source of jobs as more and more peasants came to the city.

The building of middle-class housing in response to the expansion of the urban middle classes contributed significantly to a restructuring of the boundaries between the private and public spheres along class lines. The maintenance of a middle-class culture promoted the incorporation of rural migrants into the interiors of the domestic spheres of middle classes, creating a powerful physical and symbolic space shared by urban and rural classes. While these rural migrants became an increasingly indispensable part of middle-class existence, the middle class came to define itself in contradistinction to the peasants. Indeed, contact between these groups gave rise to intensified forms of boundary-defining activity. The emergence of an occupational role for migrant men also helped to consolidate the definition of the housewifery role for middle-class women, who performed tasks of homemaking, nurturance, and sociability within the confines of the domestic arena. This arrangement generated a gender division of labor that implicitly limited opportunities for women to act and interact within the streets, shops, and markets of the public sphere. Although not ostensibly designed to exercise patriarchal power over female spatial mobility, these structural reconfigurations have often perpetuated it. Doorkeepers who stood between middle-class housewives and the street not only saved the women from the mundane chores of purchasing and daily provisioning but also "protected" them from the outside world and encounters with strangers, all the while reinforcing spatial gender boundaries.

Doorkeepers create an orderly, comfortable existence for middle- and upper-middle-class urban populations in Turkey. Doorkeepers embody the contact point of modern and modernizing populations, situated as rural "outsiders within"[7] the modern urban domestic sphere. Their status in this realm is clearly symbolized by the location of their apartments in the basements of buildings. Despite sharing the same gate, roof, and neighborhood, building tenants and doorkeeper families understand each other in the classical terms of upstairs and downstairs. The layers of experience attending this encounter make apartment houses unique points of contact that hold different meanings for each type of inhabitant. For doorkeepers and their families, the apartment house is a place of docility, containment, incarceration, and painful stigmatization. But also it offers them a sense of autonomy and the prestige deriving from contact with the middle class and distinction from other rural migrants who reside in squatter settlements.

Doorkeeper families are not scattered haphazardly throughout middle- and upper-middle-class areas. They migrated in patterns that transposed kinship and geographic communities to the new urban environment. This reconstitution of regional communities in middle- and upper-middle-class urban space is clearly reflected in my survey. Eighty-three percent of the domestic workers interviewed, for example, reside near male relatives or former neighbors also working as doorkeepers in the immediate neighborhood. As doorkeeping became an occupational enclave for migrant men from rural areas, their wives were increasingly employed as domestic workers in the same neighborhoods. The doorkeeper wives, unlike their sisters who settled on the margins of urban space and became full-time housewives, began immediately to work in the homes of tenants. Such employment gave husbands control over their wives' experiences with waged work and choice of employers. These women now hold a monopoly over the domestic service industry: only 14 percent of the doorkeeper wives interviewed reported never having worked as a domestic. Although apartment house doorkeeping integrates the supply and demand sides of domestic labor, doorkeeping does not insure employment for wives. Recruitment of wives is never the direct result of a formal, legally binding agreement between employers and doorkeepers. In fact, at the time of my survey, 23 percent of domestic workers had no in-house employers but worked exclusively for out-of-building employers in the surrounding neighborhood.

SHELTERING TRADITION.   The structure of doorkeeping both confirms and denies continuity with tradition. The apartment building constitutes a spatial zone where tradition can persist: it acts as a container of traditional action along with important social transformations in terms of gender roles. In this book, I explore the complex ways in which the organization of doorkeeping inhibits possibilities for becoming modern and reimposes traditional forms of class and gender servility upon these migrants.

The migration of peasant women often results in their "housewifeization" (Ayata and Ayata 1996; Şenyapılı 1981b). In migrant communities women, especially married women, are not allowed to work outside the home. Squatter settlements would seem to offer an abundant domestic labor pool, yet few squatter women seek employment as domestic workers.[8] Patriarchal opposition to women's paid work, rooted in deep-seated anxieties about perceived threats to female sexuality and modesty and to men's honor, drastically limits the sorts of work women can perform and the contexts in which they can work. The institution of doorkeeping, however, spatially unites the supply and demand sides of domestic labor and thus insures the continued presence of the protective paternalistic gaze. In effect, women can undertake paid domestic labor without leaving the home or the oversight of their husbands. And the payment of the domestic worker's wages may even go directly to the husband.

Tradition is also maintained by the imprecise boundaries between work and home that ultimately involve all household members in the labor experience of the doorkeeper. Despite its formalization as a service occupation, the institution of doorkeeping does not allow the doorkeeper to become an individualized wage laborer. On the contrary, it reconstitutes the migrant family as a laboring unit whose male head directs its combined labor processes. Doorkeepers' wives partially retain their former unpaid family worker status and attain a new independent earner identity as domestic workers.

Yet, the same institution, by tying the husband to the home, generates changes in the traditional gendered division of labor, especially with regard to childcare. As I show in Chapter 2, most domestic workers with young children are able to work full-time schedules (five to seven days a week) because of their husbands' availability to meet the demands of young children. However, the objective condition of the doorkeeper's domestic availability is not effective in breaking the strong link between household work and gender role identity. In fact, I argue that this link becomes even stronger in such families because the door-keeper's very occupational role (subservient and feminized) is likely to generate gender anxiety in him.

EXPERIENCING STIGMATIZATION.   The doorkeeper always lives with his family, always in the dingy basement apartment of the building for which he works—a job "benefit" that precludes any sense of profes-sional pride and any sense of shared space with tenants. Further, these housing conditions constitute an important element in the formulation of stigma and contempt. Many of the apartment houses I visited, new and old, confine doorkeepers to damp underground chambers with lit-tle light and poor ventilation. The majority consist of two rooms with a half kitchen and often no adequate bathing facilities. About 18 percent have one room and only 11 percent have more than two rooms. The average household includes 4.3 people. Doorkeepers and their wives complain that they "are stuffed underground" and that their "children do not see the face of the sun." Moreover, conditions seldom vary according to employer status. Although my sample group was drawn equally from middle- and upper-middle-class districts of Ankara, there was no correspondence between the luxury of the apartment building and the condition and size of its doorkeeper apartment. Substandard housing conditions are the norm, regardless of the class or location of the apartment building.

Although the layouts of doorkeeper dwellings, like those of squatter settlement houses, display some variety, all have the same unsettling qualities. The typical apartment, for example, has huge, exposed pipes running through the living room. Passage from one room to another often requires that one step around the building's heating-system burner, through which coal dust or refuse are carried to the domestic quarters. Windows, typical of those found in basements, are too small and placed too high to admit light. Such conditions create and perpet-uate a sense of discomfort, alienation, and confinement, providing a home often described by its occupants as a prison.

Doorkeepers' feelings of alienation are mirrored in contempt and stigmatization by the upstairs residents. This stigma permeates the doorkeeper's life, extending to his job as well as his family. I argue that this stigma results from the day-to-day proximity of the doorkeeper to the middle-class residents whom he and his family serve. Following Mary Douglas (1989), I argue that the stigma is the residents' symbolical protective barrier against what they perceive as pollution of their dwelling. Not only do doorkeepers have a low status, but, by occupying the physical and cultural margins of middle-class dwellings, they challenge the ordering of class- and status-based inequalities as well as urban-rural-based divisions within the Turkish city. The middle class keeps these dangerously close "outsiders within" in place by acts of contempt. Stigmatization, by structuring the interactions among members of each class, affirms the social distance that the middle class feels is undermined by physical proximity and the lack of ritualized social contacts, especially among children.

The following comments by doorkeepers' wives reflect the contempt they feel from the middle class, especially toward their children and their segregation and alleged uncleanliness.

The main problem is with children. As they grow up they become unhappy. They start asking how we became doorkeepers.

They belittle and humiliate doorkeepers' children. They look at doorkeepers as unclean peasants. They treat us with contempt.

They despise doorkeepers. They warn their children, "Don't play with doorkeepers' kids. They will contaminate you with microbes." We're humans too, only our appearance does not fit with theirs.

Regardless of how well you dress and groom your kids, they are still identified as the doorkeeper's kids. They still don't play with our kids.

Through these and other such testimonies the doorkeeper families in the study voiced their profound sense of being stigmatized. To the middle class, perceived poor hygiene is the symbol and symptom of a deeper character structure, sign of an essentially contemptible existence. Their accusations of uncleanliness go beyond aesthetics and reflect on the moral character of both the doorkeeper and his family. They are especially hurtful to wives, who are held responsible for family hygiene.

As Douglas (1989) points out, stigma is attached to those persons and groups that reside at the margins of society and thus define those margins. Douglas says that witches, novices, and unborn children, for example, are threatening, because they have no official place in the patterning of society. Marginal persons, those whose status is ambiguous or weakly defined, are dangerous because margins are the most vulnerable point in any social structure. By policing the margins, the center strengthens itself. Viewed from this perspective, doorkeeper families are marginals in the city because they belong neither in the apartment house (in the same sense that tenants do) nor in the squatter settlements.[9] They are seen as carriers of pollution and disorder.

Even when relegated to the bottom of the class hierarchy and made a subordinate group in cultural and economic terms, doorkeeper families are still feared and avoided because of the symbolic threat of close contact with them. Urban classes worry about the confusion caused by the blurring of class boundaries. This worry, along with the fear of "pollution," seems greater among members of the middle class whose concern with status distinctions stems from a particular class insecurity that Barbara Ehrenreich (1989) calls "fear of falling." Social distancing from the doorkeeper families is, in this sense, a typical practice in the self-definition of middle-class identity.[10] But under what conditions are boundaries perceived to be threatened? The location of doorkeepers' homes at the bottom of apartment buildings and the role of the doorkeepers as order takers do not seem to satisfy middle-class tenants' need to demarcate social boundaries. I argue that social boundaries are perceived to be undermined when they are permeable, as they are in Ankara with the cross-class interaction of children and the doorkeeper families' claim to a fair share of city resources and opportunities.

The threat of mixing is countered by established rituals. Social contacts between doorkeeper families and tenants are highly ritualized, asserting and reasserting class and status differences through asymmetrical participation in systems of exchange. For example, tenants put doorkeeper families in a low-status position by giving unreciprocated gifts to doorkeepers. During religious holidays, when social visits are common between relatives, friends, neighbors, and acquaintances, doorkeepers visit the tenants but their visits are not reciprocated. This practice stems from a long-established cultural norm that allows superiors not to reciprocate without appearing rude.

Among children, however, either there are no routinized forms of exclusion or they are more difficult to implement and hence the threat established by the unregulated mixing of the doorkeepers' children with the middle-class children of the neighborhood. The children attend school together, share desks, play at the same playground, hang out at the same neighborhood corner, get haircuts in the same barbershop, ride the same school bus, and walk the same routes to school.[11] This mixing of children, which may even lead to cross-class romantic attachments, is a function of the structural conditions of the occupation of doorkeeper. Tenants respond to this perceived "pollution" by creating elaborate symbolic means for segregating doorkeeper families.[12] Odor, manners, demeanor, and uncleanliness constitute the terms of a symbolic distancing vocabulary, provided by the stigmatized group's actual involvement in "dirty" work, their unhygienic housing conditions, and their peasant background.

Although doorkeeper households establish and maintain communities among themselves, they are physically isolated from squatter settlement communities. And although the two groups have similar patterns of migration and class origin, only doorkeeper families possess a collective, occupation-based identity. Their unique position within the city generates distinctive grammars of life for these people who would otherwise possess a common migrant identity. If we use the metaphor of "outsider" to define the marginalized position of the migrant in urban space, then the doorkeepers appear as "outsiders within" because of their marginality within middle- and upper-middle-class space. Squatter settlement migrants, however, remain mere "outsiders" because their community-based collective experience is distanced from the "within."

Third Space: Women of the Squatter Settlements

The social and spatial structure of apartment house living and the interconnected hierarchical worlds of doorkeepers and tenants within this structure differ drastically from the structure of squatter settlement neighborhoods. Migrant families in Turkey establish neighborhoods in squatter settlement areas that are highly homogenous in terms of family, kinship ties, and village or town of origin (A. Ayata 1989; Ayata and Ayata 1996; Duben 1982; Heper 1983; Karpat 1976; Kartal 1978, 1983; Şenyapılı 1981a). Often an entire neighborhood of squatters originates from the same town. My study confirms this pattern: 74 percent of domestic workers had female relatives or fellow migrants from the same town of origin currently working as domestic workers living in the same squatter settlement neighborhood.

The Turkish word for squatter settlements, *gecekondu* (settled overnight), originated in the 1940s when waves of peasants came to the city and built shelters by night on public land belonging to the State Treasury. Squatter settlement neighborhoods continued to proliferate in the major cities of Turkey throughout the 1950s with diversification of type and method of house building. Local and national governmental response to the housing problem of rural migrants and demands for the legalization of homes was varied and often contradictory, with alternating policies of construction pardons and outright demolition. In an effort to prevent creation of a large proletariat, for example, the government employed a pragmatic politics of containment and responded to the demands of squatter settlements for improved services and public facilities with pardons for houses built illegally. Successful grass-roots initiatives by squatter settlement residents as well as voting power played a significant role in these processes. Through the creation of neighborhood associations called Gecekonduyu Güzelleştirme Derneği (Association for the Beautification of the Squatter Settlement), the new urbanities demanded schools, bus service, public utilities, street improvements, and the legalization of individual dwellings. The associations provided an important instrument for political action by linking squatter settlement dwellers, political parties, and the local and national governments. Yet access to basic public services within the city remains very uneven. According to some estimates, more than half of all families in squatter settlements lack some or all of the amenities of water, electricity, decent streets, and accessible schools (Keleş and Danielson 1985). This statistic is especially striking because in 1995, close to 60 percent of Ankara's population lived in squatter housing (Keleş 2000:387).

Despite these problems, urban experts agree that squatter settlements in Turkey should not be considered slums (Keleş and Danielson 1985:183) and that migrants in squatter settlements are "far from a destitute mass" (Özbudun 1976:191). These interpretations are based on the observation that a high proportion of migrants were able to move into urban occupations and that some others joined the urban working class—a pattern reflected in my own work. About half of the husbands of the domestic workers in the squatter settlement group I studied are public service workers: janitors, gardeners, messengers, night watchmen, heating operators, street sweepers, garbage collectors, and government employees. About 13 percent of the husbands are unemployed and 7.4 percent are semi-skilled industrial workers. Another 13 percent are retired. Only a small percentage (7.4 percent) are informal workers, such as construction workers, and an even smaller group include microentrepreneurs. In short, the majority of husbands of domestic workers I studied possess low-prestige, low-paying but high-security government jobs.[13]

Until recently, two dominant perspectives informed the debate about squatter settlements and their inhabitants: the modernization and the Marxist perspectives. The modernization perspective views the squatter settlement buildings and their inhabitants as undesirable, disruptive forces in the imagined orderliness of the city—transitional forms of living that will soon change into modern urban modes. Marxists, in contrast, tend to romanticize this urban migrant space as fertile ground for revolution. Gülsüm Baydar Nalbantoğlu (1997) offers an alternative perspective. She urges us to understand this place as a space where "the languages of the city and the village clash, and other languages emerge [in] a space of translation across the urban-rural boundaries" (192). It is indeed a third space, and a disruptive language, because the squatter buildings and settlements "interrupt the conventional meanings of such terms as boundaries and walls, inside and outside, and public and private" (206).

Panoramic views of squatter settlement neighborhoods suggest immaculate suburban neighborhoods, while masking the diversity of housing conditions and shifting meanings of home/street, inside/outside, and public/private contained within. On a warm day, one might glimpse a woman bent over washing her husband's tired feet in their small garden, just off the neighborhood's only paved road—to an outsider an act of private intimacy performed in the street. One might also encounter scenes of reciprocal aid—services that are not easily afforded in the market and part of what social scientists call the moral economy of the poor. A domestic worker, for example, gives her neighbor's adult son a haircut in the open courtyard; women take turns helping one another with the arduous task of storing coal for the winter. On wet days, mazelike muddy roads hinder mobility and threaten clean interior spaces. During winter, dwellings shrink as residents move to central rooms, leaving colder outlying rooms vacant. Coal stoves, usually placed in the living room, dictate the rhythm of daily life, inverting notions of public/private and intimate/distant spatialities.

This is not a place where village life is recreated. Nor is it a place that assumes the social and material forms of urban modernity. The squatter settlement creates new roles and values, sometimes mixing incompatible categories, appropriating markers of peasantry and urbanism and merging traditional practices with new ones. This is an interactive and visible community, one that always seems to be open to the moralizing gaze of insiders and outsiders (A. Ayata 1989).

One striking characteristic of squatter settlement communities is that most women, especially married women, in these communities are not allowed to work outside the home. Squatter settlements present an abundant potential labor supply for domestic work, yet because of patriarchal opposition to women's employment they show the lowest urban female participation in wage labor (Ayata and Ayata 1996). In the following chapters, the women who deviated from this pattern by joining the ranks of domestic workers describe their own circumstances and the ways in which they managed to overcome patriarchal constraints.

The social relations of neighborliness and kinship embedded in these communities structure and regulate the domestic labor market and social relations within it, especially with regard to recruitment patterns and development of a work culture. Domestic workers' communities constitute a vital base of symbolic and material resources. Each domestic worker is situated at the center of an extended network in which the members interact frequently and reciprocally. The durability and intensity of these networks result from the low degree of mobility within squatter settlement neighborhoods. Domestic workers use informal networks to control recruitment patterns, develop job and wage standards, and create a work ethic, as well as to play on their employers' class and gender guilt. We should not, however, romanticize these networks as models of egalitarianism. They are simultaneously egalitarian, competitive, negotiable, and always prone to creating their own internal hierarchies. My analysis leaves little doubt that there is no such thing as an objective law of supply and demand. Ankara's domestic labor pool grows from a deeply rooted social context of knowing subjects who recognize a complex system of rules and exercise substantial control over one another's behavior.

COMPARATIVE PROFILES

Basement and squatter women have in common their class and rural origins along with their employment in domestic service. With a few exceptions, domestic workers come to Ankara with no previous urban experience. Only two of the domestic workers I spoke with were city-born. Even so, during the time of my survey, a majority of these migrant women had lived in Ankara for a fairly long time, roughly eleven years on average for the two groups combined. Most of that majority came from the squatter settlement group. Also, more squatter settlement domestic workers (28.1 percent) had lived in Ankara for over twenty years (having arrived in Ankara during the 1960s with the first wave of rural migration). To put it differently, 40.6 percent of the doorkeeper domestic workers had arrived in Ankara within the last five years of the survey as compared with 12.3 percent of the squatter domestic workers. In sum, close to half of the domestic workers in the doorkeeper group are recent migrants to Ankara. Old and new migrants, however, are equally represented in the total sample.

The domestic workers range in age from 18.5 to 66.0 years with a mean age of 33.2. The domestic workers in the squatter settlement group are, on average, 6.4 years older than the domestic workers in the doorkeeper group. In the squatter settlement group, the greatest concentration was in the 31-to-40-year-old category, which represented 52.6 percent of the total number of the workers in this group. In the doorkeeper group, the 21-to-30- and 31-to-40-year-old categories show an equal concentration, representing 42.7 and 39.8 percent, respectively, of the total. The mean age of marriage is 17.6 years for the doorkeeper group and 16.7 for the squatter settlement group.

Length of domestic employment ranged from one month to 37.0 years with a mean of 7.7 years. The domestic workers in the squatter group had, on average, 4.7 years more experience in domestic service than those in the doorkeeper group.

Nearly half of the domestic workers are illiterate and only 3 percent have as much as a middle school education (eight years of schooling). Of those who are literate, 38.6 percent are graduates of adult literacy programs. Although the two groups are similar in terms of number of years in primary school and literacy rate, they differ in the proportion of participation in the adult literacy programs. While only 12 percent of the workers in the squatter group participated in these programs, the corresponding figure for the doorkeeper group is nearly twice that. The education level attained by husbands is also low but higher than that attained by their wives. The great majority of husbands had completed primary school (79 percent of the doorkeeper and 71 percent of the squatter settlement husbands). About 9 percent of the doorkeeper husbands were illiterate; the corresponding figure for the squatter husbands—14 percent—was slightly higher. Only 10 percent of the doorkeeper husbands and 12 percent of squatter men had schooling beyond primary school.

The two groups have similar household characteristics. No household in this study included nonrelated persons and the majority of domestic workers lived in nuclear units. Eighty-nine percent of the doorkeeper households and 81 percent of the squatter settlement households were nuclear, and the remainder were households of extended families that included various combinations of husbands' or wives' widowed fathers and mothers and unmarried sisters and brothers. The doorkeeper households were smaller, with an average of 4.3 members compared with 5.3 members in squatter settlement households. The average size of doorkeeper households was the same as the national average and slightly higher than the urban average of 3.7 persons (HIPS 1980). Doorkeeper families have an average of 2.6 children living at home, while squatter families average 3.1. One-third of the squatter families have more than three children, compared with 10 percent of doorkeeper families, reflecting their respective stages in the family life cycle.

A REAL-LIFE IRONY

At the center of this book lies a real-life irony. It is more specifically about an unexpected parallel between experience of a traditional form of subordination in one sphere and of autonomy in another. Control over women's labor through patriarchal subordination of women within the family creates a waged domestic labor market in Turkey in which domestic workers' labor is expensive and scarce. In Ankara this structure affords domestic workers autonomy in the workplace and negotiating power with regard to middle-class women, complicating simple accounts of the uniformity of gender subordination in economic, sexual, and familial relations. Parallel readings of basement and squatter women's stories illuminate the odd connection between the empowering structure of domestic employment and migrant women's lack of autonomous access to employment. Women's position in the labor market in Turkey is linked to the unequal power relations embodied in the patriarchal structures of marriage and family, where women cannot assert their right to decide their own destiny in the world of work.

Recognizing this patriarchal dynamic is central to understanding domestic service and its configuration of gender and class relations. The Turkish case constitutes an instance in which patriarchy, by not releasing its control over women's labor, has modernized Turkish domestic service, while in other cases domestic workers must struggle to transform themselves from traditional maids into employees. It is also ironic that middle-class women's access to cheap, readily available labor is circumscribed by this patriarchal design. In the following chapters, I demonstrate that at different levels micro and macro forces work together to generate this unique dynamic. Although a parallel reading of the stories of basement and squatter women reveals many similarities, it also exposes differences in the lives of these women. Control over women's labor, for example, is stronger where the challenge to patriarchal relations is perceived to be greater. The contrast between squatter workers and the women of the basement also allows us to explore the ways in which interpretations of women's wage labor and its effects play out within two different social and spatial settings, especially in the realms of gender division of labor at home and relations of money and authority. By bringing their differing perspectives into focus and revealing circumstances under which women resist or refrain from resisting control over their labor, and earnings, I hope to contribute to the refinement of concepts such as "women's subordination" and to add some concreteness to the abstract concept of patriarchy.

TROUBLING ENCOUNTERS BETWEEN "SISTERS"

An important aspect of this study is its recognition of the agency of women, even when it means an agency for their own subordination. I focus on the self-perceptions and perspectives of domestic workers that emerge from their experiences in the home, workplace, community, and urban space. Migrant women's own responses and self-images are often displaced in accounts of the impact of development on Turkish women by descriptions of their subordination to structures of patriarchy and its intimate ally, capitalism. In such accounts, domestic workers are considered the most oppressed group of Turkish women, subject to the domination of men and of the middle-class women for whom they work. This view of double subordination in terms of gender and class— at the domestic worker's own home and at the home of strangers—misrepresents these women's lives and fails to acknowledge their agency. In opposition to these simplistic and homogenizing accounts, my data offers a more nuanced portrayal of the interactions of class, gender, and patriarchy in domestic workers' lives. The complexities manifest in their stories defy any simplistic account of oppression or emancipation.

In Turkey, as elsewhere, waged domestic labor takes place at an important junction of gender and class inequality. Waged domestic labor is central to the processes of both the reproduction of class and the traditional gender division of labor. It allows middle-class women to escape domestic work and avoid confronting the traditional gender division of labor within the household. Thus, scholars have argued that one class of women escapes some of the constraints of gender stratification by using the labor of those women who are most severely limited by class, race, and ethnic inequalities (Glenn 1986; Rollins 1985; Romero 1992). Women who buy other women's labor are criticized for not contesting patriarchal gender division of labor and, thus, perpetuating it (Hartmann 1981a).

Waged domestic labor creates a new class of women who perform the heaviest, most repetitious household tasks. In *Servicing the Middle-Classes,* Nicky Gregson and Michelle Lowe (1994) describe this process: "Household cleaning in middle-class households is no longer just a gender-segregated task. . . . It is also being constructed as an occupation for working-class women. The corollary of this position is that in certain middle-class households cleaning is no longer being seen as a suitable use of middle-class women's time-space" (110). What is crucial about this process is that waged domestic labor plays a pivotal role in the creation of polarized middle-class and working-class versions of femininity.

These generalizations, however, miss the lived realities of workplace interrelations. Domestic workers' diverse and often ambivalent responses to proletarianization and new versions of femininity undermine some of these polarizing tendencies. The role played by the domestic service in the construction of contrasting class-based femininities is further complicated in the Turkish case by the fact that class relations between women are also articulated within their urban/modern and rural/traditional roles. In this book, I look at the relationship between domestic workers and their employers in the context of an absence of race category and of a muted sense of ethnicity as the main source of inequality. The main axes of difference and inequality in Turkey are based on class and the strong distinction drawn between modern, urban women and modernizing peasant women.

My data on domestic workers' employment patterns reveals that the transformation of peasant women into working–class women is by no means uncomplicated or complete. Ninety-one percent of the workers in this study (145 out of 160) work for multiple employers; only a small number of workers are tied to a single employer. Domestic workers can be distributed on a continuum between "specialists" (proletarianized house cleaners), who sell their labor for rigidly defined tasks, and "generalists" (traditional maids), based on days worked, number of employers, and frequency of work for a given employer. The majority of domestic workers were situated toward the specialist end. Among specialist positions, the most advantageous involve multiple weekly visits to a single employer; these offer shorter work hours, more variety of work load, and better chances for patronage benefits. In contrast, complete specialization—laboring in a different home every day—allows greater autonomy over the labor process but involves repeatedly performing the most dirty and physically exhausting labor. Furthermore, this level of proletarianization in domestic service confers a menial identity to the worker and fosters an image of the physically strong, resilient working woman reminiscent of how they were defined as peasant women. I show in Chapters 3 and 4 that domestic workers do not embrace this proletarianized peasant image, although they equally avoid association with a single employer. Furthermore, domestic workers' preferences for different modes of employment have significant implications for middle-class women. In carving out a work identity between the two undesirable extremes, domestic workers choose those employers who can afford their labor most frequently. This means that middle-class employers are less desirable than, and thus in competition with, upper-middle-class employers.

The central theoretical issue addressed by any study of domestic service is how to conceptualize the relationship between women on either side of the labor relation. Domestic service is an occupational domain that historically has brought members of different races, classes, and nationalities together, not in factories or offices, but within the private spheres of the dominant classes and races. These often troubling relationships tend to defy a conventional class- and race-based analysis, and the actors in them have been described by phrases, such as "domestic enemies" and "distant companions," that evoke the simultaneous experience of distance and closeness (Fairchilds 1984; Hansen 1989). This book raises the question, How do increased contractuality and employers' social position affect this distance and closeness? Under conditions in which domestic work resembles rational wage labor should we study these interactions as class struggles (Romero 1992) or must we employ new metaphors closer to "maternalism" (Glenn 1988; Katzman 1978a,b; Rollins 1985)?

The issue of how domestic workers and employers perceive, deal with, and manage class inequality, and how gender identity mediates this class tension in their daily interactions is a focus of this book. I diverge, however, from most other studies of employer-worker relations, which attribute usually oppressive power to the employers and view workers as capable only of resistance. The employer woman is often defined as the actor who has the effective means of eliciting compliance while her domestic worker does not. I do not deny this power imbalance, but I do try to understand the interpersonal processes by which interclass social relations are produced. The social sciences usually analyze power macrosociologically, assuming that individuals' responses to specific interactions express and reflect social-structural forces beyond the boundaries of their immediate encounter. I approach this relationship as a mutual construct in which both domestic workers and employers participate equally, thereby offering a relational concept of power and a less mechanical and less dramatic understanding of resistance. Power relations are enacted in face-to-face encounters between superiors and their subordinates. The latter can respond to domination in mundane, informal, diffuse, and individualistic ways. James Scott (1985) calls such tactics the "weapons of the weak." Developing a vocabulary for understanding confrontations between the powerless and the powerful, Scott attempts to understand the structure of inequalities between agrarian landlords and wage laborers and concludes that peasant resistance is routine and a "constant process of testing and renegotiating of relations between classes." I employ his notion of "resistance as a routine action" here because it is helpful for understanding the dynamics of the relations that I observed in Ankara. I am especially interested in how both groups of women deploy their understandings of women's gender subordination and patriarchal constructions of women's identity in the management of their own day-to-day relationships. I examine the relations between women and how the two groups of women (middle-class and peasant) relate to men and demonstrate how these relationships comprise an interactive relationship of power.

Domestic workers' class subordination is grounded in a tense relationship between two women who are at once "sisters" and antagonists. Class-bound expressions of gender are constructed and class-based inequalities are actively dealt with by both groups of women in the management of their relationship. By examining some concrete instances of what I call the "class" and "intimacy work" done by these two groups of women, I hope to provide a better understanding of the relations between different classes of women. This question is of critical concern for feminist movements in Turkey and elsewhere. The increasing participation of women in the labor force, with or without equality to men, means that class distinctions become a central source of division among women. Clearly, a feminist politics based on an assumed common identity among women, independent of race, class, and culture is untenable. By bringing these women together, domestic service allows us to examine the lived experiences of class inequality and the implications of difference.

THE POWER OF BINARIES:
TRADITION AND MODERNITY REVISITED

The study of industrialization and modernization in third world countries has undergone considerable change over the past three decades. Emphasis has shifted from a preoccupation with individual mentality to the study of the internal and external obstacles to structural development. While the modernization approach[14] focused on the extent to which self-oriented individuals, free from the bonds of traditional attachments exist, the dependency perspective,[15] informed by Marxist social theory, focused on the study of the economy and on broad structures of inequality between and within countries.[16] The introduction of gender by feminist scholars as an axis for understanding the interaction between individual practices and experience on one hand and structures on the other and the redefinition of urban economies by scholars working on globalization and the informal sector have significantly altered approaches to studies of women in third world societies. The growing preoccupation with women in third world societies has occurred in the midst of gender theorization in social theory and a rapidly changing international system since the mid-seventies.[17] The new attention to gender as an important organizing principle of society and a source of personal identity (Connell 1987; Scott 1988) has become a major ground for rethinking or launching criticisms of Marxist and neo-classical theories of labor, markets, class, race-based stratification, statehood, development, labor migration, work, and household.[18]

Recent scholarship expresses extreme discomfort with distinctions between "modern" and "traditional" as a major framework for studying economic and social transformations in industrializing societies and particularly for examining emerging modalities of life and identity (Abu-Lughod 1998; Adam 1996; Luke 1996; Ong 1988; Thompson 1996). It has been argued that this polarity precludes consideration of important sources of difference, complexity, and diverse meanings of modernity and fails to recognize the changing face of modernity. Students of Turkish modernization have also started seriously to interrogate the project of modernity in Turkey and have called for employing the distinction between modern and traditional not as an organizing assumption but rather as a topic for intense investigation (Bozdoğan and Kasaba 1997; Kandiyoti 1997). These scholars seek to study "the specificities of the 'modern' in the Turkish context" (Kandiyoti 1997:113): How is modernity variously understood and experienced? What aspects of elite notions of modernity are accepted, reworked, or changed by so-called traditional segments of society and in which domains of life and how? How is the tension between the modern and the traditional expressed concretely in the daily organization of women's lives and conduct, lives said to be caught between these forces?

These questions have only recently made an impact on the discourses and research agendas of social scientists. It is no accident that the development of feminist theory, on one hand, with its insistence on gender constructions as fundamental aspects of social order and cultural change, and the demise of modernizing and developmentalist projects, on the other hand, have placed these questions on the agenda. These significant questions are largely ignored by the dominant paradigms of Marxist and modernization thought, which focus on changes in judicial, political, and institutional spheres but fail to explore the cultural consequences of these transformations. Marxist and modernization perspectives also fail to recognize the various unequal and contradictory forms of modernization and the "life worlds" (Mardin 1997) of those people whose subjectivities and social lives were to be transformed by the project. Deniz Kandiyoti (1997), for example, notes that "the assumed inexorable march of society from traditional, rural, and less developed to modern, urban, industrialized, and more developed, or, alternatively, from feudal to capitalist, meant that complexities on the ground could be dismissed as 'transitional forms'" (129). In the classificatory systems of the social sciences, these rural migrants were placed in a position of liminality and were understood as if in transition or in the process of moving from one fixed status to another and therefore are studied from the perspective of integration and assimilation into modern, urbanized structures and institutions of life.

Now, more and more scholars take a pluralist stance, accepting that fragmentation and multiple combinations of forces of modernity and tradition are indispensable for considering Turkish social order at the end of the century. They call for more intense studies of the new identities and modalities of life engendered by the modernity project. To this end, Joel S. Migdal (1997) suggests that "the effects of the modernity project . . . can be found not in examination of elites and their institutions exclusively, nor in a focus solely on the poor or marginal groups of society, but on those physical and social spaces where the two intersect" (253–54). He draws our attention to the significance of interactive processes, suggesting that the "challenge" is to illuminate "the encounter" of those formerly excluded groups "with the modernity project—the changes in them that this encounter produced and their surprising ability to transform the project itself" (259).

The experiences of domestic workers and doorkeepers reveal important dimensions of cultural change and raise questions about the lives of people who occupy the new social territories formed by the rapid social transformations in Turkey. Apartment buildings and middle-class homes constitute physical and social spaces of intersection and interaction between "traditional," "modern," "rural," and "urban," where rural migrants encounter urban classes through their work as domestic workers and doorkeepers. The "critical tale"[19] I offer in this book provides a context for close examination of the consciousness of class inequality and how migrants—with a past identity as peasants—imagine, understand, and practice what they perceive as modernity and tradition. I argue that in the process they invent new forms of cultural difference in the Turkish urban landscape that do not fit neatly into the binary categories of "modern" and "traditional." Yet, the tension between "traditional" and "modern" permeates the lives and subjectivities of the people in this study. They reinscribe this binary opposition even as they change its form. I wish to advance the debate about the opposition between tradition and modernity by suggesting that these forces exercise a special potency in people's lives, organizing class, gender, experience, and consciousness. I agree with those who argue that modernity and tradition, as categories of analysis, often fail to explain the complexities of cultural change, but we must not ignore the centrality of the opposition in the constitution of the subjectivities of margin dwellers. How, then, can we simultaneously abandon this opposition yet preserve it within analysis?

I also believe that the time has come to explore the diverse meanings of tradition, the conditions in which traditional practices are sheltered, nurtured, or reconfigured and the meanings attributed to tradition by those who are thought of as its bearers. I examine these questions with particular reference to the relationship between tradition and locality. I follow John B. Thompson (1996) in arguing that traditional practices are not only temporally defined but also spatially specific and spatially defined. What I seek to emphasize is the significance of space and locality in the articulation of traditional practices with regard to gender and authority relations. The experiences of doorkeepers and their wives illuminate alternately inhibiting and enabling aspects of location and how tradition is maintained in practice.

THE CONFLUENCE OF LABORS AND IDENTITIES IN THE INFORMAL SECTOR

An extensive informal labor market in which a sizeable portion of the urban labor force engages in various income-producing activities characterizes the economies of many developing countries. Such economies have been called "pre-capitalist," "traditional," "petty commodity production," "subaltern," "shadow," and "informal sector" (Arizpe 1975; Bawly 1982; Bromley and Gerry 1979; Illich 1981) and cover a wide range of production and distribution activities, such as small workshops, domestic service, industrial homework, and petty trade and services.

Social scientists and development agencies examining the informal sector as it touches upon fundamental problems of poverty, unemployment, and proletarianization within the context of third world industrialization, as well as participants within the informal sector themselves, have had great difficulty in defining the boundaries, activities, and class locations of workers in the informal sector. The ongoing expansion of informal activities and the decentralization of work in postindustrial countries contribute to this difficulty (see Castells and Portes 1989 for comparative figures of this expansion). Alejandro Portes and Saskia Sassen-Koob (1987) define composite informal work as "all those work situations characterized by the *absence* of (1) a clear separation between capital and labor; (2) a contractual relationship between both; and (3) a labor force that is paid wages and whose conditions of work and pay are legally regulated" (31). Defined this way, the informal sector includes all income-earning production and exchange activities outside the formal and state-regulated economy. The role of state control is particularly emphasized: the informal sector is "unregulated by the institutions of society, in a legal and social environment in which similar activities are regulated" (Castells and Portes 1989:12). Thus, the boundaries of the informal sector move according to changes in state regulations.

The fact that most displaced agricultural laborers enter the informal sector and remain there (see Portes and Walton 1981 for evidence from Africa, Asia, and Latin America of this persistent trend) contradicts the predictions of modernization theory. The experience of Western development predicts that informal activities should disappear. Scholars writing during the last two decades of the twentieth century on the informal sector (Benton 1990; Bromley and Gerry 1979; Bujra 1978; Gerry and Birkbeck 1981; Portes and Benton 1984; Portes and Schauffler 1993; Portes and Walton 1981; Portes, Castells, and Benton 1989) share the following observations and premises: informal activities are not essentially separate from the rest of the capitalist economy, informal workers exist within the major axis of production and exchange relations, informal activities do not exist under capitalist social and economic relations as an isolated and anachronistic survival, and workers in the informal sector do not constitute poor, marginal subpopulations with secluded lifestyles.

These authors point out that capital accumulation on a world scale has played a key role in determining the conditions and direction of industrialization in developing countries. They link the persistence of small-scale production and the proliferation of the informal sector in third world cities to these countries' integration into the world market. Their studies, conducted from the point of view of structural articulation, emphasize the integration of formal and informal sectors and analyze various links between the two. The results illustrate the two basic functions performed by the informal sector. First, it provides cheap labor power in backward capitalist production, which includes small enterprises employing unprotected wage labor and disguised wageworkers hired by larger national or international corporations on a casual or subcontracting basis. It also provides inexpensive goods and services to urban classes, with the effect of subsidizing their costs of reproduction as labor force, thereby enabling the formal sector to keep wages and fringe benefits down for its own workers and to subsidize some state provisions necessary for social reproduction (e.g., self-building rather than public housing, domestic workers rather than formal childcare systems). While this literature has made significant theoretical contributions to our understanding of the informal sector by rejecting its transitional and traditional character, it overemphasizes the functions of the informal sector with regard to national and international economies. This overemphasis leads to a tendency to assume an essential and unchanging functional connection between the informal and formal sectors. Emerging research in this field shows, however, that the linkages between these sectors are neither predetermined nor constant.

To understand the social and economic effects of the informal sector on its participants, the differential impact of state policies that regulate them, and the ways in which the informal sector interacts with the capitalist sector we must distinguish between the large variety of groups and types of activities within the informal sector. Furthermore, analysis of gender stratification in the informal sector would greatly enhance our understanding of the workings of this sector and its shifting boundaries, but the question of gender has not yet been integrated in studies of this worldwide process of informalization. Paid domestic work, for example, sits uneasily between "formal" as distinguished from "informal" work at home. Unlike many other informal occupations carried out within the household, paid domestic work does not allow women to combine their work activities with their own domestic tasks and childcare.

Women are incorporated into informal labor and exchange processes in different and unequal ways (Arizpe 1975; Beneria and Roldan 1987; Mies 1982; Moser 1978; Portes, Castells, and Benton 1989; Redclift and

Mingione 1985; Roldan 1985). Gender-based hierarchical relations resulting in the division of labor and the continuation of domestic patriarchy
keep women confined to particular branches of the informal sector.
Women are excluded from activities that require mobility, flexibility,
and independence and provide higher earnings while they are concentrated in those activities that are compatible with their roles within the
domestic sphere. The organization of women's work in this sector and
its articulation within the social and economic processes of the capitalist sector are ultimately mediated by men.

Furthermore, access to paid work through informal activities does not
produce the emancipatory effects one might expect. Such activities generally occur within the home and, therefore, isolate workers from one
another, thereby sustaining, naturalizing, or elaborating patriarchal
notions of womanhood. Informal activities generally enhance women's
domestic roles and reinforce women's dependent status as wives and
mothers rather than as income earners. In Günseli Berik's (1987) study
of women carpet weavers in rural Turkey, Mine Çınar's (1988) and Jenny
White's (1994) studies of subcontracted home workers in İstanbul and
Bursa, and Maria Mies's (1982) study of women lace makers in India,
we see how women often underestimate their own indispensable contribution to household and to national economies because they consider
their productive labor a mere extension of their domestic responsibilities. As Çınar (1988:22) reports, almost all the women she interviewed
viewed their subcontracting as temporary and their knitting as a hobby,
even though some of these women had done this type of work for over
ten years.

A broad range of studies have shown that the dominant pattern of
labor participation in developing societies places women in predominantly informal activities, such as sweatshop employment, subcontracted homework, unpaid family subsistence production, and domestic work and small trades in the informal sector (Beneria and Sen 1981;
Boserup 1970; Deere 1976; Mies 1982; Moser 1981; Safa and Nash 1976;
Sen and Grown 1987). Another pattern—one particularly dominant in
South Asia and the Caribbean—involves massive incorporation of
young, single females into the wage labor market as a result of the relocation of export-oriented manufacturing to these countries where the
cost of labor is lower than in advanced industrial countries (Lim 1983;
Elson and Pearson 1981; Ong 1987; Ward 1984). Women's incorporation

into the labor force either as unprotected, disguised laborers or as wage laborers is associated with what is often called the globalization of production or the new international division of labor (Frobel, Kreye, and Heinrichs 1979). The globalization of production involves a redivision of labor within the world capitalist system as well as a restructuring of the capitalist economy in the advanced industrial countries. This new phase involves transferring the labor-intensive phases of production to third world countries where high urban employment and massive female migration to regional industrial zones creates a large supply of cheap labor (Khoo, Smith, and Fawcett 1984; Lim 1983; Sassen-Koob 1981, 1984).

The globalization of production has affected primarily third world women's employment. Research in Latin American countries has shown that most export-oriented manufacturers employ large amounts of informal female labor. They reduce production costs by "utilizing more vulnerable segments of the labor force, such as women, and by circumventing labor legislation designed to protect workers such as minimum wages, fringe benefits, and adequate working conditions" (Safa 1986:135). Beneria and Sen (1982) point out that women are vulnerable because of their role in the reproductive sphere.

> The masses of third world women are indeed integrated into that process, but at the bottom of an inherently hierarchical and contradictory structure of production and accumulation [because of] their primary responsibility for the reproductive tasks of childbearing and domestic work. . . . In a system that makes use of existing gender hierarchies so as to generate and intensify inequalities, women tend to be placed in subordinate positions at the different levels of interaction between class and gender. . . . The significance of this argument is that women's role and location in the development process is conditioned by their role in the reproductive sphere. (161, 162, 167)

The earlier investigations of whether women are integrated into the development process have thus evolved into studies of the relations and mechanisms through which they are integrated. The analytical framework of Marxist-feminist perspectives (Beneria and Sen 1981, 1982; Lim 1983; Mies 1986) has guided much of the research in the area of women and development and has established the main parameters for looking at the problem (see Brydon and Chant 1989 for a secondary analysis from this perspective of existing research on women in the third world).

The reproductive sphere, as a critical set of social relations concerned with the sexual division of labor and control over women's labor within and outside the home, emerged as the main focus of scholarship concerning women and development. The investigation of interconnections between women's positions in the productive and reproductive spheres, the two being systematically structured by patriarchy, has become a productive research agenda. This approach poses important challenges to traditional Marxist perspectives and the dependency paradigm, both of which define the gender question outside the gender- and age-based hierarchies of social and economic relations within the household.

Yet, this broad Marxist-feminist perspective, in turn, takes for granted the nature of the reproductive sphere and patriarchy (Jelin 1991). Questions concerning the sphere's construction and how its boundaries and activities culturally and historically change have not yet been fully analyzed. Instead, changes in the reproductive sphere, including those involving family, are explained by their presumed functionality within the structure of global capitalism. An assumption is made that women's reproductive roles are necessary to the creation of a cheap, flexible, and docile labor force in order to explain women's present role as either wage laborers or informal workers in the global capitalist network.

Recent research demonstrates the limitations of this accepted theoretical framework and reveals its overgeneralization of particular trends in some countries. It becomes evident that the boundaries between single and married women on one hand and participation in the informal sector and formal sector on the other are more permeable than thought and that the growth of the informal sector is not always intrinsically tied to global capitalism.[20] These cases tell us that the concentration of women in certain sectors or branches of the economy cannot be explained without a detailed examination of the interactions between varying forms of gender dynamics and global capitalism. The relationship between the economic position of women and their subordination can be understood only through reference to internal dynamics and the immediate material, cultural, and institutional practices in which they are embedded, not by reference to global forces or categories. Recognition of the variety of household forms and of historically and culturally shifting notions of patriarchy helps frame the link between women and economy in a less deterministic way than that achieved by Marxist-feminist analysis.[21]

THE GLOBAL LANDSCAPE OF DOMESTIC SERVICE

Domestic service as an occupational domain was long ago declared obsolete in the landscape of industrial societies by evolutionary sociological perspectives (Coser 1973) that noted a decline in the number of domestic workers in the United States after the Second World War.[22] Lewis Coser argued that domestic service was doomed to extinction for two reasons: the servant role was no longer necessary because modern household technology and an expanding market eradicated the need for traditional homemakers, and the power imbalance manifest in employee-employer relations was incompatible with democratic society. This unilinear assumption of modernization theory has also been applied to domestic service in developing countries with the prediction that domestic service in these societies also will fade with time (Chaplin 1978; McBride 1974).

The content, structure, and organization of domestic service have indeed changed radically with industrialization and have assumed a more contractual form. But the modernization of domestic work is multifaceted and does not closely fit the evolutionary model.[23] The decline of the domestic work force and other changes in the status and nature of domestic work was the result of a complex interplay of racial, ethnic, and economic dynamics and involved changes in women's relationships to work as well as changing definitions of domesticity. The modernization perspective—which argues that housework ceased to be demanding work following the complete transformation of household work services and childcare into a capitalist labor arena—does not accurately explain this decline (as documented in detail in Cowan 1983). Furthermore, the proposition put forward by Coser (1973) that the servant role as a mode of work and behavior extrinsic to democracy also has been challenged by many case studies that document the survival of master-servant relations under democratic conditions (Rollins 1985; Romero 1992; Ruiz 1987). Moreover, a growing body of qualitative and quantitative evidence indicates that domestic service is far from extinct. On the contrary, it is increasing in both postindustrial and developing societies. Domestic work is a major occupation for women in many third world countries, and in the United States and in many other countries legal and illegal female immigrants constitute a large part of the domestic labor pool.[24]

Gregson and Lowe (1994) document this resurgence of waged domestic labor in the homes of middle-class dual-career couples in Britain beginning in the 1980s. (For most of the postwar period in Britain domestic labor has been performed without pay by middle-class women.) The authors argue that the increased demand for two specific categories of waged domestic labor, cleaners and nannies, was generated by the growth of women's participation in the managerial labor force. Furthermore, they demonstrate that, unlike the situation in the United States, there is no close association between domestic work and transnational female migration and ethnicity. Nonetheless, differences between women based on class and life cycle play a major role in creating the two distinct types of female waged-labor: "The nanny in contemporary Britain is an occupational category characterized predominantly by young, unmarried women from white collar, intermediate status households, whereas cleaning is the domain of older, married, working-class women" (Gregson and Lowe 1994:124). Moreover, the social relations of waged domestic labor continue to be governed by ideologies of motherhood, caring, and false kinship relations, which, when combined, reconstitute a traditional domestic service in Britain, in which class-based definitions of womanhood are sharply defined.

Globally, inequalities that persist in the gender division of labor sustain the growth of those classes who employ domestic workers. But the first world woman's relationship to domestic service is different from that of her third world counterpart. According to Isis Duarte (1989), the prohibitive cost of domestic service in post-industrial societies puts such services out of the reach of many middle-class women, thereby rendering "second-shift" work a necessity for these women. Their third world counterparts do not carry the burden of the "second shift," however, because of their access to a large pool of cheap domestic labor.

In third world countries, the structure of domestic service continues to be shaped by the dissolution of rural traditions and framed by patterns of gender-specific migration, according to which, women migrate more easily than men because of the availability of domestic work (Jelin 1977). This pattern of migration sustains a live-in mode of domestic service that inhibits the development of a more contractual employer-employee relation. Some studies of domestic service in Latin America (e.g., Chaney and Castro 1989), however, point out an increasing tendency toward "casualization," or a live-out mode of domestic service.

Yet, although live-out domestic work removes some of the oppressive dimensions of domestic service, as noted in Kuznesof 1989, it can become much less regulated and usually less secure than a live-in position when there is a large labor pool.

In the United States, the growing numbers of immigrant women who enter domestic service are stratified along lines of race, ethnicity, and migrant status. In this occupational domain, race, class, gender, and ethnic differences not only structure the labor process but also frame the nature of exchanges between mistress and maid. These differences are reflected in domestic workers' wages and conditions of employment. A dual wage system reflects the racial and ethnic differences between domestic workers. Undocumented immigrants are paid far less than other groups of domestic workers (Romero 1992).

Current immigration patterns seem to support the continuation of live-in arrangements. Pierrette Hondagneu-Sotelo and Ernestine Avila's research (1997) among Latina domestic workers in Los Angeles signals the reemergence of this old pattern of participation in domestic service. They argue that live-in nanny arrangements attract the most vulnerable segment of the immigrant population, recent arrivals without immigration papers, and encourage temporal and spatial separations of working mothers and children. "Transnational mothers" work in the United States to support their children at home in Mexico or Central America, creating new meanings and practices of motherhood in these families. Thus the institution of domestic service not only has endured but continues to grow and transform under different labor regimes. The interplay between the internal structures of third world countries from which immigrants originate and the international structures within which they operate constitutes the critical starting point for an understanding of the processes restructuring domestic service and the emergence of multiple domestic worker roles. These new categories of domestic worker include Mexican immigrant women who commute daily across national borders in El Paso (Ruiz 1987), live-in West Indian childcare workers in New York City (Colen 1986, 1989), Chicana day workers with multiple employers in Denver who fit the role of petit-bourgeois (Romero 1988, 1992), Central American immigrant workers who are members of housecleaning cooperatives (Salzinger 1991), live-in Latina workers who work in the United States and practice "transnational mothering" (Hondagneu-Sotelo and Avila 1997), and female and male employees of cleaning companies (Bickham Mendez 1998).

We are confronted with an occupational domain in which several different labor processes and work relations coexist and in which boundaries of work relations are shifting. Although most workers sell their labor in informal ways with terms, wages, and conditions, negotiated orally, informality can no longer be considered the defining characteristic of domestic labor. In the United States, for example, and in some third world countries, such as Peru, Brazil, and Martinique, social security benefits have expanded to include domestic workers, though state enforcement of this policy remains uneven (Colen and Sanjek 1990; de Oliveria and da Conceicao 1989). In several Latin American countries, domestic workers have even formed unions and associations (Chaney and Castro 1989).

Domestic service is changing in both the first and the third worlds, but sociologists of work and occupation have not yet developed a consistent and integrated model to account for these transformations and their effect on work structures and to interpret their meaning for those involved. In what way and to what extent do the workers themselves shape the emergence of different work structures? How are the structural changes expressed and experienced by different groups of domestic workers? In the United States, for example, for immigrants with skills who need to learn a new language, employment in domestic service may be a transient stage; for others it may become an occupational ghetto. We must ask whether the work trajectories of third world immigrant women will be similar to those of the Issei studied by Evelyn Nakano Glenn (1986), of the African American women who filled the ranks of domestic service for so many decades, or of white European immigrant women. Recent historical studies demonstrate that racial and ethnic origins affect domestic work careers in different ways, in terms of life changes, work conditions, and cultural characteristics. Furthermore, as mentioned above, the legal and cultural conditions under which current labor movements occur are very different from those of earlier domestic worker cohorts as well.

We must also examine the relationship between domestic work and the general trend of informalization, which, according to its leading theorists, is structural and universal rather than cyclical (Portes, Castells, and Benton 1989). This phenomenon invites a rethinking of the imagined course of industrial development and employment structures. If conventional employment based on the centrality of rationalized labor is declining and class and social markers such as "blue collar," "white collar," "menial," and "manual" are collapsing, then where does domestic service stand in this new ordering of the relationship between work and its bearers? It might be appropriate to suggest that employment in domestic service is becoming more like other jobs in terms of deskilling, falling wages, and the absence of institutional evaluation of skills, autonomy, and job security in the present situation of postindustrial societies.

RESEARCH CONTEXT

Industrialization and Modernization in Turkey

This section presents a brief history of industrialization and modernization in Turkey to explain the context in which migration and recruitment of migrant women into the informal sector of the economy occurs. It outlines the key structural transformations that have taken place since the foundation of the Turkish Republic and the main consequences of these processes for the social and economic status of women and the family structure.

Turkey is a large developing nation undergoing social transformation so rapidly that it has been described as a society "on the brink of a social mutation" (Tekeli 1990:3). One aspect of change is an ongoing urbanization that is drawing the rural population into the big cities in a process one social scientist calls "depeasantization" (Kıray 1991). The impact of these social and economic transformations on women and gender relations is not uniform in Turkey.

Two historical processes have made Turkey unique in the third world: it has never been colonized, and it was the first Islamic country to accomplish the transition to a secular state. Turkey does not readily fit a postcolonial society model. The absence of influence by an outside, colonial power means that the indigenous dynamics and politico-cultural meanings attached to modernization should be given weight in an explanation of the Turkish socioeconomic structure and its gender relations. Students of Turkish modernization, in emphasizing the distinctiveness of the Turkish experience, often point out that modernization is considered synonymous with Westernization, a process that began with the Tanzimat reforms of 1839 and the subsequent adaptation of western European norms, styles, and institutions. Such characteristics as "elite-driven, consensus-based, [and an] institution-building process that took its inspiration exclusively from the West" (Bozdoğan and Kasaba 1997:3–4) have been cited as evidence of the viability of the project of modernity even in an overwhelmingly Muslim country. In addition to making the transition to a secular state, Turkey was among the first countries in the world where the political rights of women as citizens were recognized. These events initiated irreversible processes that positioned Turkish women in a far more Westernized context than the women of other Islamic societies.

Industrialization, since the establishment of the Republic in 1921, has provided the means to build a modern nation-state out of the ruins of the Ottoman Empire. Turkey, like its Latin American counterparts, employed two main strategies in its project of industrialization (Barkey 1984; Eralp 1990; Keyder 1987). Between 1960 and 1970, the government adopted an import substitution model characterized by protectionist economic policies aimed at achieving independent industrialization. Later, in 1980, austerity measures were passed to help initiate export-oriented manufacturing, with the aim of integrating the Turkish economy into the global market and in the hope that Turkey would be admitted to the European Economic Community. The export-oriented industrialization strategy was directed by Turgut Özal, who was the economy czar after the military coup of 1980 and then became the democratic leader of the vastly liberalized economy. He promised not only to avert economic crises and high inflation but also to usher Turkey into a new era of economic development by transforming the protectionist state into a liberal one. Most interpretations of Turkish modernization emphasize the fundamental and active role of the state both in economic and social development and in the production of regulatory discourses and policies on modernity, especially concerning gender relations and private life (Kandiyoti 1997).

The early years of the Republic were devoted to nation building. The 1920s constituted a period of economic reconstruction characterized by state-centered development of an essentially inward-looking economy (Keyder 1979). Until the Second World War, large increases in production and industrial employment were achieved through adapting a doctrine of statism controlled by the military bureaucratic elite. The omnipotence of the state, which inhibited the emergence of a strong industrial bourgeoisie, has been attributed to the tradition of Ottoman bureaucratic rule. The economic practice of statism led to an increase in industrial production while the peasants' real wages and terms of trade declined (Boratav 1988; Keyder 1979). Not only did the surplus obtained from peasants go to the bureaucrats and the industrial bourgeoisie but militant secularism also antagonized the peasantry and the petty bourgeoisie of Turkey's small towns.

The founding of an opposition party—the Democrat Party (DP)—in 1946 and its accession to power with the votes of peasants after the 1950 election marked the beginning of a new period in Turkey. Çaglar Keyder (1979) sees it as a transformation from elite rule to full class rule and from "one pattern of capitalist modernization to another" (20). The DP lessened state control over the economy, privatized some of the state economic enterprises, and created capitalist agriculture. During the early 1950s, the agricultural sector experienced a boom through the commercialization of agriculture, which increased export earnings. Within four years, the area of land under cultivation increased by more than 50 percent (Keyder 1979; 1987). The dramatic change in agriculture resulted from extensive mechanization and changes in production methods. Small land-holding peasants were no longer able to secure their subsistence by farming. The vast majority became agricultural wageworkers or migrated to urban areas. The large-scale internal migration increased the urban population from 18.5 percent to 25.0 percent (Keyder 1979). A period of stagnation ensued that was due to a decline in agricultural exports followed by government restriction on imports in the early 1960s. Here began the import substitution period in Turkey, which lasted until the late 1970s. During this period industrial production was directed exclusively toward the internal market and the industrial sector was allowed to develop in a well-protected environment. Agriculture continued to undergo rapid change, and even though there was not a trend toward concentration of land, the existence of properly capitalist forms and the domination of capital in agriculture predominated. Displaced agricultural laborers continued to move into services and industry.

Rural out-migration has been one important response to the mechanization of agricultural production and the decline of agricultural employment accounting for the rapid growth of cities in Turkey. The percentage of people who live in urban areas rose from 18.5 percent in 1950 to 33.2 percent in 1970, 45.4 percent in 1980 (Keleş and Danielson 1985),[25] and 65.0 percent in 1997 (KSSGM 1998). In more rapidly expanding urban centers (such as İstanbul, Ankara, İzmir, Adana, and Bursa), the population increase outstripped these cities' capacity to provide housing, employment, and other infrastructural elements, forcing migrants to build their own houses and to create their own employment opportunities.

As peasants came to the city, the number of squatter settlement houses mushroomed rapidly from 100,000 units in 1950 to 1.25 million in 1983 (Keleş and Danielson 1985:41). Although during the past decade this upward trend has slowed down—there were 450,000 squatter houses in 1995 (Keleş 2000:387)—the majority of Ankara's population, 60 percent, live in squatter housing. In Turkey, as elsewhere, squatter settlement housing continues to represent a low-cost solution for the state, both economically and politically.

Modernizing Gender

During the early years of the Republic, women as a focus of the radical Westernist program represented the crux of modernity (see Kandiyoti 1989; Göle 1997). The most important social reforms of this period centered on women. The conception of women's emancipation and the construction of women as citizens (including a limited sexual equality) were prioritized among Kemal Ataturk's official ideology: "Our enemies claim that Turkey cannot be considered a civilized nation because she consists of two separate parts: men and women. Can we shut our eyes to one portion of a group? The road of progress must be trodden by both sexes together marching arm in arm" (quoted in Abadan-Unat 1991). The early republican state under the leadership of Ataturk passed laws and implemented policies aimed at redefining women's social and legal status and the relationship between men and women.

Polygamy, the segregation of sexes, traditional arranged marriages, and divorce laws leading to easy repudiation of wives were seen as the major obstacles preventing the enlightenment and liberation of women (Sirman 1989). As the leaders of the nation tried to create a Turkish as opposed to an Ottoman identity, they contended with the power of Islam. These reforms were directed at undermining the basic Islamic way of life that formed the legal basis of the Ottoman state (Tekeli 1981:144). Thus, in 1926, a modified version of the Swiss civil code was adopted. Monogamy was declared the only officially recognized form of marital union, and women were given the right to initiate divorce.

Gender relations, however, were conceived of in terms of complementarity, not equality. This distinction appears clearly in the civil code. According to the code, the husband is the head of the family and he alone has the right to choose a domicile. Furthermore, according to a clause that, thanks to feminists, was revoked by the constitutional court in 1992, a woman may not obtain gainful employment without the consent of her husband. Compulsory universal primary education—for both sexes—was introduced early on, and in 1934 women received the right to vote and to seek election in general elections (Abadan-Unat 1990, 1991). Legal reforms and the granting of political rights to women were the products of efforts by the modernizing elite, not the women themselves. The strong point of Kemalism was that it drew on educated, modernized, Westernized cadres to represent and impose modernity. The existing state machinery and the popular conception of the state as an authoritarian protector of the populous also helped solidify modernity's hold on Turkish society, despite its contradictions and despite, as Sibel Bozdoğan and Reşat Kasaba (1997) comment, "how shallow Turkey's 'civilizational shift' from Islam to the West has actually been." "Institutional, ritual, symbolic, and aesthetic manifestations of modernity," they point out, "have become constituent elements of the Turkish collective consciousness since the 1920s" (5).

The emancipation of women from the constrictions of tradition was a prerequisite to the successful transition to the modern nation that the Kemalists envisioned. Since women themselves did not consciously seek such major modifications in the position of women, however, this reform is referred to as "state feminism." During the debate about the value of these reforms that began with the resurgence of fundamentalist Islam in the 1980s, it was generally agreed that women were used as symbolic pawns in the process of nation building (Kandiyoti 1989; Sirman 1989)[26] and that women—excluding the urban elite—did not benefit from legal efforts to improve their position in society. As the experience of masses of women from different quarters reveals, these imposed reforms did not in any simple way guarantee the liberation of women.

Despite free and compulsory primary education, the literacy rate still reflects a wide gender gap: 72 percent of women are literate, compared with 89 percent of men (KSSGM 1998:5). This gap increases at higher levels of education: 54 percent of middle-school graduates are women, compared with 75 percent of men, and only 42 percent of those with higher education are women. Yet, the proportion of female students in universities is large (39 percent in 1996–97, according to Women's KSSGM 1998:8), indicating a growing number of university-educated women. Also, a significant proportion of women pursue training for professions in medicine, engineering, and communications. In 1997, women represented 41 percent, 23 percent, and 56 percent, respectively, of those enrolled in these subjects (KSSGM 1998:8–9). The proportion of women in academia is also high (33 percent).

Although Turkey has seen a shift from rural to urban employment for both men and women over the past three decades, women's participation in economic production still occurs predominantly in agriculture, where they work as "unpaid family laborers." In 1955, 96 percent of women were engaged in agriculture. This figure dropped to 79 percent in 1985 and 37 percent in 1997. Nonagricultural participation rose to 21 percent in 1985 from 5 percent in 1955 (Özbay 1990).

According to statistics, women's labor force participation declined significantly, from the 72.1 percent of women economically active in 1955 to 32.7 percent in 1985 (Özbay 1995). This decline can be attributed to such factors as the decreasing significance of agricultural production in the Turkish economy that led to the massive migration of rural populations to urban areas in the 1960s and 1970s. Yet the conclusion that women's participation in the labor force has declined might be unwarranted, because there is no reliable information about the extent and forms of women's unregistered participation in the informal work force. Studies conducted in the 1980s on women's informal occupations in urban settings do suggest that the labor of migrant women was becoming increasingly informalized (Çınar 1991; White 1991). Piecework and workshop production of textile and leather garments for international markets boomed in that decade under export-oriented economic policies (White 1991).

The Turkish urban labor force shows a marked gender differentiation. Only 16.5 percent of the female population in metropolitan areas was employed in 1994. This distribution of the female urban labor force suggests, on one hand, a high proportion of unskilled female labor (about half of the total), and, on the other hand, abundant highly qualified professional female labor. In 1985, 29.4 percent of those employed in professions were women (UNICEF 1991), but women were relatively absent from semi-skilled occupations. One study (Öncü 1981) suggests that one in every five practicing lawyers in Turkey is female, and that one in every six practicing doctors is female. About one-third of the lawyers listed in the İstanbul Bar Association in 1978 were female.

Ayşe Öncü (1981) argues that the higher proportion of professional women found in Turkey than is found in most Western industrial countries can be explained by recruitment patterns initiated by the Kemalist reforms and state policies that aimed at expanding the professional classes and actively filling the ranks of the professions with women. This initiative perpetuated itself through the systematic recruitment of professional women with elite backgrounds. Kandiyoti (1997) adds, however, that recruitment of these women into professions was a way of preventing the recruitment of men of humble peasant origin and thus to insure the continuity of a homogenous state elite. Öncü (1981) also links the significant number of women in professions to the availability of a large pool of female migrant labor in cities. Inexpensive domestic workers enable middle- and upper-class women to combine their career and family roles without disrupting the existing gender division of labor in their family (see also Erkut 1982).

As studies of squatter women conducted in the late 1970s indicate, migration of peasant women often results in their "housewifeization." In one author's harsh words, they become "[self- and] home-decorating machines" (Şenyapılı 1981b:214). During the first wave of migration in the early 1950s, the demand for male labor was low because of the insufficient development of the industrial and service sectors in urban areas. Some squatter women therefore had to work in domestic service for the expanding numbers of newly employed middle-class women. This work was generally considered temporary, ceasing once the women's husbands found secure and stable jobs. Two representative surveys conducted in the squatter settlements of Ankara and Istanbul in 1976–77 found that only four out of eighty-one employed female members of the Istanbul squatter households and two out of sixty in the Ankara households were working as domestic workers in private homes (Şenyapılı 1981:211, table IX). Women's participation in both formal and informal sectors was low —only 5.5 percent of women between 15 and 64 years of age in Istanbul and 6.0 percent in Ankara. The low level of employment among women is explained partly by the concentration of working women 25 years old and younger. Female participation in the work force was limited to unmarried daughters of migrant families, who entered and then left the work force after marriage (Kandiyoti 1982). This trend is further explained by the low pay and low prestige of women's jobs and by the relatively stable and high income of factory-worker husbands, who owed their good wages to successful labor movements. In Turkey, during the 1970s, unionized workers received higher wages than civil servants. Furthermore, wages in the organized sector in Turkey were probably higher than those of any comparable developing country in that period (Keyder 1979).

Women's positions in Turkey's agricultural sector have become more diverse since the 1950s with increased mechanization and the commodification of production.[27] Studies of rural women in agricultural production systems offer similar descriptions of the organization of production and women's places within these systems (Berik 1987; Kandiyoti 1990; Sirman 1988). All reveal that although female labor is central to the production process in a predominantly household-based peasant economy, this production system is characterized by the absence of autonomous female economic activity and independent female earnings. Women's many economic activities, whether in the form of agricultural production, small-scale manufacturing, or husbandry, are organized under a patriarchal structure of authority. Women are central actors in the formation and maintenance of the kinship and intra-household relationships upon which production operations rely, but they have no independent access to the market and depend on men's representation. Furthermore, when women are employed as wage laborers or in small-scale manufacturing, such as carpet weaving, their wages are negotiated by and paid to the head of the household, and, as a result, women have no control over cash flow.

Since the early 1970s, Turkish scholars interested in the question of modernization and its impact on the family have focused on the replacement of a posited traditional extended family with a nuclear one deemed the epitome of modernization (Kıray 1964; Kongar 1972; Magneralla 1972; Timur 1972). This approach reduced the description of the family to an enumeration of the number of individuals living together, confusing the concepts of family and household. Furthermore, authority relations within this unit were taken as a given. The main goal of these scholars was to gauge the extent of modernization, measured in terms of similarities between the Turkish family and a presumed Western model. Thus, the widespread existence of nuclear family households, especially in urban areas, has been taken as a sure sign of the modernization of the family structure.

According to the results of the first nationwide survey conducted in 1968, the patriarchal extended family constituted only about one-fifth of all households in Turkey (Timur 1972). They were relatively more common in the villages (25.4 percent) than in metropolitan areas (4.6 percent), indicating a change of family structure with urbanization and modernization. Furthermore, it was pointed out that the ownership of land was the determining factor encouraging the constitution of extended patriarchal families of two generations in rural areas. While landless agricultural families were predominantly nuclear (79 percent), extended patriarchal families were more common among rich landholders (58 percent).

Data concerning past forms of family and household structure in Turkey have only recently been studied systematically, however, and many of the early assumptions about changes in family structure associated with modernization were based on conclusions drawn from a few monographs on villages written in the 1940s and early 1950s (Berkes 1942; Boran 1945; Yasa 1953), all of which reported that patriarchal extended family life was the norm in Turkish village households. More recent historical work on the demographic and structural trends of Ottoman and Turkish families between 1880 and 1940 (Duben and Behar 1991), however, offers a detailed description of family and household structure and debunks the patriarchal extended family argument. These researchers found that households in preindustrial Turkey had a rather simple structure and, in fact, mostly included nuclear families (Duben and Behar 1991). Patriarchal extended families, in both Istanbul and Anatolia, were common only among upper-class families.

Nationwide studies undertaken in the 1980s indicate an increasing proportion of nuclear households in Turkey (Esmer, Fişek, and Kalaycıoğlu 1986; HIPS 1989; Özbay 1989). The most distinctive factor differentiating present patriarchal extended families from past examples is that they are found predominantly among lower classes, indicating that the social and economic basis of patriarchal extended families has changed.

Ferhunde Özbay's extensive review (1989) of studies undertaken in the 1980s on household and family structure led her to conclude that household size, structure, and composition in Turkey is now contingent upon changing economic circumstances and that the establishment of extended households should be regarded as a survival strategy. She argues that the emergence of such households was prompted by the need to overcome economic uncertainty and does not represent a "traditional life style," especially in urban areas (16). She further demonstrates that the nuclear family is the normative choice of the majority of the Turkish families. Yet, beneath the nuclear family structure, mutual aid and affective kinship ties remain very strong in Turkish households (Duben 1982; White 1994).

All of these studies make clear that nonfamily households are extremely rare in Turkey. Marriage and the family are the only legitimate institutions within which sexual and reproductive relationships can take place (Tekeli 1990:151). Very high marriage rates and low divorce rates corroborate this conclusion. Turkish divorce law is one of the most permissive in the world, yet the proportion of divorces in Turkey has never exceeded 2 percent (KSSGM 1995:4) and is lower there than in any other Mediterranean Muslim country (Levine 1982:325). Thus, the family with its economic foundation and patriarchal ideology constitutes a major structural obstacle to women's achieving an identity apart from that of wife and mother.

Even so, the social transformations initiated by the transition from state-controlled capitalism to a privatized and liberalized market economy since the early 1980s have restructured women's relation to the home and altered their traditional ties to domesticity. The structural transformations most relevant to an examination of the relations between middle-class women and domestic workers include the development of the modern public sphere, the rise of new forms of consumption, and changes in the education system (Özbay 1995). This is not to say that old sources of identity, including mothering and housekeeping, have given way to radically new ones. Attention to these changes is necessary to understand the divide between public and private and the changing roles women play in the articulation of class distinctions and social mobility.

By the mid-1980s the liberalized market economy, with its expansion of advertising, mass communications, consumer credit, and commercial leisure, had cultivated an important change in the Turkish urban classes' relationship to consumption, both quantitatively and qualitatively. Changes in consumption are dramatically altering the way in which middle-class women now use their labor and time. The emergence of new consumption sites, such as malls, mega-markets, shopping centers, and department stores that combine leisure, entertainment, and shopping, represent an important example of how an expanding global market economy is changing women's activities outside the home while recasting definitions of female sociability. The immense increase in packaged foods available in Turkey, for example, has led to a corresponding decrease in the amount of time women spend in the kitchen.[28] Women's activities increasingly take place outside the domestic sphere, marking the end of women's sociospatial exclusion from urban public life.

Another equally important transformation taking place in modern Turkish society is the growing privatization of education at all levels, with enduring effects on class stratification and middle-class social mobility. Fierce competition for entrance to the best schools demands parents' close attention to their children's curricular and extra-curricular activities. Parental oversight of education, which now includes identifying and securing private tutors and finding the best prep-class schools, has become a primary preoccupation for both housewives and working mothers.[29] All these activities take women away from the home, expand the public sphere in which they perform motherhood, and put them into new relations of sociability and competition with their peers. It should be stressed here that these new roles entail new definitions of good, successful motherhood while strengthening women's identity as autonomous actors in the public arena.

> The fact that women acquire identity through the family is more clearly defined with the expansion of capitalism. As women shoulder additional responsibilities connected with the social status of the family in 1980s Turkey, they appear to take over from men the capacity to act as family representative. . . . As women identify their social status with that of the family, the rise or fall in status of any member of the family confers new status on them, and gives the impression of social mobility. They consequently direct their activities toward increasing the status of the family, especially that of its male members. (Özbay 1995:109–10)

There is yet another trend, however, that is potentially at odds with women's family-bound class identification: women engage in a very individualized process of self-construction in their focus on bodily health and beauty. The focus for women's consumption is no longer limited to family and class. A growing emphasis on cosmetics and other beauty

products, reinforced by the proliferation of advertising, advice literature, and health and beauty magazines has increasingly changed the
terms of the cultural constitution of female identity. The proliferation of
private gyms (*jimnastik salonları*) and diet centers that cater mainly to
women, especially housewives, also marks an increasing body-cen-
teredness. It signals the emergence of a new feminine self that is centered
on the body. Middle-class women's investments in this domain are made
possible, in large part, by the availability of domestic workers who save
them from physical labor. Moreover, these new cultural practices of femininity also play a key role in accentuating differences in appearance
between "traditional women" (domestic workers) and modern women.
Domestic workers who are deprived of the means of participating in
this individualized body-focused culture do not, however, remain unaf-
fected by it. As I illustrate in the following pages, middle-class women's
investment in modern feminine identities powerfully affects their daily
relationship with domestic labor. It is with such contexts in mind that
we must view the emergence of new modes of femininity and new ways
in which gender and class are articulated through domestic service.
These changes speak to the rapid socioeconomic reconfiguration of
Turkey and, in turn, individual responses to them.

EMPIRICAL FOUNDATION

Four sources of field data—a survey, participant observation, in-depth
interviews, and focus group research—provide the foundation of this
book. The absence of any previous study or data on domestic workers
and the structure of domestic service in Turkey influenced my method
of investigation in important ways. It called for a survey of domestic
workers that would provide a significant amount of reliable information regarding the earnings, work schedules, recruitment patterns, and
household organization and dynamics of domestic workers, about
which very little was known. My aim was not limited, however, to
obtaining information about the extent and forms of women's unregistered participation in domestic service. I wanted to understand subjectivities and self-definitions of domestic workers that emerge from their
experiences with earning wages, confronting modernity and urbanity,
and working for middle-class women. I also wanted to examine the
ways in which gendered social and economic relations embedded in

family-kinship and neighborhood networks regulate the operation of domestic service. These two important dimensions of the study required my collecting intimate accounts of domestic workers and maintaining a sustained involvement in their daily lives. While a survey questionnaire with structured questions is a useful and efficient tool for discovering and accounting for patterned, structured aspects of people's lives, it is limited in two important respects, as stressed by the proponents of qualitative research (Statham, Miller, and Mauksch 1988). A survey cannot easily account for processes, and, by imposing preconceived categories that may have no meaning to the individual, it disregards the individual's definition of the situation. Participant observation and open interviews as well as focus group interviews allowed me to move beyond these limitations.

The fact that a majority of domestic workers in Turkey are wives of doorkeepers allowed me to draw a representative sample. The apartment buildings that house this group of domestic workers and employers provided me with a frame for random sampling (see Appendix for a discussion of sampling procedures).

Avoiding Husbands Who Know Better:
Interviews with Doorkeepers' Wives

Efforts to obtain agreement for interviews with doorkeepers' wives began with an introductory statement that included a brief description of the purpose of the research, emphasizing confidentiality and the scientific nature of the study. I explained the sampling procedure in lay terms to assure them that they were not particularly chosen but selected randomly, "as in a lottery" (*kurada çıkmak*, a common Turkish phrase).[30] Although my fear of rejection never ceased to haunt me throughout the study, the response rate was quite high; the proportion of domestic workers who were contacted and agreed to be interviewed was 93 percent in this group.[31] In fact, initial contact for the survey interview led to many invitations for subsequent visits and sustained interactions with some of the families. Six women from this group later became the subjects of in-depth interviews.

An early consideration in interviewing doorkeepers' wives was the problem of privacy. Because the doorkeeper's job requires him to be home, it was inappropriate to ask the doorkeeper husbands to leave while the interviews were conducted, especially considering that they live in small apartments with one or two rooms. Besides these practical considerations, some of the husbands suggested that they should be the ones interviewed by asserting their authority and superiority, using such reasons as, "I know better than my wife," "I can give better, more correct, reliable answers," or "She's ignorant, illiterate." In some other instances we met husbands who wanted to stay and listen to the interview by invoking the notion of oneness—"We don't have any secrets from each other." Women's own responses to their husbands' attempt to silence them also varied. Some simply remained silent while others hinted at their agreement with their husbands by exhibiting self-doubt about their abilities, mostly conveyed by the expression, "But what would I know?" The latter group of women at the end of the interview usually asked whether their performance had been satisfactory. Yet there were some others who took the initiative and told their husbands that they should leave. It is also important to note that this group of women's responses marked a sharp contrast with those of the women in the squatter settlement group, of whom all but one felt no need to ask their husbands' permission to be interviewed or to explain my presence in their homes in instances when the husband happened to be home.

In response to comments suggesting that the husband should be present, we reemphasized the nature of the research and how important it was for the purpose of the study to get the wife's own account. I also instructed my research assistants that if the husband insisted on staying, they should change the order of some questions, posing, for example, questions about fertility and birth control early on so that the husband would become uncomfortable and leave on his own account. This strategy proved successful, and in no case did we have to complete the entire interview in the presence of a husband. The interviews with door-keepers' wives started in November 1989 and ended in July 1990. All the interviews, with few exceptions, took place in the home of the respondent. The interviews lasted on average ninety minutes and ranged from forty-five minutes to three hours.[32]

Interviews with Squatter Settlement Women

The interviews with the squatter settlement women were completed between May and July 1990. My initial plan was to start interviewing the squatter settlement group on Sundays in early January. However, weather and the practical constraints of squatter settlement life made this plan impossible. After several visits to the squatter settlement neighborhood Nato Yolu in early January, I realized that achieving privacy would be impossible. At that time of year, when all the homes in squatter settlement neighborhoods are heated with coal stoves, only the room with the stove, usually the living room, is habitable because of the bonechilling cold. Since I was treated as a guest, I was unable to persuade the respondents to move to another room or the kitchen so we could conduct the interviews in private. Even if I had been successful, the relocation would have created an uncomfortable situation in which respondents would have been inclined to give quick answers.

Besides, I realized that Sunday visits were not always appropriate. In most families, Sundays are set aside for heating the thermosyphon (if there is one) so the family can have running hot water for baths and the women can do laundry.

During the cold-weather months, although visiting and interviewing went on as the research progressed and friendships formed and consolidated, making contact seemed to be especially difficult in Nato Yolu and Oran, because the women from these neighborhoods spend long hours traveling to and from work. When they get home, it is already dark, and so in a few instances when I did stay late, the male members of the family escorted me to the bus stop, despite my gentle objections. To avoid imposing this extra burden, I decided to wait until early May to continue the research when the days would be longer and transportation easier.

In this group, only two domestic workers out of a total of sixty-one, to whom I was referred by their friends, refused to be interviewed. One of them declined because of the length of interview and the other one, a Kurdish woman who was a recent migrant, feared that I might be researching her political views.[33]

The interviews with this group averaged a little over one hour and ranged from twenty minutes (an incomplete interview) to two hours. The majority of the interviews took place in the homes of domestic workers and most were completed in a single visit. I also conducted in-depth interviews with four women in this group.

Participant Observation

For another source of field data, I took part in many informal gatherings of domestic workers for drinking tea and chatting. I was also

invited to circumcision and wedding ceremonies and to women's periodic "acceptance-day" (*kabul günü*) gatherings. I spent a considerable
amount of time in their homes, casually socializing, watching television, and eating meals with them, their husbands and children, and
their neighbors. Some of the domestic workers also visited my home.
My interaction with these women, in some important respects, resem-
bled the kinds of interaction carried on between close neighbors. I
became a "neighbor" by virtue of my constant presence in their communities. This status allowed for considerable informality: participating in daily routines without setting-up particular meeting times and
without radically interrupting the rhythm of work or leisure. For example, I assisted women as they folded laundry, prepared food, and bar-
gained with the street peddlers. On a few occasions I accompanied
them on visits to a doctor's office or to stores. As they shared their
lives with me, I told them about my life. They often questioned me
about life in the United States and my anomalous position as a married but childless woman. Their comforting remarks, such as, "Who
knows, Gul, one day you might find yourself pregnant," made it clear
to me that I was not able to convince them that I chose to be childless.
All these interactions not only allowed me a deeper understanding of
the fabric of their lives but also provided valuable information on the
establishment and maintenance of informal social networks among
domestic workers.

Focus Group Interviews

I used focus group interviews with domestic workers to corroborate
data developed in the survey. I planned two focus group interviews,
one with the doorkeeper group and the other with the squatter settlement group, but only one was successful. Both times I invited a group
of wives of doorkeepers to my apartment no one came. Why they did
not attend, whether because something indeed came up as they claimed
or their husbands did not allow them to go, will remain unknown. The
focus group interview with eight domestic workers in the squatter settlement group whom I previously had interviewed, however, took
place in one of the participant's home. My role was to bring up certain
key issues that had emerged in the preliminary analysis of the survey
data and to generate discussion on these issues, rather than to pose specific questions.

Focus group interviews were also conducted with eighteen employers representing three different groups of employing women, with six women in each group. I designed focus group interviews with employers as an ancillary aspect of the study to explore a range of issues entailed as women of different classes come into contact in domestic service, as well as to explore the effect hiring a domestic worker has on gender role negotiations in her family. The questions dealt with the privatized nature of the labor relations, social security benefits, and issues of wages, patronage, recruitment, and the double day.

I conjectured that work relationships and how the domestic worker comes to define herself with respect to her employer would be different for each of three main groups of employers, feminist women, professional women, and full-time housewives. The six, self-identified, feminist women are all active in the feminist movement in Turkey. Three are university professors, one is a housewife, and two hold executive positions. The six professional women included an architect, two lawyers, a high school teacher, and two executives. Of the housewives, all from the upper-middle class, two had had paid work in the past but were currently full-time homemakers.[34]

Although it is not possible in any measurable way to determine the level of sincerity achieved in the survey, I believe that a high degree of sincerity and openness on the part of the respondents was achieved. The traditional sociological insight on this crucial aspect of the data-gathering process tells us that people have a tendency to confide in a stranger in ways they never would with those they know and, therefore, the position of the researcher as a stranger produces sincerity when it is coupled with assurance of complete discretion. I believe that the openness and sincerity of the respondents in this study can be explained by this general principle in only a broad sense. There is another factor to be considered.

Mirra Komarovsky (1967) argues that the respondents' openness and sincerity signifies the absence of what she calls "the capacity to be an object to oneself" (15), a kind of psychological sophistication that allows one to imagine the attitude of the other. In the course of an interview, it describes the respondent's strategy: responding to a question while at the same time taking on the role of interviewer, imagining the interviewer's attitude and reaction and thereby manufacturing the answer accordingly. While I would not venture to attribute lack of such sophistication to my respondents, it still seems that the possibility of manufacturing insincere answers by the respondents was reduced by the fact that for all the women in the sample, this was their very first experience with a scientific study. They had no preconceived ideas about how to "properly" present themselves to me and no knowledge about my position to guess what constituted a desirable answer.

2 Husbands, Households, and Other Determinants of Women's Work

"Let's eat less rather than you work." With these words Sevim Belgan's husband conveyed his discontent when five years ago she first expressed her desire to join the ranks of domestic work to help him financially.[1] Sevim's husband, a driver in a government office, finally gave in but allows her to work only for a particular employer who is from the same city as he. She now commutes twice a week from her home in one of the squatter settlement districts to a middle-class neighborhood. Meral Kazan's husband, a postal worker, used the phrase "Women's employment equals prostitution" to make the point that he will never consent to her employment outside the home. She now has a busy, clandestine work life: five times a week she traverses boundaries of her squatter neighborhood to work in several middle-class homes, without the knowledge and consent of her husband, who thinks that his wife is at home making and selling lace for neighborhood clients. In contrast, Fatma Gülseven, wife of a doorkeeper and a veteran domestic worker who for fourteen years has been taking the stairs from her basement apartment to the apartments upstairs, recalls that her entry into domestic wage work was a predictable and natural step for her after she and her husband settled down in one of the middle-class apartment buildings of Ankara. "My husband asked me back in the village whether I would do household work in the homes of tenants if we moved here and he became doorkeeper. I said yes. And then when he was asked by a tenant, he came and asked me again."

Other women of the squatter settlements in this study recounted tension-filled conversations like those of Sevim Belgan and Meral Kazan and even violent incidents that occurred when they sought to persuade their husbands to allow them to earn wages in domestic service. The difficulty they had in obtaining their husbands' consent figured prominently in the narratives of every woman in the squatter group when they talked about how they became domestic workers. The stories illustrate powerfully that poverty is not a great dissolver of patriarchy. Economic hardship in many urban households does not erode deep-seated male objections to women's employment. Furthermore, husbands' opposition to their wives' employment effectively restricts the supply of domestic labor from squatter settlements. Despite the high demand for their labor by middle-class households, women of the squatter settlements, a logical and abundant pool of domestic workers (in 1980, 70 percent of the population of Ankara lived in squatter settlements), overwhelmingly remain outside both the formal and the informal work force.

Fatma Gülseven's unproblematic incorporation into domestic service is directly related to her being the wife of a doorkeeper. In stark contrast to the squatter settlement husbands, doorkeeper husbands mediate their wives' recruitment into domestic work. Indeed, Fatma's easy incorporation provides the answer to a larger question of this study: why doorkeepers' wives monopolize the domestic supply market in Turkey. Husbands' doorkeeping jobs, by virtue of their residential base, bring the "supply" and "demand" sides of domestic labor closer spatially and allow husbands to maintain protective and paternalistic control over their wives' participation in this area of informal work. The intimacy of their connection to urban classes—their "outsider within" position in the urban space—does not challenge constraints on female spatial mobility and conventional male objections to women's waged employment. Thus, migrant women are available for urban work when restrictions on their spatial mobility remain undisturbed and their husbands can directly regulate their labor. It is not striking, therefore, that during the time of the study 86 percent of doorkeepers' wives (selected according to a representative sample) were employed as domestic workers. The strong link between the doorkeepers' wives' entry into domestic service and their positioning in the urban middle-class neighborhoods is also underscored by the entry profiles of domestic workers I studied from the squatter settlement group. In fact, twenty-five of them had a doorkeeper past: they had begun working when their husbands were employed as doorkeepers.

Turkish women's low level of participation in the work force has been amply documented. What I seek to emphasize here is that opposing voices of husbands in the migrant households give shape and form to far wider societal processes. The centrality of male power in generating particular configurations of gender and class dynamics is particularly apparent in the organization of domestic service and its social relations. Patriarchal control over migrant women's labor makes their labor expensive and scarce and actively reduces middle-class women's ability to purchase cheap, readily available domestic wage labor. In a sense, husbands "protect" their wives against blatant forms of class exploitation. Migrant women's gender subordination affords them that "protection." In other third world countries domestic service is performed primarily by young, single women who migrate alone to urban centers and constitute a large supply of cheap labor (Chaney and Castro 1989; Duarte 1989; Hondagneu-Sotelo and Avila 1997; Jelin 1977; Kuznesof 1989). The abundant supply of labor in these countries sustains live-in domestic service and inhibits the development of contractual employer-employee relationships. Patriarchy in Turkey, however, by controlling women's labor, has helped to modernize domestic service. Prohibitions on female mobility, wage earning, and independence that have limited the labor supply have rendered live-in domestic help impractical. Domestic labor, therefore, is performed as day work for multiple employers and organized more on a contractual basis than is domestic work in other developing countries. Tradition in Turkey engenders modern forms of labor relations.

In this chapter I focus on the individual characteristics of domestic workers and the characteristics of their households. My examination of their work schedules and histories shows that employment in domestic service is stable and continuous: it is not a mere survival strategy or a transition to other occupations. I also look at the relation between doorkeeping and migrant women's entrance into the labor market and demonstrate that the key factor prohibiting women's participation in domestic service or any other form of employment is the husband's traditional opposition rather than women's childcare or other domestic responsibilities. By bringing together the supply and demand sides of domestic labor, the institution of doorkeeping allows doorkeeper husbands to oversee their wives' participation in the domestic work force. Thus, the wives' urban employment is experienced as a continuation of, rather than a radical departure from, traditional (rural) work.

BECOMING A DOMESTIC WORKER

Doorkeepers' Wives' Story

For rural migrant families, a doorkeeping post provides a secure livelihood with social insurance coverage, rent-free accommodation in a middle-class neighborhood, and access to jobs in which a wife can earn wages under carefully defined conditions.[2] These families are drawn to urban areas by word-of-mouth news about doorkeeping jobs. New openings for door-keeping jobs are neither advertised in newspapers nor registered in the Labor Placement Office, and therefore when the possibility of a job open-ing arises, doorkeepers pass on the information to relatives or neighbors from their hometown who have been searching for such a position (see Levine 1973a). In this way, each middle- and upper-middle-class neigh-borhood in which doorkeeper families settle develops a "regional" iden-tity. The territorial concentration in the urban landscape of migrants from a single village, town, or region is similar to the pattern observed in squat-ter settlements, where each district or neighborhood is composed of rural migrants from the same region (A. Ayata 1989; Duben 1982).[3] These net-works not only facilitate migrant men's entry into doorkeeping jobs but also provide community standards supporting migrant women's employ-ment in domestic service. Sisters, sisters-in-law, aunts, cousins, and other relatives, close or distant, who earlier joined the ranks of the domestic work force help newcomers enter the domestic labor market. The experi-enced workers become role models for the new workers as they frame their own work and family lives in the new urban environment. Paralleling the incidence of doorkeepers' working in the immediate neighborhood of rel-atives and fellow townsmen, a high proportion of domestic workers (79 percent) also have female relatives or fellow townsmen working nearby.[4] In short, the prior existence of these relationships and constitution of domestic work as an acceptable occupation for wives of doorkeepers prove to be crucial for shaping the terms in which new migrant families think about their situation and strategize about their changing life circumstances.

Although the high demand for household labor plays a critical role in encouraging the wives of doorkeepers to enter domestic service, migrant families also actively seek such opportunities. There is no hap-hazard elective affinity between the doorkeeper's job and his wife's working as domestic worker. Half of the domestic workers reported that when their husbands became doorkeepers they had already planned to take domestic work. In fact, the availability of wage work for women in the form of employment in domestic service under these specific conditions might be a strong motivation for a family's becom-ing a doorkeeping family in the first place. It might also extend to their migration decisions; some families must have migrated specifically with the objective of finding doorkeeper and domestic work. Although this study does not include an analysis of the dynamics of migration, a multidimensional and complex issue, some in-depth interviews suggest that the availability of domestic work for wives did play a central role in the decision to migrate and become a doorkeeping family.[5]

The near simultaneity of the husbands' entry into doorkeeping and the wives' entry into domestic work in two- thirds of the cases supports the claim that these families came to settle down with the intention of securing wage work for the wife. Sixty-five percent of the domestic workers entered the occupation within one year of their husband's entry into doorkeeping. Twenty-one percent entered between one and five years after their husbands became doorkeepers. In only 10 percent of the cases did six or more years elapse before wives entered the domestic labor force.[6]

In doorkeeper families the wife's employment in waged domestic work is part of a planned strategy rather than an accidental extension of the husband's job. The hiring of doorkeepers does not also entail hiring a domestic worker for the apartment building. First, recruitment of the wives as domestic workers is never the direct result of a formal, legally binding agreement between employers (owners or managers of the apartment building) and the doorkeeper husband himself. That is, his wife's availability and willingness to work as a domestic worker for the tenants is not a precondition for the husband to secure his job.[7] The relatively high percentage (23 percent, or 24 cases out of 103) of domestic workers who have no in-house employers but work exclusively for employers in other buildings in the surrounding neighborhood suggests that informal pressure is either absent or effectively countered. And in some cases there may be no demand for in-house domestic workers at a given time.

To understand the interactions between doorkeeping, domestic service, and middle-class tenants it is instructive to look at some situations where in-house employment is absent. The following examples illuminate the kind of strategies employed by domestic workers and their husbands in responding to perceived pressure by tenants seeking domestic help. One of the workers explained that she does not work for tenants in her own building to avoid possible conflicts: "My husband does not allow me to work for the tenants. He said, 'If you work for some and not work for others, they will get annoyed [darılırlar].'" He

informed his tenants at the outset: "My wife is already working for outside employers; she cannot work for you." The doorkeeper's mediation
reflects his desire not to jeopardize his relationship with some of his own
employers (the tenants). Another domestic worker's explanation reveals
a concern on the part of the husband that working for the tenants might
transform the pattern of his wife's employment: "My husband does not
want me to work for the tenants because he says they could call you any
time (night or day), whenever they need you, to do dishes, et cetera.
They would make you work on a task basis." In contrast to the preceding cases, one domestic worker talked about receiving pressure from
her husband to work for the tenants. She stated, "My husband says that
[tenants] pressure him because I'm not working for them, and he thinks
I ought to work for them, because he says our bread is provided by
them." Another domestic worker described her direct confrontation
with the tenants: "They keep pressuring me to work for them. I already
have enough employers. I told them I have a small kid; I can't take up
more work. But they are so ruthless and selfish. They say lock up the
kid and work also for us, as if my child is not a child like theirs."

   All of these comments make clear that there are continuing tensions
in this husband-mediated encounter between the two sides of labor
supply and demand.

Squatter Settlement Women's Story

When we examine the ways in which squatter settlement women enter
domestic service we see a very different pattern. Many squatter settlement women remain outside both modern and informal labor forces
because they lack permission from their husbands for employment
(squatter settlement women's labor force participation in Ankara was 6
percent, according to Senyapili 1981b:209).[8] Of the fifty-seven women I
studied in the squatter settlement group, twenty-five (44 percent)
entered domestic service when their husbands worked as doorkeepers
and continued to work after their husbands changed to a different occupation. In fact, many of these women continue to work for the same
employers in the apartment house in which they had worked and
resided as part of a doorkeeping family. This group's work history is
similar to that of the majority of domestic workers in the doorkeeper
group, who entered domestic service about the same time that their
husbands began doorkeeping.

Two distinct profiles emerge from the work histories of the squatter settlement workers. The dominant profile consists of nineteen cases (60 percent): six or more years elapsed between the time these women arrived in Ankara and the time they entered domestic service (between six and twenty-five years, with a mean of thirteen years). The second profile consists of eleven cases (34 percent): these women entered domestic service immediately upon arriving in Ankara. Sevim Belgan, Hatice Feryal, and Nazmiye Demiral fit the dominant profile.

Sevim Belgan, introduced in the opening paragraph, continues to hear her husband say, "Let's eat less rather than you work." Only when she found an employer through her cousin who is also a domestic worker, however, did he consent but on the condition that she not work for other families. Although Sevim wants to increase her workdays, her employer does not need her more than twice a week. She thinks that she could persuade her husband to let her work full-time with social insurance coverage if she could find work in a traditionally female-dominated field, such as seamstress work in clothing manufacturing.

Sevim Belgan's decision to work has been limited by special conditions that dictate for whom she can work, where she can work, and the hours she can work. In this case the husband's consent for the wife's employment is not given once and for all but is subject to specifications and further negotiation. Indeed, employment in domestic service offers the flexibility of choosing and changing employers, but this flexibility assumes that the women in fact choose their own circumstances of work and elements of work situations in a way that eliminates the conditions that would be incongruous with their husband's definition of proper employment.

Hatice Feryal's husband, like Sevim Belgan's husband, initially opposed his wife's seeking employment. Hatice Feryal migrated to Ankara fifteen years ago but started to work only three years ago when her children were aged 14, 11, and 10. Her entry into domestic service coincided with her oldest son's graduation from middle school and a time when the family faced severe economic hardship because of the cost of building their house. Her husband, who is a night watchman in a government office building, did not want his son to further his education. Instead, Hatice's husband decided that his son should earn wages to contribute to the family finances. Hatice Feryal says this decision created a turning point because she very much wanted her son to have an education. She decided that she rather than her son should earn wages. She found her first job with the aid of a neighbor who was also a domestic worker. But she spent a month in constant struggle to get the consent of her husband.

Hatice Feryal, like Sevim Belgan, is working but with conditions. Her husband monitors her travel to and from work. He calls her work in the morning to see whether she arrived on time and again later to learn at what time she will leave and arrive home.

The dynamic and fluid nature of the husband's consent is also illustrated in Nazmiye Demiral's case, where we more clearly see that permission to work is not given in response to financial pressures but is produced by the configuration of different factors over the course of the life cycle. Nazmiye Demiral, a young woman (aged 31) with three children (two daughters aged 11 and 8 and a son aged 5), is the wife of a welder. She first came to Ankara right after her marriage thirteen years ago. For three years her husband could not find work in his trade but had to work in a small bakery (*fırın*) until finally obtaining a job in one of the largest construction companies in Turkey that took them to a small eastern town for eight years. Two years ago the job brought them back to Ankara. During their first three years in Ankara, when the family was economically insecure, Nazmiye Demiral wanted to work but her husband would not allow her to. Although her family got by with difficulty after their relocation in Ankara, she never thought again about working until she had an encounter with a street peddler a year later from whom she wanted to buy a warm-up suit (*eşortman*) required for her daughter's physical education class. She described how this encounter galvanized her decision to pursue wage work: "I was bargaining with this street peddler [*eskici*—one who goes door-to-door to buy and sell second-hand goods, mostly clothes] for a lousy set of warm-ups, [but] he did not want to sell them to me. I felt so humiliated. At that moment it occurred to me that if I worked I could have bought a brand-new warm-up suit for my daughter."

This time she faced no opposition from her husband, a change she attributed to his having the right kind of (*makul*) friends at work. His consent must also have been due to his having two sisters and two sisters-in-law who already were employed in domestic work by that time. Her husband does not get involved in her choice of employers, but he threatens to withdraw his consent if she comes home late from work.

There are also two cases among women who entered domestic service six or more years after moving to Ankara but whose strategies of entry into paid employment are not typical. Because of their husbands' fierce opposition to their employment, these two women hide their employment from them. This strategy is not possible for women in the doorkeeper group and for most women in the squatter settlement group.

Nurten Hanioğlu, a 31-year-old woman, is the only domestic worker in the study who has a middle-school diploma. Her family came to Ankara when she was 6 years old. She married when she was 20. Her husband is a state employee who spends his salary on drinking and gambling. His irregular contribution to the household budget is insufficient to cover the cost of basic food. She says that every time she demands his permission to work (because her children eat nothing but bread), he repeats his motto, "If I bring home money then you eat, if I don't then you starve." She manages to work two days a week in order to feed her three daughters (aged 11, 9, and 6) but whenever he suspects that she is working, he beats her.

Meral Kazan, a 37-year-old woman, has also been working without the knowledge of her husband, who equates women's employment with prostitution. Like Nurten Hanioglu's husband, he rarely gives his wife housekeeping money and spends his earnings on his mistress. Meral is currently working secretly five days a week while also making lace, on the side, at home (with the consent of her husband).[9] Her oldest son (20 years old) is a technician in a government office. She also has a 19-year-old daughter who is trying to get into a college and a 15-year-old son who goes to high school. In both cases, the husband's absences from home—Nurten Hanioğlu says her husband uses their home only as a hotel, and Meral Kazan's husband sometimes does not show up for days at a time—allow these women to maintain their clandestine work lives.

All eleven of the squatter women who began domestic work immediately upon migrating to Ankara (with less than one year mean difference between arrival in Ankara and entry into the occupation) began working between 1988 and 1990, a period when the job market for men was very tight, especially for illiterate men. Seven of these women are Kurdish and most belonged to "late-stage" households with a large pool of potential labor. Since there were no employment prospects for male members of the household, the women became the sole earners of the household through their access to employment in domestic service. There is no discernible pattern of difference in men's attitudes about women's employment in these households. Men still oppose their wives' working and allow them to do so only under closely defined circumstances.

Kezban Tur's case highlights various dimensions of entry into the occupation by these recent migrants and provides insights into the nature and expression of the husband's opposition to the wife's employment in cases where deployment of female labor is less problematic. Kezban Tur, a 43-year-old woman who came to Ankara eleven months ago with her newly extended family, including a new daughter-in-law, is a novice domestic worker. Her illiterate husband has not found work since their arrival. Her married son, who is 19, is also unemployed, though he has worked sporadically on construction sites and in a grocery store and is about to depart for his mandatory military service. She has three daughters, aged 18, 16, and 12. Her oldest daughter has a job as a childcare worker in a private home. Her 16-year-old daughter, who had employment caring for an elderly woman, was forced by her father to leave when he refused to let her accompany her employer for the summer vacation in a sea resort town. She is currently looking for a similar job, but one that her father will favor. Kezban Tur's new daughter-in-law is also in the process of becoming a domestic worker; she recently began accompanying her mother-in-law to work with the dual purpose of receiving training and easing Kezban's work schedule. Kezban described taking a firm hand to make her entry into the occupation.

> The first time I came to Ankara to take my daughter to the hospital to arrange for her eye operation, we stayed with relatives and saw that women like me were working and earning wages. I thought I could also work. So I decided to accompany my husband when he came to Ankara, although he did not want me to. He still regrets my coming here and working and keeps saying, "Why did you come, you should have stayed back in the village." I say I came, and I am going to continue to work and have my daughters work. You men should also work to provide your own bread. I told him each one of us should work for ourself.

Compared with the wives of doorkeepers, the majority of the women in the squatter settlement group find entry into paid domestic worker more problematic. Even though they are compelled by financial necessity to work, undertaking paid labor entails conflict between the wife and the husband and complex negotiations and conflicts concerning gender and authority. In struggling to insure the familial and economic authority of their patriarchal positions, husbands try to redefine the meaning of work by constricting the domain of their wives' wage-earning activity.

Undoubtedly, one of the most important manifestations of men's patriarchal control is the power to sanction or forbid their wives' work outside the home. Once a woman enters the domestic labor market, the informal nature of domestic work, with multiple employers and changing schedules, repeatedly presents her husband with opportunities to exercise control over her work. The issue of consent surfaces every time the woman attempts to replace one employer with another or add or delete workdays. Men's authority to grant or withhold consent is part of the micro-social dynamics of work-gender negotiations in all the cases in this study, albeit in different forms of expression and to different degrees. I suggest that we can properly understand such consent only as a process, rather than as something once and for all given or withheld by the husband. Even in cases in which the woman's employment is fully accepted and normalized, the husband still maintains real and symbolic control over the conditions of her employment. Through these repeated instances of wifely obedience and resistance, male assertion of dominance and normative structures of gender are activated and negotiated.

URBAN WORK HISTORIES

Only 4 out of 103 women in the doorkeeper group and 11 out of 57 women in the squatter settlement group had some employment experiences outside domestic service after migrating to Ankara. According to their work histories, these women had very similar experiences. Their stories show with striking clarity what binds women to domestic service by detailing the reasons for their short tenure in other jobs.

Two of the domestic workers in the doorkeeper group who had employment experiences outside the domestic service, Furüzan Baba and Bahriye Tek, tried nondomestic jobs before their husbands became doorkeepers. Furüzan Baba, after moving to Ankara, employed herself making clothes for her neighbors for about four years. One year prior to her husband's entry into doorkeeping, she started stitching jeans in a clothing plant, during which time her mother-in-law took care of her 2-year-old daughter. After working one year, she left the job because, she said, the plant's great distance from her home caused her often to be late for work and thus to receive docked wages.

Bahriye Tek moved to Ankara ten years ago and settled down in a squatter settlement neighborhood with her husband and her two sons (then aged 11 and 10). For three years her husband worked in a government office as a combination cleaner and messenger (*odacı*). During those years, she had two different jobs. She first worked briefly in a crèche and later worked for three months as a cleaning woman in an export-import firm. She left both jobs for the same reason: like Furüzan Baba, she had to spend long hours commuting. To remove their children from the "bad" influences of squatter settlement life, her husband took a doorkeeping post the fourth year of their residence in Ankara. Almost immediately after her husband became a doorkeeper, she moved into domestic service.

Eleven women in the squatter settlement group also had distinct, yet related, experiences in employment outside domestic service. Some started working for wages in jobs outside domestic service and then later entered domestic service, whereas some others took other jobs after having worked in domestic service and later re-entered their former occupation. They all encountered similar constraining circumstances that affected the direction of their work lives and all had to mediate patriarchal constraints.

Aysel Karadeniz, a 33-year-old mother of four children and a stepson, left two jobs in compliance with her husband's wishes. She left an international export firm where she worked six months as a tea maker and server and an association of artists where she worked two years as a cook when they wanted to give her Sosyal Sigorta (Social Insurance) coverage. Her husband's rationale, she said, was, "If you get Sosyal Sigorta coverage, you permanently commit yourself to work; you would never quit but want to work forever." When the family first moved to Ankara seventeen years ago, she also worked as an apprentice for a seamstress for a year in the neighborhood where her husband was a doorkeeper, before moving into domestic service.

Furüzan Doğulu, the mother of a 9- and an 11-year-old, moved to Ankara as a newly married woman twelve years ago. She went straight to work as a domestic worker while her husband worked as a doorkeeper in a job that lasted five years. After they moved to a squatter settlement neighborhood, she continued to work while her husband vacillated between jobs until, with the aid of his wife, he found stable employment as a garbage collector. Last year, despite her husband's fierce objections, which he often expressed by beating her, she worked for six months in a small construction firm answering telephones and cleaning. She left that job because she never received the social insurance coverage and fringe benefits the firm promised her. She decided that a job without social insurance coverage was not worth the unending physical abuse she suffered. She continued to search for a job with social insurance coverage. She found what she called the perfect job—cleaning in a laboratory in a state hospital. One morning in the second month of her new employment, she found that her husband had turned in her resignation without her knowledge. She returned to domestic service.

Kezban Bati also had a short-lived employment experience outside domestic service. Seven years ago she worked as a secretary and receptionist in a tennis club in an upscale neighborhood. Although the job came with social insurance coverage and her husband did not initially have any objection to this kind of employment, he forced her to quit after two months. She explained that her husband could not stand the pressure exerted on him by his father and his older sister, who thought that working in a tennis club among strange men was inappropriate employment for Kezban.

Tülin Kentli's family moved to Ankara when she was 6 years old. She married in Ankara at the age of 19 and a year later had her first child. In the sixth year of her marriage, when her second child was 2 years old, she started her first job as a domestic worker. Three years ago, she found a job in a construction firm making tea and doing light cleaning. A year later she left the firm and moved back into domestic service because the job, though it provided social insurance coverage, paid poorly and irregularly.

This group also includes three domestic workers, Peri Kalp, Aksu Genç, and Zeliye Küçük, who before moving into the domestic service tried other kinds of informal work to earn wages. Peri Kalp did piecework for a clothing company (*konfeksiyon*) for two months. She knitted sweaters but found the work very tiring; she explained that it was even more exhausting than cleaning other people's houses because her arms ached so badly when she knitted all day. Aksu Genç tried self-employment for a year. She did knitting along with embroidery, but her main clientele were friends and neighbors who, like her, were poor and could not provide many orders. Zeliye Küçük made lace for her neighbors when her children were small, but the work provided only supplementary income.

The accounts above reveal two important elements common to the urban employment experiences of the fifteen women: their experiences were all confined to a very narrow range of occupations and their employment in these positions was short term. The major type of employment was cleaning offices. None of the women had any employment experience of a nondomestic character. Cleaning and making and serving tea in modern workplaces (offices, hospitals, clubs, crèches, and dormitories) are the only areas of employment outside of domestic service open to these women who have limited educations.[10] The kinds of jobs they held well reflect the type of labor demand available for "unskilled" female workers in Ankara, where there is a marked absence of industrial employment.

Before entering domestic service, a few of the women also created their own income opportunities by practicing their gendered skills in knitting, lace making, and sewing. Such work is unprofitable, however, given a clientele of low-income neighbors and relatives. Unlike Istanbul, where export-oriented industries make use of home-based female labor (women producing products in their homes) in squatter settlement neighborhoods, Ankara lacks subcontracting work.

Most of the women worked in firms (almost invariably construction firms) situated on the border between the informal and the formal sector, operating outside of labor regulations in their hiring of unskilled migrant labor. They were not protected by minimum wage legislation and did not have access to social insurance coverage. Despite the similarity of much of the work to domestic work in private homes, these women distinguish between work that is protected by labor legislation and provides social insurance coverage and work that remains outside the framework of government legislation. Access to social insurance coverage that entails the fringe benefits of health coverage and severance pay is provided only by a formal job. As I show in Chapter 3, such benefits are profoundly important even though domestic service is better paid. Conditions prevailing in the firms in which these women worked—irregular payment, low wages, and broken promises about social insurance coverage—diminished the worthiness of this type of employment compared with domestic service and were a prime determinant of women's short tenure and their subsequent re-entry into domestic service.

Women's unpaid work and other responsibilities in the reproductive sphere, conventionally thought to be important determinants of married women's movement into and out of paid work, do not emerge as significant factors in shaping the work histories of these women or of any of the other women in my sample. More specifically, their short job tenure did not stem from a conflict between family and work roles, from a failure to design a better strategy of combining those roles. Instead, patriarchal constraints entangled with certain characteristics of employment impose significant obstacles on the direction of their work lives. The absence of lasting, permanent employment in their work histories is frequently related to the male resistance they encountered in their attempt to define their employment strategies autonomously. In some instances, husbands manifested a deep ambivalence, if not outright opposition, toward their wives' employment in those areas and, thus, the women were forced to return to domestic service.

PROTECTING WOMEN: PATERNALISTIC CONSTRAINTS ON WOMEN'S WORK

The stories of squatter women who overcame their husbands' objections and became domestic workers raise many questions. Why is women's employment such a contested issue among rural migrant families? Why are women not allowed to sell their labor power for a cash wage? Why are women unable to take on fully the classic attributes of a free wage laborer, defined by Marx (1976:273) as possessed of the ability to "dispose his labor power as his own commodity"?[11] Why are women discouraged and even banned from taking some form of social insurance that entails security for old age? Why is the discussion of women's employment focused on women's sexuality?

Patriarchal control over female labor has often been explained as a result of the breadwinner system, under which a woman's life-long domesticity and her economic and social dependence on her husband are based on the masculine role of provider. While I do not deny the importance of the relationship between performance of a provider role and the power deriving from that role, the breadwinner model becomes problematic when applied to the families I studied. First, as many other scholars have noted, we cannot take the breadwinner/housewife system as the universal family form (Tilly and Scott 1978; Davis 1988). The model is particularly inapplicable to formerly rural families who relocate in urban centers. The breadwinner husband who earns a "family wage" and the full-time housewife are not features of rural society in Turkey. Turkish peasants do not oppose femininity and motherhood to women's paid work. On the contrary, although differentiation of spheres of work and sociability by gender is prevalent, the Turkish peasantry stresses the complementary productive roles of women and men. In many parts of the rural Turkey, peasant women are key workers in agricultural production (in addition to their domestic activities) but not independent economic actors, deferring to men in the productive sphere (Berik 1987; Kandiyoti 1990; Sirman 1988). Women's multitude of economic activities, whether in the form of agricultural production, small-scale manufacturing, or husbandry, have been founded on a kinship- and household-based economy organized under a patriarchal structure of authority characterized by the absence of independent female ownership, economic activity, and earnings.[12] Women have no formal role in the politics of village society and economic decision making. Their informal influence is often considerable, however, because women are central agents in the formation and maintenance of kinship and intra-household relationships upon which production operations rest, especially in the realm of recruitment and mutual exchanges of labor among peasant households (Sirman 1995).

Second, following Weber, if we define authority as legitimate power, the source of a husband's authority is familial, and his ability to dominate does not derive from a provider role. Men get their legitimate status to dominate women by virtue of their position in the patriarchal family. Thus, I suggest that we must pose this question of male control first at the level of normative patriarchal gender order and the concepts of gender identity in order to account for the persistence of male control over women's labor, even when the male head of the household (husband) is not in a provider role. But we must also pose the question to explain why the husband's dominance can operate without any conflict (or force) and in many situations either goes unrecognized as such by wives or is evaluated in positive terms (for example, when male prohibition of women's paid work is conceptualized in terms of male jealousy expressed as love and care). Women's compliance rarely occurs in a context of force. In such situations of systematic "misrecognition," the issue of legitimacy becomes central, for legitimating ideologies provide subordinate individuals with subjectively meaningful reasons to comply and show deference.

Central to what Deniz Kandiyoti (1988) calls "classical patriarchy," where senior males hold authority and women's labor and reproductive capacities are appropriated by the patrilineage into which they marry, is a gender system based on paternalism. The boundaries of male authority are diffuse and intimate: male authority permeates all aspects of a subordinate's life, rather than confining itself to a more specific set of activities. As Carol Delaney (1991:172) succinctly puts it, "Authority, except for the elder male (and even that is relative), is always outside the self." In the context of Turkish culture, the male authority manifests itself in the concept of permission or consent (*izin*) as the cause of action,[13] implicating different categories of women and men by age differentially. "Young men need their father's *izin* [permission] to leave the village, but girls and women need it to go anywhere outside the home" (Delaney 1991:172). In this system, women, to be virtuous, should be legally, economically, and morally dependent on men.[14] Paternalism manifests itself through both protection and responsibility. A husband's claim to manhood is supported by his ability to protect and support his dependents, primarily his wife and children and his mother in her old age. Men, as fathers and husbands, bear responsibility for the security, honor, and reputation of their family. But men's honor is dependent on the behavior of women. Paternalistic gender norms construct femininity as dependence and submissiveness and situate this femininity in a protected environment away from autonomous action and movement. Kandiyoti (1988) describes women's relation to this system of male domination as "bargaining with patriarchy." Women receive "protection and security in exchange for submissiveness and propriety" (280).

The breakdown of material bases of "classical patriarchy" with the commodification of agriculture, urbanization, and migration has generated a situation in which men's unquestioned authority as fathers and husbands have become less taken-for-granted and less secure, creating "new areas of uncertainty and a renegotiation of relationships based on gender and age" (Kandiyoti 1995:307).[15] The displacement of at-once authoritarian and protective patriarchy does not mean, however, a general transformation of the relations between men and women or a radical reframing of what it means to be a man-husband and a woman-wife. Indeed, a cross-culturally and historically common response has been to reproduce familiar traditional practices in new social contexts and to preserve patriarchal organization of gender relations and identities.

Women's employment in urban areas, characterized by female mobility and an individual wage, is a realm of experience that directly challenges the basis of paternalistic domination, protection, and women's gender identity. In an urban context, husbands' control (and protection) over their wives is undermined by occupational situations, working conditions, and labor relations that are not organized by ties of kinship, community, and neighborhood. Employment in the modern labor market, characterized as impersonal, rational, and legalistic with centralized control and fixed work scenarios, constrains the role of the husband. There is limited flexibility in such work systems that precludes the husband's involvement and takes the wife out of the home and necessitates her interaction with nonkin and strange (unrelated) men as fellow workers, employers, or clients in contexts free of the social controls characteristic of rural environments.

I argue that employment in domestic service, especially in the prevalent form of workers' having multiple employers, provides conditions under which husbands can maintain the traditional forms of control over women's work and their work-related conduct. The organization of domestic service with multiple employers entails greater ability to choose suitable employers. Also, the effect of losing an employer deemed undesirable by the husband is financially inconsequential in the long run. The husband can easily afford to pick and choose for whom the wife will work. Although a woman's work in domestic service brings her in contact with people outside the family and kin, it does so in a context that can be potentially controlled by the husband. Moreover, employment in domestic service is consistent with traditional interpretations of women's work: the workplace is the employer's home; the employer is herself a woman; the worker interacts with her employer as an individual; the recruitment of domestic workers is organized by kinship and neighborhood-based networks, the relations between employer and worker are frequently grounded in personal ties; and the payment of the domestic worker's wages might even go to the husband.

For these reasons it is possible to conclude that as long as her work is confined within the circles drawn by the husband, employment is not experienced as being problematic and is seen as an extension of traditional work rather than a radical departure from the latter. This pattern of continuity between peasant women's work and migrant women's work in urban domestic service is best realized when it is associated with the institution of the doorkeeping. To put it differently, the door-keeping institution provides the social structural conditions under which traditional patriarchal gender relations can be sheltered and nurtured.

WORK SCHEDULES

What determines the work schedules of domestic workers? Their schedules can be broken down into three groups: full-time, "semi-full-time," and part-time. In the total sample (doorkeeper and squatter settlement groups combined), 55.6 percent of the workers work full-time, or five days or more a week, and thus constitute the largest component of the domestic work force; 23.8 percent work semi-full-time, or three or four days a week, and 20.6 percent of the workers are true part-timers who work one or two days a week (see Table 1). The comparison of the weekly work schedules of the doorkeeper and squatter settlement groups shows that the percentage of workers with five or more work-days is slightly greater for the squatter group (63.2 percent compared with 51.5 percent), whereas the percentage of workers who occupy a middle position between the full-timers and the part-timers, with three or four workdays, is significantly greater for the doorkeeper group (27.2 percent compared with 17.5 percent). There is no marked difference between the two groups for part-timers.

Comparisions of weekly work schedules raise several questions. Are these "part-time" workers different from their "full-time" and "semi-full-time" counterparts in terms of their individual characteristics, such as physiological status; that is, are they different in terms of constraints posed by whether they are in the childbearing stage or a lactation stage,

TABLE 1.   Weekly Work Schedules

	Doorkeeper		Squatter		Total Sample	
	%	N	%	N	%	N
1–2 days	21.4		19.3		20.6	
3–4 days	27.2		17.5		23.8	
5–7 days	51.5		63.2		55.6	
Total	100.1	103	100.0	57	100.0	160

Note: Percentages may not total 100 because of rounding.

or do they have the kinds of constraints that are intimately linked with household structure and household characteristics? Do they differ in terms of gender and age composition of the household and whether they can pass on childcare and domestic work to others? Or can they, because of the material characteristics of their households, rely on the earnings of kin and children and thus afford to work less and earn less? Is their working part-time related to the gender relations at home, where these women have husbands who are reluctant to let them work with a full-time schedule? Or do all these "supply"-related factors play out in an uneven and complex manner, representing an accommodation of various interests and priorities in their work and family lives? Or, alternatively, can their position as part-timers in this work force be attributable to "demand"-related factors? Simply put, do they work with less than full-time schedules just because they cannot find more work?

An examination of the different structural conditions of work for squatter settlement women and doorkeeper wives provides insight into the relative importance of these various factors in determining the level of the participation in the domestic work force and the diverse patterns of work-family interaction. Three structural conditions are especially relevant here: the homebound nature of the work of the doorkeeper and its implications for participation in childcare, household structure, and composition (and their implications both for internal gender division of labor, especially with regard to childcare, and for the economic position of the household) and access to employers.

Determinants of Work Schedules

DEMANDS OF YOUNG CHILDREN.   Are domestic workers with young children (defined as children 5 years of age or younger)[16] more likely to have part-time schedules than are domestic workers who have no young children? Are domestic workers with husbands who take on care of the young children more likely to have full-time schedules?

Among domestic workers in the doorkeeper group, a greater proportion of women without dependent children work full-time (60 percent) compared with domestic workers who have dependent children (40 percent). However, having young children is not associated with minimal work schedules. Indeed, a greater proportion of women with dependent children work semi-full-time schedules (40 percent) compared with those who do not have dependent children (18 percent).

Although the subsample size of the squatter settlement group is too small to establish a meaningful association, the same pattern can also be observed among these workers.

Having small children does not alone predict whether a domestic worker will work part-time. The existence or absence of an alternative care-giver is more closely correlated with the work schedules of these women with small children. Hence, the household structure—whether the household is at an "early" or "late" stage in the life cycle—the internal divisions of labor in the household, and the age and gender of children each play a role.

One would expect that the "homebound" nature of the work of the doorkeeper would produce an objective condition that would reduce the importance of the management of childcare as an obstacle to a woman's having a heavy work schedule. The doorkeeper's homebound work should be an important structural factor regulating the family and work interaction of domestic workers who are wives of doorkeepers, which is absent in the case of squatter settlement workers.

When we examine in the doorkeeper households the effects on a domestic worker's work schedule of having assistance in childcare provided two different ways—by the husband and by an individual other than the husband—we observe that working between five and seven days is significantly associated with having childcare provided by a husband (45 percent). Those whose source of help for childcare is "other than husband" are concentrated in the three-to-four-days schedule (58 percent). In other words, childcare provided by "other than husband" allows only a "semi-" full-time schedule, and the number of workdays increases when the childcare help is provided by the husband.[17]

Among the doorkeeper group, the availability of husbands for childcare reduces the incompatibility of full-time schedules with having dependent children and makes full-time or semi-full-time employment possible for women with dependent children. It is difficult, however, to arrive at definite conclusions with regard to the squatter settlement group because the subsample is too small to make a statistically meaningful comparison.

THE ECONOMIC POSITION OF THE HOUSEHOLD.   How does the economic standing of the household affect the work schedule of domestic workers? The economic standing of households in this context is discussed in terms of two variables: the relative importance of a domestic worker's income to household subsistence ("Can the household subsist without her income?": do without it / do without it but would be difficult / cannot do without it); and the proportion in a household of nonearners (dependents) to earners (the "dependency ratio"). The dependency ratio is obtained by dividing the number of nonearners by the number of earners in a household.

For both groups of workers, there is a strong positive relationship between the household's dependence on a domestic worker's earnings and the woman's work schedule. In households that attach great importance to the domestic worker's income, the largest percentage work full-time (66 percent). In households in which subsistence can be secured without the domestic worker's income, however, the largest percentage work part-time (60 percent). Thus, a household's economic standing is significant in predicting whether a domestic worker from the household will work full- or part-time.

Domestic workers in the squatter settlement group belong to larger households (on average, 5.3 people) than do those in the doorkeeper group (on average, 4.3 people). Because the mean difference in household size within each of the three work-schedule groups for both doorkeeper and squatter settlement groups are marginal, however, there is no identifiable pattern of relationship between household size and work schedule. Perhaps, in considering the interaction between domestic workers' work schedules and household size, the dependency ratio is more relevant than household size because it takes into account the existence of other members of the household with earnings relative to number of dependents. We expect that differences in dependency ratios among domestic worker households would produce differences in work schedules. Overall, doorkeeper households have substantially lower dependency ratios than squatter settlement households (0.96 compared with 1.31), reflecting the fact that earners in the squatter settlement households support a greater number of dependents than do those in the doorkeeper households. In the doorkeeper group, as might be expected, there is a greater tendency among domestic workers with higher dependency ratios to work semi-full-time (1.08) and full-time (0.96) schedules than there is among those with lower dependency ratios (0.83). However, there is a converse relationship between these two variables in the squatter settlement group. That is, domestic workers in households with a relatively high dependency ratio (1.41) work part-time, contrary to the expectation. This converse relationship indicates the salience of other determinants of work schedules, such as the absence of childcare options and the husband's opposition, a point that I consider in depth in the following pages.

LABOR DEMAND. In the absence of any systematic data on labor demand, I use "years of experience in domestic service" as a proxy variable to gauge the role played by this factor in determining work schedule. One of the basic arguments of this study is that for workers in the doorkeeper group "tenure in domestic service" does not have any effect on the intensity of participation in the domestic work force because of the spatial convergence of the supply and demand sides of this labor arrangement in the middle- and upper-middle-class neighborhoods. This convergence prevents the occurrence of any expected difference in the access to the demand pool between newcomers to the occupation and the old-timers. Thus, we do not expect that newcomers will have a greater tendency to have fewer workdays than old-timers. Indeed, differences in work schedules in this respect are negligible: part-time workers have, on average, 6.06 years of experience and full-time workers have 6.13 years of experience, indicating that work schedules are not affected by years of experience.

Among the squatter settlement group (who have no direct access to the demand pool), there are significant differences between novice and veteran workers in terms of work schedules. The years of experience of those workers with full-time schedules (11.70 years) are on the average substantially higher than those of the semi-full-timers and part-timers (8.41 and 6.39 years, respectively). A meaningful explanation of these wide differentials is complicated by the nature of the sample. Any generalization on the basis of this non-probabilistic sample inevitably will be tenuous. However, it still could be suggested that kinship and neighborhood-based networks in squatter neighborhoods that function as recruitment channels do not easily and quickly integrate newcomers.

How do semi-full-time and part-time workers explain their less than full-time participation in the work force? Is there an identifiable pattern that is common to both semi-full-timers and part-timers?

First, there is no single, dominant factor that explains being in a less than full-time position for all the workers in this subsample. Instead, many different factors influence the work strategies of women. "Lack of demand," "ill health," " young children," "exhaustion," "too many responsibilities at home," "pregnancy," "no financial need," and "lack of permission by husband" were mentioned as reasons for working less than full-time. Second, these determinants of work schedules are not markedly different in the doorkeeper and squatter settlement groups. Third, a clear pattern of distinction between the semi-full-timers and the part-timers is absent.

Lack of demand is the most frequently stated reason for working fewer than five days a week among workers in the doorkeeper group. This factor, although less pronounced, also constitutes a significant factor for workers in the squatter settlement group (fifteen compared with five). However, the meaning of the absence of demand is quite different for domestic workers from the doorkeeper group. It is, in fact, a supply factor because it is associated with the lack of a husband's permission. To put it differently, in these cases "absence of demand" meant that there was no "in-house" demand defined as the type of employer required by husbands. The demand factor thus speaks more directly to the division between privileged and undesirable demand pools. For squatter settlement workers the demand factor is associated with their dual status as "recent migrants" and "newcomers" to the occupation; they all expected to increase their number of workdays as they became more familiar with the domestic labor market through the recruitment channels of the community.

Ill health, a factor that is not captured by the aggregate analysis of the data, is a significant determinant of "less work" in both groups. Workers identified as having ill health have the kinds of chronic health problem, such as high blood pressure, asthma, and hernias, that preclude the performance of some tasks. Therefore, for these workers ill health is a major cause of a reduced work schedule (eight cases in the doorkeeper group and six cases in the squatter group).

The data on the effect of having young children on the work schedules of the doorkeeper group suggests that the demands of young children do not reduce the intensity of domestic workers' employment because "daytime" childcare is taken over by husbands. The eight cases in the doorkeeper group, where the presence of small children is given as the only reason for less work, represent women with husbands who depart from the general pattern by not taking on childcare responsibilities (eight workers in the doorkeeper group and four workers in the squatter group).

Changes in the Work Schedules

Having examined the current work schedules and the various individual and household factors affecting domestic workers' schedules, we can address the question of continuity. To what extent do these schedules remain stable? What causes domestic workers to modify their schedules? I explore these questions by focusing on the changes in work schedules from the previous year.

Of the total sample, 52.5 percent reported that they currently have the same work schedule as in the previous year and 36.2 percent reported that they have different schedules than in the previous year; of those, 20.6 percent decreased the number of workdays, while 15.6 percent increased the number (see Table 2). A small percentage (11.3 percent) were not working at all in the previous year. Before discussing the circumstances under which these women make schedule modifications, we should note that the changes in work schedules are minor and have no substantial impact on the welfare of households. For example, of those workers who decreased their number of workdays, more than half of them (63 percent) did so by one or two days. Similarly, 62 percent of those who increased the work schedule added only one or two days. The corresponding figure for those who increased by one or two days is the same (62 percent). Only a small number of cases reported a drastic change from between five and seven days to one or two days or vice versa.

TABLE 2.   Changes in Work Schedules from the Previous Year

	Doorkeeper		Squatter		Total Sample	
	%	N	%	N	%	N
No change	49.5	51	57.9	33	52.5	84
Decrease	18.4	19	24.6	14	20.6	33
Increase	18.4	19	10.5	6	15.6	25
Did not work previous year	13.6	14	7.0	4	11.3	18
Total	99.9	103	100.0	57	100.0	160

A broad range of factors was cited as influencing the decision to add or delete workdays, reflecting changes in individual and household circumstances. The most common reason given for schedule change was the changing financial need of the household. The second and third most common reasons were ill health and the demands of young children. The absence of labor demand (deemed suitable by the husband) is also a significant factor. In a small number of cases in this subsample, the decision to reduce or increase the work schedule is related to some other factor, such as a second job (being a female doorkeeper) or exhaustion.

A greater number of women (27 percent, or fifteen cases) in this subsample have expanded or shrunk their work schedules in response to the changing financial needs of the household. Although the definition of increased or decreased financial need varies with the family, in most cases, the expansion or contraction in the volume of work is a direct outcome of structural changes in the internal household economy, arising during times of, and in response to, transitions in the family life cycle. Such changes frequently include, but are not restricted to, the addition of new earners to the household or the marriage of a daughter or a son. In other cases financial need results from purchases of new household goods (appliances, kitchen gadgets, television sets, VCRs, small electronic goods, or a telephone connection) bought on installment or investment on a house or a plot of land.

In one case the increased need for additional income was due to the establishment of a new, independent household for an adult child.

> Yeşim Tez, a 38-year-old woman, has four grown-up sons (aged 23, 22, 21, and 18), one of whom is severely disabled, and a daughter (aged 17). Her 45-year-old husband retired four years ago and currently is not working. Her newly married son is a driver at a private company and her youngest son works as a busboy in a pastry shop. Her other children are unemployed. Following the "semi-extension" of the household by her eldest son's marriage last year, Yeşim Tez started to work as well, on Saturdays and Sundays. Although her newly married son and pregnant daughter-in-law have a separate house, actually an extension of the main house, they continue to eat with the family because her son's entire monthly salary goes to pay off installments on furniture, a refrigerator, and other household items.

In contrast, the reduced need for the earnings of the domestic worker is often associated with the multiplication of wage earners in the household. The earnings of daughters rather than sons are channeled more often into the household income. Gülgün Zer is a case in point.

Gülgün Zer, a mother of six children (three daughters and three sons, aged 20, 19, 17, 16, 13, and 12), who has been in the ranks of the domestic work force for twenty years, was able to decrease her workdays from five days a week in the previous year to two days in the current year. This reduction was made possible by her two eldest daughters' recent employment as private childcare workers. Although the addition of new contributions to the household economy did not allow her to retire completely from the work force, it still represents a significant change in that her daughters released her from the responsibility of being the primary earner. The permanency of her new work schedule depends on further changes in the household structure (such as the marriage of her daughters) and is representative of a volatile situation shared by many households that have reached a "late" life-cycle stage.

A second example of the decreased financial need is provided by the case of Tülin Yat.

Tulin Yat is one of the older women in this study and a veteran of domestic service with fourteen years of experience. She belongs to a late-stage household in which there are multiple earners and that at the time of the study was on the brink of reconstitution as an extended household with the addition of her new daughter-in-law. She has two adult sons (aged 21 and 18) at home with stable employment and a daughter outside the household. Tulin Yat's husband, who is 52 years old, has a stable job as a government employee. Her household also incorporates her elderly widowed father-in-law. Although she has had a regular four-day-a-week schedule over the years, during the previous year she worked six days a week. Her increased work schedule was a response to the need for more cash to go toward paying expenses associated with the marriage of her oldest son. In the current year, she was able to return to her original work schedule by eliminating two workdays, since all the expenditures associated with preparation of her son's living quarters and wedding had been paid off.

Financial need is sometimes dictated by changes in household or transitions in the family life cycle but defined in abstract terms. In these cases, additional income is needed to reduce the impact of high inflation and to maintain comparable standards of living in the face of the erosion of real wages. We should not assume, however, that worsening economic conditions are always and uniformly responded to by increasing the number of days worked. Households may adapt in different ways to increased economic hardship by deploying more members into the labor force, by eating less, and by decreasing consumption of certain goods. For example, an increased number of workdays cannot be sustained, especially in situations where young children are present, and childcare cannot be passed on to others. Oya Taşan's case illustrates how two important determinants of work schedules are interrelated and interactive.

Oya Taşan, a 31-year-old woman and mother of three (aged 13, 12, and 5) from the squatter settlement group, has been working for ten years. She is one of the few women in this study whose childcare strategy is to take her youngest son with her to work. Although she explained that she has increased her workdays from three to five because the family needed more income in the current year, her son's reaching an age where he is more manageable at her workplaces must have influenced her decision to expand her schedule.

The presence of small children at home and ill health emerge as equally important reasons for changing work schedules (21 percent and 20 percent, respectively). In some cases, pregnancy and birth are cited as reasons for working less in the previous year or to be working less in the current year.

Among those in the doorkeeper group who increased their hours from the previous years, three had temporarily reduced their workdays as a result of advanced pregnancy or the demands of infants. Once the fathers could take over childcare, however, they returned to work full-time.

Aysel Zetten is the wife of a doorkeeper who has an 18-month-old son. Last year, after the birth of her son, she worked only two days a week. But now she works five days a week. During the day, when she is out to work, her husband takes care of the child. The situation of 32-year-old Taze Kaslı is very similar to that of Aysel Zetten. She has a 30-month-old son. When he was an infant, she worked only two days; this year she expanded her work schedule by adding four more days. Another first-time mother is Sevtap Candan, who last year worked two days a week, except during the last two months of her pregnancy and immediately after giving birth. She has a 1-year-old son and maintains a heavy seven-day-a-week work schedule.

An important point is that these cases are all "early-stage" nuclear households, in which couples are having their first child and where no extended kin is present. As documented above, having an extended family is uncommon among doorkeepers and therefore most families have no older children or female kin who can take over childcare responsibilities. These cases differ from "late-stage" nuclear households, in which childcare is taken over by one or more children (almost invariably by daughters) or by both daughters and the father. The majority of primary and secondary schools in Turkey are half-time, operating with two shifts. This arrangement makes possible a division of labor between fathers and daughters; if a daughter goes to school in the morning, the father takes care of the small child, and she takes over when she comes home in the afternoon.

The number and ages of children determine the degree to which a doorkeeper husband can help with childcare. The husband's wage work can conflict with the care of many young children.

The change in the work schedule of Fedaye Hüseyinoğlu, a 39-year-old woman and the mother of two daughters and a son (aged 8, 6, and 4), illustrates this point. In the previous year, although her husband took care of children, she worked only three days a week. This year she added two more days because her two daughters reached an age where they need less constant attention. In addition, her older daughter can help her father care for her younger siblings before or after her shift at school. Thus, Fedaye's increased work schedule is linked to progress through the developmental cycle of the family to a stage where daughters begin to take over some of childcare responsibilities.

All of these cases highlight the links between the nature of the husband's doorkeeping job and the women's ability to work even when a small child is present. Given the household structures they have, these women could not have accommodated a full-time work schedule without their husbands' becoming "daytime" primary care-givers of children. It should be emphasized that the physical proximity of "workplaces" is also a contributing factor in some cases of domestic workers with newborn babies in which the mother can return home to nurse her infant a number of times during the workday, if she works for an "in-house" employer. This strategy, however, is not available to domestic workers from the squatter settlement group. On the whole, domestic workers in the doorkeeper group are in a better position to minimize the negative effect on their work schedules of having small children.

The significance of the nature of the husband's doorkeeping job as an "objective condition" for releasing women with small children for full-time work can also be observed when we examine the changes in the work schedules of the domestic workers from the squatter settlement group. Because of the constraints posed by childbirth and early motherhood, women in the squatter settlement group reduced the number of workdays and were unable to bring them back to the previous level after childbirth. Hence, in a marked contrast with the doorkeeper group, the presence of small children entailed a reduced number of workdays. Nur Gezer exemplifies this pattern.

> Nur Gezer is a first-time mother with an 18-month-old daughter, but she is slightly older (28) than her counterparts in the doorkeeper group described above. She is a veteran of domestic service with ten years of experience. Her husband, who is a janitor at a military air base, has a stable full-time (nine-to-five) job. In contrast to the women in the above cases, after having her daughter, she has reduced her workdays from six to two. She can afford to work only for two days, when she leaves her daughter with a sister-in-law who lives in another squatter settlement neighborhood.

The case of Aliye Ali, a mother of five, not only demonstrates the same pattern of work schedule reduction in the absence of alternative childcare options but also highlights the importance of looking at the gender composition of the household.

Aliye Ali's three-and-a-half-year-old daughter, who needs to be looked after, is the major barrier to Aliye's exercising her desire to increase her workdays from three a week. She desperately needs to work more because her income is the only regular income the family receives. She is a member of a household whose material conditions of life are uncertain. Her husband works only sporadically, whenever he can find work, and her two sons (aged 19 and 17) are unemployed, usually spending time looking for jobs and hanging out in coffeehouses. Her other children, an 11-year-old daughter and a 13-year-old son, are in school. When she is out at work and her other daughter is in school, her neighbor (also her landlady) minds her younger daughter free of charge. But it was becoming increasingly difficult to maintain such an arrangement because of her strained relationship with the neighbor. She will be better able to cope with childcare when school is out and her 11-year-old daughter can take over. Yet summers, when employers go away on vacation, are not the best time to increase one's work schedule.

The case of Zehra Col is an example of a sudden and drastic change in the work schedule as a result of ill health.

Zehra Col is a 45-year-old woman and a mother of three children (aged 23, 19, and 14). Two of her children are employed and one of them is about to get married. She has been working for thirteen years but was forced to make a drastic change from five days to one day because she has a fractured spine. Despite her doctor's warning that she must absolutely not engage in any strenuous activity, she continues to work one day a week to help pay the debts they have accumulated while preparing her son's new household and wedding.

As pointed out above, the "demand factor" is the determinant of work schedules most difficult to measure and evaluate. In the context of the current structure of domestic service in Turkey, there is a continuous demand for domestic work, but jobs considered desirable may be hard to find. As the following chapters reveal, domestic workers evaluate potential jobs carefully, considering several key factors. However, husbands also play a crucial role in determining whether a domestic worker is employed in a particular household. Thus, in cases in which a domestic worker reports that she wants to work more but can't find more work because her husband does not permit her to obtain employment from outside, labor demand as a determinant of her work schedule is fused with supply factors. Among the doorkeeper group, desirable jobs are limited to those supplied by the apartment house residents and the residents of the surrounding neighborhood. Not in a single case in the doorkeeper sample, for example, does a domestic worker choose employment that would require her to commute. The husbands' screening of the labor demand characteristics also affects the level of work schedules. For example, as a general rule, domestic workers are not allowed to work for single men, even if they constitute "in-house" demand.

The following case illustrates the critical role played by husbands' restrictions on women's employment options.

Narin Çalışır, a 29-year-old woman, has three children (aged 13, 10, and 7) who are all in school and who look after themselves after school. She joined the ranks of the domestic work force only a year ago with two workdays. But since her husband does not allow her to work for "outside" employers and there is insufficient "in-house" demand for her to work full-time, she had to shift to single-family work—five days a week for a family in the same apartment building. This meant that she had to settle for lower pay. Thus, although she now has three more workdays, she is making about the same amount of money she was making last year when she worked only two days. Meanwhile, her husband "compensates" for her effective loss of earnings caused by his opposition to her taking up "outside" employers by working at two other apartment buildings as a doorkeeper.

UNEASY DISTINCTIONS

Profiles of domestic workers in terms of current work schedules and histories in domestic service reveal continuity and stability despite the informal structure of their labor. Through these profiles the problematic division between "formal" and "informal" work and the uneasy position of domestic workers in this division become apparent. The typical work profile of woman in this study does not fit the typical work profile of woman in the informal sector, which invokes images of women engaging in home-based income-producing activities, such as knitting, sewing, and assembly work, the kind of work that is episodic and flexible, revolving around the demands of childcare, housework, and other obligations at home. For the majority of the domestic workers in this study, work is not a supplementary activity. It is a central and significant part of their everyday lives and is not considered a mere extension of their domestic responsibilities.

The general profile of this work force complicates the received paradigms that attempt to explain the heavy concentration of women in the informal sector in terms of an easy "fit" between the spheres of "work" (production) and "home" (reproduction).[18] Employment in domestic service, like employment in the formal sector, does not easily accommodate women's attempts to combine productive and reproductive activities. It is well documented that women are segregated into certain branches of the informal sector, characterized by low remuneration, poor conditions of work, and a lack of autonomy and mobility. Men, in contrast, tend to concentrate in those areas of the informal sector characterized by higher earnings, mobility, and autonomy. Despite extensive exploration of this gender divide in the informal sector and the ways in which the informal sector articulates with the global market, insufficient attention has been paid to internal divisions within the female urban informal sector and the interactions among them.[19] The type of work women do, the space of their work, and the social context and social relations of their work have tremendous implications for how they define themselves and the meaning of work in their lives. For example, there is overwhelming evidence from the experiences of women in many different countries that when women do home-based work they conflate their income-generating work with their household activities and thus undervalue their productive labor and do not define themselves as working women. Lace makers in Narsapur India (Mies 1982), industrial subcontracted home workers in Mexico City (Beneria and Roldan 1987), piece workers in İstanbul (Çınar 1987, 1989; White 1994), and carpet weavers in rural Turkey (Berik 1987) all produce goods for national and international markets but see their work as a mere extension of their roles as daughters, wives, and mothers.

Jenny White's study (1994) of a group of squatter settlement women in İstanbul who engage in home-based piece work or work in family and neighborhood ateliers for export and local markets, or do both, demonstrates the shortcomings of the conventional account that explains married women's concentration in the informal sector by its easy accommodation to women's family responsibilities. White's work demonstrates the links established between women, paid work, and sexuality, similar to those found in my examination of domestic workers. More important, the women White studied also constitute would-be domestic workers. A representative survey (Çınar 1991) conducted among subcontracted female home workers in the squatter settlement neighborhoods of İstanbul, whom White studied, found that the majority of respondents (40 percent) cited employment in the domestic service as being not only the most desired job but also the most feasible one (45 percent). Yet it was found that the main reason for not becoming a domestic worker was lack of husband's permission (55 percent).

Women and girls in White's study (1994) sew clothing, knit sweaters, and stitch decorations onto shoes and garments. They also put together boxes of pencil leads, ballpoint pens, cardboard boxes, necklaces, and prayer beads (13). These activities are all considered fitting manifestations of female skills and roles, while market transactions are considered to be the domain of men. Production of these goods, exported to Europe, the Middle East, and the United States, is organized several different ways, but the most common form is the neighborhood piecework atelier where the raw material is prepared and distributed for piecework to other families in the neighborhood. The owner of the piecework atelier "takes orders from and delivers the product to an intermediary who deals with the merchant or exporter" (13).

White presents a detailed analysis of why the women she studied, although intensely engaged in income-producing activities, maintain a fiction of "nonworking " and deny that they actually "work" by conflating their labor for income-producing activities with household labor. This conceptualization of the self as "nonworking " becomes even more striking for those women who work away from home, in neighborhood ateliers, and are employed as nonfamily workers. They, too, insist that they are not working women, because, White explains, capitalist small-scale commodity production, even when intimately tied with the global market, operates with a kinship logic in Turkey, where labor is organized "according to the ideology of the traditional family, which links labor with role identity and social responsibility" (14). Thus, she argues, "profit is extracted from the labor of some group members by others through relations of production that emphasize open-ended reciprocity and social solidarity" (149). Since for these poor and low-income families the family and community constitute a substantial source of support and security, giving labor or other resources without expectation of immediate monetary return is seen as the basis for forging firm bonds of mutual aid and indebtedness. But more important, within this framework, not only is women's labor seen as the property of the group but women's gender identity is largely defined by her labor, in the sense that her income-producing labor is conflated with her social roles. A woman's identity is inextricably linked with her role as wife, mother, and daughter. And thus women's work cannot be exchanged for money. "The women see these income-producing activities," according to White (1994) "as being an expression of their identity as good women and of their consequent membership in a defining group as wife, mother, neighbor, and muslim, rather than as work for which they can demand a fair financial return" (8–9). Thus, the unpaid or poorly paid nature of women's labor is legitimized by a cultural construction of "giving" labor as a contribution to family and community and an expression of identity. There is also an important link established between the loss of reputation as a good woman and working for money. A woman who engages in capitalistic wage-labor relationship, not organized by family and kinship means, is involved in an impersonal relationship and deviates from the model of womanhood that entails giving without expectation of immediate return as a wife, mother, and daughter. Such a betrayal of femininity can also betray her reputation as a good woman. Women employ this patriarchal code of honor to judge themselves according to the same standards of sexual purity and womanhood. By conflating their labor for money and their family duties and household work, they maintain their sense of self-respect and dignity in the face of the degrading status of working for wages. "As long as individual production, piecework, and atelier labor are seen to be an expression of group identity and solidarity, rather than "work," they remain morally and socially acceptable" (113).

White's analysis (1994) demonstrates that the existence of widespread decentralized capitalist economic activity cannot be understood in economic terms. Cultural constructions of womanhood, motherhood, and women's sexuality are crucial in shaping the nature of the informal sector and its ties to the global capitalist market in Turkey. As graphically illustrated by other cases around the world, the ideology of the naturalness of women's skills and capabilities and the cultural conceptualization of labor as an expression of women's identity form "the basic mechanism by which international business takes advantage . . . to create a pool of cheap, expendable, primarily female labor" (2).

White (1994) concludes, "If women (and men) do not recognize a difference between women's income producing labor and household labor, there is no obvious way for income-earning activities to substantially affect their lives in terms of greater control over resources and decision making. Women gain no individual control over their economic or productive lives from the work they do because their labor is in a sense the property of the group" (16). Whether this conclusion is applicable to the domestic workers and how domestic workers understand their labor can be addressed by an examination of the ways in which they shape their modes of employment in domestic service, their perspectives on future work strategies, their encounters with employers, and their conception of wage earning. The experiences recounted in this chapter do make clear, however, that, unlike the identities of their sisters in the squatter settlements of Istanbul and in major cities around the world, the identities of Ankara's domestic workers are not structured to exclude wage earning.

An upper-middle-class neighborhood of Ankara

A doorkeeper's wife washing windows in
an upstairs apartment

A mother and son with their upscale furniture in their squatter settlement home

A domestic worker with her employer

A squatter settlement neighborhood

A squatter settlement mother with her children in front of their house

A young squatter settlement family

A doorkeeper couple in a typical basement apartment

Women and their children in a leisure moment outside their squatter settlement house

A group of domestic workers having tea after work

A doorkeeper's wife visiting a neighbor

A domestic worker giving her neighbor's son a haircut

A multi-functional squatter settlement room

A relatively modest kitchen of a squatter
settlement house

A squatter settlement family portrait; missing are two older sons, who were out

A doorkeeper's wife with her two daughters

A group of domestic workers with the author (*seated on the floor on the right*)

3   Neither Maids Nor Cleaners

BY THE TIME Zehra Karamanoğlu's workday ended at three o'clock one Tuesday afternoon, she had washed breakfast and lunch dishes, cleaned the kitchen cabinets and refrigerator, made the beds, ironed the two loads of laundry she had washed the day before, and vacuumed and dusted the living room. In between her major chores, she changed the cat's litter, watered the plants, cleaned some spinach, and served tea to her employer. She will return to the same house the next day to perform similar tasks.

Gülsev Zeynel, on the same day, spent most of her eight-hour workday down on her hands and knees cleaning the rugs and floors of four rooms in a large house and washing the windows and doors. She will work in a different house the next morning but return to this workplace in two weeks.

Zehra Karamanoğlu's and Gülsev Zeynel's work represents two paradigmatic modes of domestic service. Zehra Karamanoğlu is a "single-employer" worker who goes to the same "workplace" five days a week. She is paid monthly and uses the expression "I'm monthly" (aylıkcıyım) to refer to her work. Gülsev Zeynel, in contrast, is one of 145 multi-employer workers out of the 160 domestic workers in the study. Her pattern of work represents the most common form of employment in Turkish domestic service. She receives daily wages and calls herself a "daily" (gündelikci). Multi-employer workers work for different employers on a weekly, biweekly, or more frequent schedule.

As Gülsev Zeynel's day suggests multi-employer workers' jobs involve a narrower set of tasks than those performed by single-employer workers. Multi-employer workers usually perform heavy cleaning on a routine, repetitive schedule. Their work is in some respects more like the services of commercial agencies that perform specific tasks in private homes than the work of traditional maids. They are, in this sense, specialists, whereas single-employer workers are "generalists"—maids of all work. Single-employer workers perform a much more loosely defined set of tasks. In addition to performing regular heavy cleaning, they also wash dishes, cook, do laundry, and render personal services to members of the employer family, such as serving tea, setting the table, and answering the door. Thus single-employer workers carry out all the daily household work to keep the household functioning and sustain a degree of domestic comfort and luxury for their employers. The salient distinction between single- and multifamily work lies not only in the type of work sold. Multi-employer workers sell their labor for specific *tasks*. In contrast, single-employer workers sell their *time* for unspecified or loosely defined responsibilities.

Defining these two paradigmatic cases of employment in this way is useful for making an analytical distinction between traditional maids and cleaners, though not all "multi-employer" workers in this study can be defined easily as cleaners. The division between single- and multi-employer work is relevant when we use it to compare these two groups by flexibility of choosing and changing employers, weekly work schedule, and wages (a single-employer worker makes about two-thirds less than a multi-employer for the same number of days). But when we examine the frequency of visits to each employer, this distinction between multi- and single-employer becomes unsatisfactory. The "multi-employer" label lumps together all the workers who have more than one employer without taking into account the frequency of repeated visits to the same employer. For example, Gülsev Zeynel works five days a week for twelve different employers with different cycles. She has biweekly cycles for three of her employers and she works for the remaining nine every third week. Zerrin Yasaz's schedule is less complex: although she works four days a week, she has only two employers, working for each one twice a week. Thus, in terms of what she does on the job, her work more closely resembles that of the single-employer worker Zehra Karamanoğlu than that of Gülsev Zeynel. Frequency of work for a given employer affects the intensity and variety of tasks performed. Thus, we need to conceptualize modes of employment in domestic service on a continuum between exclusively *specialist* (modern domestic worker-cleaner) and exclusively *generalist* (traditional maid). These positions change according to the configuration of a worker's schedule, including the number of days a week she works, the total number of employers she has, and the frequency of repeated visits to the same employer. Moreover, a worker may be in a traditional maid position in relation to one of her employers but also in a modern worker position in relation to her other employers at a given moment.

This chapter focuses on characteristics of employment in domestic service. First, I distinguish and conceptualize modes of employment in domestic service and then examine job contents, control over labor process, and work hours for different modes of employment and employer women's social status. A crucial finding in this chapter is the striking uniformity of the wage levels, especially given the absence of any legislation and collective bargaining in domestic service. This finding raises several questions. What factors account for this uniformity and relatively high wages? How are wages and wage increases determined? Absence of worker protection and security is one of the defining features of employment in domestic service. How is this absence understood and experienced by domestic workers? I examine this question in relation to domestic workers' future work strategies and the "demise of patriarchal bargains" (Kandiyoti 1988) at home. In the last section I turn the analysis of mode of employment and autonomy in the labor process in a slightly different direction to consider the larger implications of mode of employment in the formation of work identities and in the emergence of polarized identities of womanhood. Widening my discussion on work identity also provides underpinnings for Chapter 4, in which I discuss the complex world of cross-class relations between women.

MODES OF EMPLOYMENT IN DOMESTIC SERVICE

I distinguish four modes of employment by using three variables—the number of days worked per week, the total number of employers, and the number of repeated visits to the same employer in a week. One mode ("daily") identifies workers with a single employer; the other three modes identify multi-employer workers. Domestic workers with weekly cycles (those who work for the same employer once a week) constitute the largest percentage of workers in the sample (42.5 percent), and workers with multiweekly cycles (those who work for the same employer less than once a week) constitute the next largest (24.4 percent). Workers with multiday cycles (those who work for the same employer more than once a week) make up the final 23.8 percent of the group (see Table 3). The majority of domestic workers (66.9 percent; i.e., the multiweekly category combined with the weekly) work as "specialists," or "modern" domestic workers, who sell their labor for specific tasks.

TABLE 3.   Modes of Employment in Domestic Service

Modes of Employment by Frequency of Cycles to the Same Employer	Doorkeeper		Squatter		Total Sample	
	%	N	%	N	%	N
Daily	6.8	7	14.0	8	9.4	15
Multiday	17.5	18	35.1	20	23.8	38
Weekly	51.5	53	26.3	15	42.5	68
Multiweekly	24.3	25	24.6	14	24.4	39
Total	100.1	103	100.0	57	100.1	160

Shifting our focus from domestic workers to the *distribution of the employers* by the frequency of visits, we can look at the same data from another angle. Domestic workers in the sample have a total of 691 employers. Half of the employers (51 percent) hire a domestic worker once a week, 9 percent every two weeks, and 18 percent less frequently. In contrast, only 3 percent of the employers hire a domestic worker full-time, and 20 percent hire a worker for two or more days a week. Thus, it could be concluded that the majority of employers buy "modern" domestic labor, while less than one-fourth of the employers employ a traditional type of maid. Another salient aspect of domestic service in Turkey is the diversity in the class profile of employers. Employment of domestic labor is not restricted to the elite and affluent but is found also among even modest middle classes because of wide availability of domestic labor in the form of multi-employer work. Hence, whether the "labor time" (generalist) or the "specific services" of a domestic worker (specialist) are bought is related to the class position of employers. This observation suggests that the ramifications of domestic help or relief from housework are different for different classes of employers. For an employer from the lower echelons of the middle class, hiring domestic help means relief from the dirtiest, heaviest aspects of domestic work, since she employs the domestic worker less frequently. For women of the upper-middle and the upper classes, who can employ domestic workers more frequently, hiring domestic help might entail the near-complete replacement of her own labor with the domestic worker's labor.

Table 3 also gives the distribution of modes of employment with a breakdown of the doorkeeper and the squatter settlement groups. With the exception of the category of workers with multiweekly cycles, which is uniform between the two groups, workers in the squatter settlement group tend to concentrate in the multiday cycle (35.1 percent compared with 17.5 percent) and are less represented in the category of weekly cycle. This distribution is also reflected in the average number of employers each group has, with domestic workers from the squatter settlement averaging 4 employers and those from the doorkeeper group averaging 4.4 employers.

Domestics who have weekly or multiweekly cycles for a given employer perform more physically demanding labor (heavy cleaning comprises 81 percent of the work load for workers with weekly schedules and 87 percent of those with multiweekly cycles). They specialize in such heavy cleaning tasks as washing windows, cleaning carpets, and scrubbing floors, and they do not tidy up, make beds, change sheets, organize closets, or clean refrigerators and stoves. Rather than straightening the house, in fact, they often find that all the obstacles that would make their job difficult and cumbersome (items on sofas, children's toys on the floor, dirty tea glasses from the night before on the table, unmade beds, etc.) have already been cleared away.[1]

These women working weekly and multiweekly cycles described their work as arduous, demanding, fatiguing, and monotonous. Despite the widespread availability of modern labor-saving devices in middle-class homes, housecleaning tasks are still labor intensive. Vacuum cleaners are used to remove dust from carpets, armchairs, and floors but all of the washing is done by hand. Floors are scrubbed by hand (without rubber gloves) rather than with the use of a mop, and rugs must be washed from a kneeling position. All these tasks require physical strength and are made more difficult by the fact that most middle-class homes in urban Turkey are furnished with heavy furniture and rugs that need to be moved around for thorough cleaning. For example, moving the rugs outside (usually to the balcony) to remove the accumulated dust underneath is an arduous task, involving backbreaking labor. Rug cleaning is generally carried out kneeling, using a cloth with soap or detergent. Hot water is not always available in most of the homes (or is used stingily because it is expensive). Workers' hands are constantly in cold water. The labor of those who do laundry (11 percent of the work load of multiweekly workers and 10 percent of the work load of weekly workers) is increased by the absence of dryers and the demand that the women iron sheets and even dish towels. Among this group of workers, only a small proportion cook in addition to doing heavy cleaning.

In contrast, a worker with a single employer has many different tasks. More than half (53 percent) of the "daily" group's (i.e., single-employer workers) work consists of cooking, routine cleaning, washing dishes, doing laundry, and ironing. Only one single-employer worker reported that her work, like that of the majority of multi-employer workers, involves only heavy cleaning. In the single-employer group, six workers' major responsibility is providing childcare, though five of those perform heavy cleaning as well. Two wash the dishes in addition to their childcare duty.

If we consider the work of an "in-between" domestic worker (the multiday group), who goes to the same house twice a week, we see that the neat division between selling one's labor time for specific tasks and selling one's labor time for many different tasks disappears. The work content of the in-between domestic worker combines physically demanding dirty work with light housework, including organizing and straightening. The work is also less repetitive, allowing for alternation of tasks. Among this group a little less than one-third (32 percent) do only heavy cleaning; the largest category (37 percent) consists of those who cook and do laundry in addition to heavy cleaning and those who iron in addition to cleaning (21 percent of the group).

CONTROL OVER THE WORK PROCESS: AUTONOMY

How should the concept of autonomy that was developed specifically to understand worker's behavior in response to the internal constraints of control within industrial and bureaucratic organizations be understood in the context of domestic service? By definition, in domestic service, unlike in most industrial jobs where controls are embodied in the organization of the work itself, the basis of control is highly personal. Rules and norms of domestic service are largely colored by values and practices associated with the private sphere, based on the understanding that the home is an arena for personal and private relationships rather than those forms of interaction appropriate for the workplace. Much of the labor relations in domestic service are structured by familial metaphors. The conception of the workplace in terms of the private sphere makes it difficult to define the boundaries between "employee" and "employer," particularly in regard to the latter's "managerial" control over the work process. Indeed, the general structure of work relations in domestic service is built around the nonwaged meaning of domestic work: "labor of love" and "caring" (Gregson and Lowe 1994).

Moreover, the home and the labor needed to maintain it are not only a woman's realm but also the most important locus for the control of pollution and the maintenance of the boundaries between dirt (disorder) and cleanliness (order). Methods of housework are governed by cultural traditions and standards regarding "pollution" and "cleanliness." The domestic worker is expected to perform her tasks in accordance with the wishes of the employer woman and her interpretation of the Turkish-Islamic beliefs about pollution. For example, things associated with the "clean" and "unclean," the dirtier parts of the body and the house, must be segregated. Bathroom sinks—rendered unclean by dirt from the body—should not be used for food; different cleaning tools (cleaning rags) should be used to clean different areas of the house. It is the employer's task to ensure that the domestic worker maintains this separation strictly.

Workers' autonomy is defined by the degree and kind of supervision to which they are subjected. In the discourse of domestic workers, this control is perceived as "intrusion on her work" and is opposed to self-directed work, where the domestic worker herself determines the organization of her workday and the coordination of her various tasks. In self-directed work, the domestic worker decides where to start cleaning first, what kind of cleaning tools to use, what pace she should set, and the manner in which she executes particular tasks. Close monitoring or the presence of somebody looking over her shoulder is perceived as a loss of autonomy. Domestic workers who are most pleased with their work conditions are the ones who feel they have autonomy. The value attached to this sense of autonomy is reflected in the common statement, "I do my job as though I am the master of this home." For workers, autonomy makes work more psychologically tolerable, more efficient, and less physically burdensome. More important, by framing their work in the home of strangers in terms of "doing my job as though I am doing it at my home," domestic workers attempt to minimize and deny the social degradation associated with doing somebody else's dirty work. A critical distance from a negative work identity is achieved by "moving this form of work away from the terrain of waged labor and onto the terrain of unwaged domestic labor" (Gregson and Lowe 1994:227). In fact, Turkish domestic workers never identify themselves as "cleaners" or "cleaning ladies" or describe their jobs as "cleaning." Instead, they describe their employment as "going to household work."

Employers can be characterized as either housewives or employed women, each controlling work of her employee in distinct ways. Although the distinction, illustrating the two main forms of control over the work process, does not necessarily constitute a clear-cut contrast in reality since it depends on whether the housewife can actually supervise (or act on her given structural position) her domestic worker directly. She may be unable or unwilling to perform supervision, a point that I discuss in Chapter 4. In this study more employers are housewives (62 percent) than women who work outside the home (38 percent).

For employees of housewives, checks of performance are built into the work routine. They are subject to an intrusive control, entailing regular checks on their pace as well as strict supervision of the manner in which tasks are performed. Domestic workers of employed women are not under constant and direct supervision; they have autonomy by default. They get on with the job without continual interference. Yet the lack of immediate supervision does not mean that their work goes unevaluated. Some have their pace controlled through telephone calls and other indirect means. Focus-group interviews with employer women revealed that an old trick, frequently mentioned in historical studies of domestic service, is still in currency. By hiding something like an olive pit under a carpet or an obscure place, an employer can test her worker's diligence. If the worker fails to notice the pit, she is cutting corners.

Regardless of the mode of control exercised by employers, there are clear production norms. When first hired, a domestic worker is given instructions about what needs to be done and how. According to the employers interviewed, the domestic worker always comes "untrained," regardless of her previous experience in domestic service, because "every woman has her own ways of doing housework" and her own standard of cleanliness. Employers aim to transform the domestic worker into someone who can be relied upon to conduct her work without close supervision. This entails learning specified work methods as well as learning the peculiarities, such as the standards of cleanliness, of a particular employer. But after a while, according to the employers interviewed, the agreed-upon rules inevitably are manipulated, redefined, or ignored by the worker.

The employers' strategy is to get more and higher quality work done by making the best use of a domestic worker's time, while the workers' strategy is to resist the expansion of their work hours by lowering the standards, slowing down, overlooking some details or forgetting a task (e.g., emptying the trash). In other words, the strategies embedded in the labor process are purposeful acts of workers who aim to limit what employers can require of them while keeping the job.

Employers try to enforce their standards by reminding the worker of what needs to be done or scrutinizing the worker's performance more closely. One frequently mentioned and disliked exercise of managerial control involves the employer's last-minute announcement of dissatisfaction as the worker is leaving, causing her to return from the front door and finish or redo the job in question. One worker angrily described such a situation in vivid terms: "You are at the front door putting your coat on. You say good-bye and she says 'Look . . . there is a spot left on that window.' Then, of course, you gotta take off your coat and redo the thing. It's a torture." From the perspective of the employer, this "torture" is not simply a means of getting the spot cleaned or reminding the worker of acceptable standards; instead, it serves as a disciplinary punishment, aimed at inculcating self-surveillance so that the worker herself takes over the job of supervising her performance.

Given the high value workers put on autonomy on the job, one would expect to observe a higher preference for employers who are working women. However, my data does not immediately support this hypothesis. More than one-third of the domestic workers (39 percent) reported that it does not matter for them whether they work for housewives or employed women. They all gave the same reason for this indifference, stating that the job definition is the same for both kinds of employer. This sense of similarity in the job definitions reflects, in part, the effects of "specialist" work, which is more clearly defined and is characterized by a degree of impersonality and distance during work. Thirty-four percent of all the workers said that they would prefer working for housewives, whereas 26 percent expressed preference for employed women.

"Autonomy" at work is almost the only basis given (90 percent) for preferring to work for employed women. Those who prefer working for housewives expressed several different reasons. About one-third (38 percent) of the workers who prefer housewives stated that housewives help them with their tasks. Absence of responsibility when something becomes lost or stolen from the house is the second most-mentioned reason (25 percent), followed by having somebody on the scene defining tasks and having food provided (11 percent). Friendship with employers and finding housewives' homes generally cleaner are the least decisive factors.

WORK HOURS

Multi-employer work is defined by tasks rather than time. In other words, the domestic worker is paid a flat rate by the apartment regardless of how much time she spends. She therefore has no motive to keep her pace slow, increase her work hours, and thereby maximize her total wages for the day. The predominant arrangement of charging by the task gives workers considerable freedom to determine the rhythm and pace of their work. Therefore, from the perspective of the domestic worker, task work entails a degree of autonomy, because she can leave the workplace whenever her tasks are completed. Flexibility of work hours constitutes another significant factor in the preference for multi-employer work over single-employer work, in which the worker has rigidly defined work hours. This rigidity is especially true for the worker whose main responsibility is childcare (she cannot leave her workplace until the parents of the child she cares for come home). The advantage of multi-employer work appears in mean hours of work per day. Single-employer workers work 8.10 hours a day, compared with 7.21 hours for multi-employer workers, who also earn two-thirds more than single-employer workers (see Table 4).

Apart from the difference between multi- and single-employer workers, an important difference appears in the comparison of mean work hours among workers in the doorkeeper group compared with mean work hours in the squatter settlement group. The latter group's mean hours of work are substantially lower than the former's.[2] The squatter group's greater concentration in the multiday cycle explains this difference.

A comparison of the mean number of hours worked by employees of housewives compared with the mean number of hours by employees of employed women reveals that employment by a housewife increases a worker's hours of work by 4 percent or 17.4 minutes. This is not an unexpected finding. The constant supervision described in the preceding section that only housewives are able to exercise means that

TABLE 4.   Mean Number of Work Hours of Domestic Workers by Category of Worker

Classification of Domestic Worker	Mean Hours	N
By group		
Doorkeeper	7.60	103
Squatter	6.59	57
By mode of employment		
Single employer	8.10	15
Non–single employer	7.15	145
Multiday	6.59	38
Weekly	7.43	68
Multiweekly	7.21	39
By social status of employer		
Working only for housewives	7.34	38
Working only for employed women	7.05	33

this group of employers control the pace of the work by interfering in the job and demanding more thorough work.

Among multi-employer workers, multiday workers' mean number of work hours is the smallest (6.59). In general, the working conditions of this group of workers combine the advantages of multi-employer and single-employer work. Their more frequent visits to the same "workplace" tend to decrease the overall volume of work and the frequency of physically heavy and dirty work performed. They have shorter work hours but still earn the same high wages as other multi-employer workers.

Even though the hours of work range from 3 hours to 10.50 hours for the total sample, there are no significant variations in the time that domestic workers spent at the work. To put it differently, 73 percent of the workers (117 cases) spend between 6.0 and 8.5 hours at work, with extreme cases equally distributed above and below this group. The examination of hours of work in relation to the content of work suggests that those workers whose job definition includes a variety of tasks, in contrast to those whose tasks are specialized, including childcare workers, constitutes the largest percentage within the category of workers who have fewer than six hours of work a day. The childcare workers make up the largest percentage within the category of workers who have more than 8.50 hours of work. In other words, extreme cases are derived mainly from generalist and childcare workers.

WAGE SYSTEM

The wage system is among the most unusual features of domestic service in Turkey. Wages are remarkably uniform and rise steadily to keep pace with inflation. Neither government regulation nor collective bargaining is responsible for the uniformity of wages of domestic workers in Turkey. It can best be attributed to the existence of community-based networking among domestic workers and to some externally imposed circumstances other than legislation.

Three interrelated factors control variations in wages, the first of which is the supply and demand imbalance giving workers leverage in their negotiation with employers. Faced with a relatively small pool of domestic workers, employers have found that they must offer competitive wages and pay increases in order to retain workers who would otherwise be lured to other employers (employers who delay wage increases lose their domestic workers). The second factor is the existence of an effective network among domestic workers that functions as an informal regulatory entity, defining and disseminating standards for equitable wages and wage increases. The third factor is the economic background of the employers, who, for the most part, are middle- or upper-middle-class employees of the state sector. Domestic workers' wage increases follow employers' own wage increases, which are adjusted twice a year.

Domestic workers' wages are higher than the wages of much of the rest of the Turkish working class. They are three times higher than the minimum wages of other unskilled and semiskilled jobs in which they might have worked. Yet direct comparisons of wages would be misleading, because domestic workers are not covered by social insurance and lack the benefits attached to other jobs. A more apt comparison can be made with wages of female informal workers in home production for export-oriented industries. A representative survey of subcontracted female workers in the squatter settlements of İstanbul (Çınar 1991) reveals that the hourly wage of these workers (28 cents in 1987) was lower than the official minimum wage (33 cents) for the period in which the survey was conducted. Thus, the domestic workers' wages were higher than these workers' wages by an even greater percentage than they are higher than wages in the formal sector.

Between December 1989 and July 1990 (the period during which I conducted the survey), the rate for multi-employer work ranged from 15,000 TL to 25,000 TL a day. These raw figures do not, however, reflect the uniformity of the wages, since they include increases in wages that took place when the survey was being conducted. Wage increases (adjustments) occur periodically, two times a year, roughly corresponding to wage increases and adjustments in the state sector of employment, where most of the employers or their husbands work. In January 1989 wages went up by 5,000 TL a day, corresponding to a 33 percent increase over the previous wage. A second wage increase of 5,000 TL (a 25 percent increase) took effect in June 1990. Although each wage increase represents a large percentage increase over previous wages, because of high inflation, the increases in wages do not mean gains in real wages.

Higher wages can be explained further by reference to the low degree of flexibility of employers who cannot easily replace one worker with another because of the supply and demand imbalance. However, a more intrinsic factor deriving from the pattern of employment better explains why wages are higher and why, despite high wages, demand is great (and why those who buy domestic labor also include a large middle-class clientele). The employment structure—day work with multiple employers—allows for a larger clientele who employ domestic workers with little financial burden.

The narrow range of wages, except the difference between those of multi- and single-family workers discussed above, suggests wages are not contingent on experience, content of duties, or hours of work. For example, the wages of long-term employees do not differ from those of short-term employees; a worker with twenty years of experience receives the same wage as a newcomer to the occupation. Nor is there any clear connection between wages and skill level. Thus, jobs involving domestic work in modern Turkey are like unskilled jobs in which there is no vertical mobility and, as a result, none of the hierarchy based on wage and status that is typical of the old servant class in western Europe.

Wage Negotiations

A relatively large number of employers raise wages voluntarily. Fifty-three percent of domestic workers reported receiving their last pay raise without their asking for it, whereas 38 percent received raises by initi-ating the wage negotiation. The remaining 9 percent reported having both employer-initiated and self-initiated pay increases. Some domes-tic workers approach their employers by drawing comparisons with what they receive from their other employers. The ease or difficulty of asking for a raise itself is related to the structure of the relationship between workers and employers and the kind of strategies both employ.

For most of the workers who ask for raises, however, asking for a raise is a routine and integral part of the labor arrangement, deriving from a tacit understanding that the employer will never give an increase voluntarily and that the worker herself should ask for it. Workers under-stand that if they do not initiate negotiation, their current wages could persist indefinitely. The domestic workers in the survey used similar phrases to express this understanding: "If you don't ask for it, they would never increase your wages"; "You gotta ask for an increase, oth-erwise they wouldn't do it"; "They never offer an increase by them-selves; they would be very pleased if you worked for 10,000 TL a day" (her wage at that time was 20,000 TL); "If it's up to them, they would never give you a raise"; and "If it's up to them, they would make you work for nothing." Domestic workers who regularly and consistently initiated the pay-raise negotiation voiced these comments. Only a small minority of workers said that asking for a raise is a source of discom-fort. Domestic workers also occasionally request advance payments, which function as loans. Workers request such payments for building houses, marrying off children, purchasing coal for the winter, or send-ing children to private prep classes for university entrance examina-tions. Some workers receive pay while the employers are away. I con-ceptualize these monetary benefits and other types of help received from employers as patronage benefits and examine them under the rubric of patron-client relationships in Chapter 4.

In explaining how they decide when to ask for a raise and how much to ask for, well over one-third of the domestic workers stated that they base their decision on shared information and comparisons of their wages with those of their friends in the community. This finding is in keeping with the discovery of the neighborhood-based networking among domestic workers that enables them to be in daily touch with one another's work lives and thus with their employers and their pecu-liarities. One worker's statement on this issue is telling: "We will warn the employers that if they do not increase wages to 30,000 TL, we will announce a strike by August." Although she made her comment half-jokingly, it reflects the extent to which domestic workers exchange information about the wage rates and the timing of pay raises.

Since the domestic workers' community is kinship and neighbor-hood based, it is also a locus of information for their husbands. A husband's access to information on other workers' wages allows him to judge the worth of his wife's labor comparatively and to pressure her to ask for an increase. Domestic workers in both groups commonly experience this pressure. One worker said, "My husband says I am going cheap; he says, 'Go ... work for the ones who pay more.'" Another worker said, "He grumbles about why I do not ask for an increase. . . . He says, 'Everybody gets more than you, why do you accept less?'" The comparison drawn with other domestic workers in the community is also reflected in the following statement made by yet another domestic worker: "He says, 'Why are you getting less, so and so gets more than you, you should speak out too.'" In a few cases, the pressure intensifies and becomes a threat in the form of, "Either you get an increase or I'm not letting you work anymore."

It is difficult to assess whether husbands' intervention in this area plays a restrictive or an enabling role in their wives' negotiations with employers. To what extent does intervention prompt a woman to initiate pay-raise negotiations? And in what ways does this pressure affect the mode or content of negotiation? As I discuss in detail in Chapter 4, workers and employers invoke their husbands' authority in their management of the worker-employer relationship. In the area of pay-increase negotiations, however, there are few cases in which domestic workers reported transmitting their husbands' messages to their employers: "If you don't increase my wage, my husband will not allow me to come to you anymore."

A more interesting question emerging from the data is whether there is a relationship between a husband's exerting pressure for a pay increase and a wife's hiding some of her earnings from him. A pay increase provides an occasion for a woman to withhold some of her earnings until her husband, using information he received through the community, starts pressuring her. Also, domestic workers receive cash wages at the end of their workday, with delayed payment occurring occasionally among the wives of the doorkeepers. The occurrence of

delayed payment among the doorkeeper group has significant implications for control and disposal of the domestic worker's earnings, since
in these cases the delayed payment often goes to the husband. Thirty-
four percent of domestic workers from this group reported that cash
wages due to them were occasionally paid to their husbands when their
husbands served the employer (the tenant). Payment to a husband for
his wife's work, however, is not a standard practice.

Wages of Single-Employer Workers

Wage differences between single- and multi-employer workers reflect
predominantly their relative work loads resulting from their differing
employment patterns. The going monthly rate for single-employer work,
which compares unfavorably with the rate for multi-employer work,
ranged from 100,000 TL to 300,000 TL a month. There is a larger wage
variation within the group of single-employer workers. For example,
during February and March 1990 we interviewed three such workers.
Their wages were 150,000 TL, 300,000 TL, and 220,000 TL, respectively.

Some of the variation in wages among single-employer workers can
be attributed to differences in work responsibilities and level of effort.
For example, two workers in this group reported that they *never* engage
in heavy physical labor; and, indeed, their employers hire additional
domestic workers for such tasks. Single-employer workers tend to have
specific characteristics that render them unable to perform the task work
required of multi-employer workers. Among fifteen single-employer
workers, three were pregnant and unable to perform heavy physical
work at the time of the interview. Two were older, widowed women
whose main responsibilities were childcare and light housework. Four
women were confined to single-employer work because their husbands
objected to multi-employer work. Since the women in this group each
work for one employer for a prolonged time, they have less flexibility
in pressing for periodic raises, and, unlike multi-employer workers,
their implicit contracts are made for the entire year. With the exception
of four women who were new workers, the women in this group
received an average of a 60 percent pay increase over the previous
year—an increase comparable to the average total yearly wage increase
among the multi-employer workers. The majority of the workers who
did receive a raise (seven out of eleven) reported that they initiated the
negotiation with their employers for the annual raise.

INSURANCE PROTECTION AND FUTURE WORK STRATEGIES: THE DEMISE OF PATRIARCHAL BARGAINS?

With few exceptions, the domestic workers I studied are not legally recognized as employees. Domestic workers and their employers are part of an informal economy not covered by existing labor legislation. Domestic workers sell their labor in informal ways, with terms, conditions, and wages negotiated orally and without legally binding contracts. Thus, there is no legislated or regulated minimum wage, employment stability, working hours, sick days, vacations, or social insurance. While the social insurance program provided by the government, which offers a relatively high degree of security for retirement and worker redundancy, is mandatory for workers in the formal sector, workers in the informal sector depend on other sources of protection and security.

There is currently no collective effort to obtain legal protection or any attempt on the part of the government to regulate labor relations in domestic service or to extend social insurance to domestic workers. In Turkey, unlike in some Latin American countries, the desirability and need for legal protection is yet to be collectively articulated by domestic workers (Chaney and Castro 1989; Hondagneu-Sotelo and Riegos 1997).

Insecurity and instability are the defining aspects of work in the informal sector. How is this absence of worker protection understood and experienced by the workers themselves? Although all the women in this study have a strong notion of the need for security, their conception of security focuses on the social insurance issues of old-age pension and how to make claims in cases of work-related injury and illness. They expressed little interest in regulation of wages and work hours. Many expressed concern about the potential danger their work presents to their health and safety, especially those who have experienced work-related injuries.[3] The majority of the domestic workers (62 percent in doorkeeper group and 76 percent in squatter settlement group) perceive the provision of social insurance coverage as an improvement in their work conditions.

Social insurance benefits can be attached to employment in domestic service through two national programs. The largest, called Sosyal Sigorta (Social Insurance), is a mandatory social insurance program that brings with it a great measure of employee protection. All the workers in the state and workers in the private sector are covered by this program, which requires employers to pay a share of benefits on workers' behalf. Workers under this program are protected by state health and safety regulations and labor regulations that guarantee old-age pensions, paid holidays, severance pay, maternity leave, pensions for disability, and medical coverage. Only a few workers in the study are covered by Sosyal Sigorta.

The second program, called Bagkur, is designed basically for self-employed workers (including housewives). Workers who are under the Bagkur are required to make monthly payments into this social insurance program, which provides a meager retirement pension and medical coverage. Still, Bagkur covers less than 2 percent of the domestic workers from both groups in the study. More than 80 percent in both groups have no coverage at all, and most of those who have any sort of coverage have, in recent years, begun paying meager premiums (about a day's wage for a month) to the mushrooming private insurances.

The dominant pattern of employment in the form of multi-employer work constitutes a considerable obstacle to the establishment of social insurance benefits. Multi-employer work does not permit the establishment of a single-employer position or institution, which Sosyal Sigorta currently requires. Those who have this type of coverage have been able to obtain it either through their primary work (in the case of women doorkeepers) or through their having been claimed as workers in their employer's business.

Of those who are not insured by any of these programs, 94 percent (from both groups) stated that they would like to have insurance coverage through Bagkur. Despite their eagerness for some kind of insurance, most choose not to invest in any program because they are unwilling or unable to pay for Bagkur premiums. Seventy-one percent from the doorkeeper group and 52 percent from the squatter settlement group stated that their current budget does not allow them to pay for Bagkur, even though they wish to have it. The second most important reason mentioned for not signing up for Bagkur is the husband's opposition. This opposition is greater among the squatter settlement workers (21 percent, compared with 9 percent in the doorkeeper group). In these cases, the husband considers his wife's having individualized social insurance coverage a symbol and symptom of her independence from his protection and control. All of these women reported a uniform response from their husbands when they expressed a desire to enroll in Bagkur: "I'm your insurance; why do you think you need other insurance?" The length of their employment also affects domestic workers' decisions against insurance coverage. Older domestic workers, while expressing their regret over not having any insurance coverage for the many years they have worked, stated that it is too late for them. They described their situation by saying that they will be long gone when they become eligible to collect their pension. In contrast to this, new and younger workers tend to subscribe to the opposite logic that it is too early for them since they have started out recently and will have insurance coverage eventually.

This issue emerged in the focus group interviews and generated some discussion. Domestic workers who are neither willing to sacrifice part of their earnings in order to obtain insurance coverage nor willing to give up the idea of protection in their old age, suggested that the financial burden of insurance coverage should be shared by all of a worker's employers. They further suggested that this sharing would not be difficult to coordinate and implement because employers know one another through referrals and friendships.

The meaning and significance of protection also came through powerfully in their accounts of the kinds of employment they would prefer to have. Eighty-nine percent of domestic workers from the doorkeeper group and 92 percent from the squatter settlement group indicated their interest in "a job with a social insurance coverage" (*sigortalı iş*). The majority of the workers from both doorkeeper and squatter settlement groups (62 percent and 61 percent, respectively) mentioned cleaning, cooking, and serving tea in a government office, a private firm, or a hospital as their choice of employment.

What meaning do domestic workers attach to these forms of employment? First, these women are fully aware of the kinds of employment avenues open to them; none expressed interest in an unrealistic employment situation, inconsistent with her educational background and marketable skills. Second, and more important, all of the preferred jobs are similar to domestic work in terms of job content and required skills. The primary difference is that they all offer social insurance and old-age pensions. The women in the survey put a high value on these jobs, even though they yield less income than informal domestic work and are marked by their low status. All consistently expressed greatest interest in government jobs (*devlet işi*) and are undaunted by the fact that all the government jobs to which they aspire pay significantly less than domestic work. Perhaps this preference reflects a persistent desire among rural migrants for the protection and security of the Turkish state, which, with its paternalistic provision of life-long employment and other privileges, has a long tradition of being the main source of employment for a sizable portion of the urban classes. It is a kind of protection the women feel they have long been deprived of as peasants, while their urban counterparts have enjoyed all the benefits from it.

These women's desire to have employment with social insurance coverage is strongly related to their changing sense of their relation to paid work, family, and home. Their testimonies defuse the widely held notion that poor women take up wage work only for the sake of the family survival in the face of economic uncertainty. Contrary to that notion, I suggest that their preference reflects their recognition of wage work as a permanent part of their lives with the implication of a high level of commitment to wage work.

Most of the women in this study were unequivocal about their paid employment in domestic service. Sixty-five percent of the women in the doorkeeper group and 58 percent of the squatter group plan and expect to continue working. In fact, most of the women articulated the strength of their commitment to work with expressions such as, "I will work until I die" and "I would like to continue working as much as I can." For the majority of the workers, paid employment, regardless of the conditions of work or occupational status, is essential to upward social and economic mobility and to the establishment of modern forms of life they desire for themselves and their children.

Only 11 percent of the doorkeeper group and 4 percent of the squatter group wished to withdraw from waged work to become full-time housewives. The housewife ideal, however, is not feasible, affordable, or desirable for the majority of them. From their perspective, focused on the realities of their circumstances, the distinction between housewife and working wife does not make sense. They are well aware that only their continuing ability to earn wages creates conditions in which their ideals and aspirations about themselves and their children can be achieved. Their rejection of "traditional" domesticity—a version of domesticity that excludes women's employment—does not mean that working undermines their identities as mothers and wives or their devotion to home and families. Their families remain the center of their lives and of their identities.

Domestic workers encounter two main models that they can emulate in their own lives. The urban middle-class women for whom they work provide an ideal, but one that is at odds with the realities of the lives of domestic workers. Their nonworking counterparts with whom they share a common background and some current life situations provide them with another model of housewifery and motherhood, representing the absence of the promise of a better life.

For about half of the women who stated that they see their work as temporary (54 percent of both groups), the conditions of work or the occupation itself, not its being paid employment, informed their desire to leave domestic service. Doing someone else's dirty work was characterized as a "futureless" job. Another group in this ambivalent category cited exhaustion and health as the reasons they would like to discontinue working (20 percent of the doorkeeper group and 33 percent of the squatter group). Many of these women's comments about their lack of commitment to work are inextricably tied up with their complaints about the consequences of being involved in domestic work for so many years. These "worn-out" workers feel that their career in domestic service has prematurely consumed them physically.

It is important to point out that although this group of women consider their work in domestic service temporary, they expressed their noncommitment in vague terms. Most of them plan to keep working until their household's economic standing improves (43 percent of the doorkeeper group and 54 percent of the squatter group), the only condition under which they would discontinue working. Withdrawal from paid work is almost invariably associated with improved economic status and "completion" of their duties as parents. Depending on the life cycle of the household, some workers imagine the completion of their children's education or their children's marriages will free them to retire.

Another group of women (11 percent of the doorkeeper group and 21 percent of the squatter group) explained that they also view their work as being temporary but qualified the statement by saying that their withdrawal from domestic service depends on their ability to obtain employment in other fields. Thus, this group of domestic workers also has a strong commitment to employment, but they do not want to make a permanent career in domestic service. They expect to leave it upon finding a job with Sosyal Sigorta coverage and in a less menial field. Their comments on their future work strategies are accompanied, however, by an uncomfortable awareness that domestic work may not prove temporary or transitional.

Although domestic workers make significant and necessary contributions to their household economies, in most instances contributing to family budgets as much as and sometimes more than their husbands and other members of the household, these women's strong commitment to earning wages cannot be explained as a survival strategy. The concept of survival strategy is problematic in many ways, treating the household as a monolithic entity and women's relationship to paid work as one dimension. My findings suggest that the survival-strategies model greatly underestimates the role of wage earning as a component of identity formation. In the context of this study, it is especially misleading and simplistic to reduce women's commitment to paid work to a survival strategy. We need, instead, to take into account the "needs" and "desires" deriving encounters with urbanity and modernity.

Women's desire for an "individualized" form of social insurance that entails pension benefits reflects their perception of the increasing fragility of the traditional protections offered by the patriarchal family. Deniz Kandiyoti (1988) describes this phenomenon as the "demise of patriarchal bargains." In patrilinearly and patrilocally organized peasant households, in which women as dispossessed individuals are totally dependent on men (with no rights to earn a living autonomously from men), women strike a bargain with patriarchy: they receive "protection and security in exchange for submissiveness and propriety" and "adopt interpersonal strategies that maximize their security through manipulation of the affection of their sons and husband" (280). Relations between different generations of women are organized around the well-defined roles of mother-in-law and daughter-in-law with the older women in an unequivocal position of authority over the younger. Women gain power through age and by producing children, especially sons. A woman is most powerless as a young wife and most powerful when she becomes a mother-in-law. Since a son is expected to provide support and security to his mother in her old age, women are preoccupied with insuring their sons' lifelong loyalty and are in constant competition with their daughters-in-law. The promise of male economic protection and the support of sons in old age that made this bargain compelling for women is no longer viable. Urban migration, male unemployment, low wages, and neolocality (the breakdown of the patrilineal-patrilocal complex) have eroded the material bases of classical patriarchy and undermined its ability to offer security and protection. Kandiyoti (1988) argues that women's responses to the breakdown of classical patriarchy are all conservative and range from passive resistance to increased religiosity, all in efforts to restore the original patriarchal bargain that promised "protection in exchange for submissiveness and propriety" (280). Domestic workers' desire for individual insurance and their commitment to wage work reflect their unwillingness to submit to the old patriarchal bargain. Unwilling or unable to restore the original bargain, women begin to depend on their own work for protection and security.

CARVING OUT A WORK IDENTITY

Domestic workers work in private homes, where the terms and conditions of their labor are not officially determined and regulated. Their "workplace" is isolated from those of their fellow workers, allowing for personalized forms of labor control. In this chapter, however, we see that these features are articulated with the mode of employment and the wage system in such a way that domestic service emerges as a highly structured and uniformly functioning occupation that shares many characteristics with "formal" employment. Yet, the analysis of mode of employment in domestic service revealed that the transformation of peasant women into "working-class" women is neither uncomplicated nor complete.

The profiles of domestic workers in terms of mode of employment and autonomy in the labor process suggest that modes of employment in domestic service have significant implications for the formation of work identities. There is no smooth modernization of domestic service through which peasant women are transformed into working-class women and the relations between the buyers and sellers of domestic labor become depersonalized.

Recall that the majority of workers in this study have multiple employers. Workers with multiple employers are not, however, a homogenous group. They differ in terms of the frequency of repeated visits to the same employer, which entails differences in work loads, variety of tasks, and physical labor involved, thus producing different worker profiles. On the continuum between traditional maids and proletarianized cleaners, the majority of domestic workers are situated toward the "proletarianized" end. However, among proletarianized positions, the most objectively advantageous mode is that of multiple weekly visits to the same employer with shorter work hours, a lower volume of work, a greater variety of tasks, and better chances for patronage benefits. This distribution of domestic workers' profiles is all the more remarkable because the unique constellation of supply and demand structures in which supply of domestic workers does not meet the demand seems to facilitate a process of proletarianization. Yet domestic workers fashion schedules that position them between the two extremes of the continuum working as neither maids nor cleaners.

The role played by the institution of domestic service in the polarization of middle and working classes and the creation of racialized versions of femininity is widely documented in feminist scholarship (see, e.g., Davidoff 1973; Palmer 1990; Rollins 1985). Victorian gender ideology assigned the home to middle-class women as their natural sphere. They were not expected to perform dirty physical tasks but instead to function as managers and guardians of the domestic sphere. The labor of domestic workers facilitated the detachment of middle-class women from physicality, the body and bodily functions, and middle-class women were defined by their purity and delicacy; domestic workers, by virtue of their association with the body, physical labor, and contact with dirt, were seen as rough and dirty and closer to nature. Phyllis Palmer in her study of domestic service in the United States between 1920 and 1945, *Domesticity and Dirt* (1990), discusses how social assignment of different tasks to different categories of women along sharply divided class and race lines generated the oppositional ideas of womanhood in which white middle-class women as the organizers of housework and domestic space saw themselves as the "mind" of the job, and distinct from black domestic workers, who represented "the body" (74).

During the years after World War II and until the 1980s, when black women left domestic service in massive numbers, middle-class women, like working-class women earlier in the century, began to take care of their own homes, performing laborious dirty housework while holding paid jobs. Recent studies of domestic service document a renewal of the dichotomy between working-class and middle-class women in their relations to paid and domestic work. Pierrette Hondagneu-Sotelo and Ernestine Avila (1997) argue, for example, that live-in nanny arrangements in the United States attract the most vulnerable segment of the immigrant population (recent arrivals without immigration papers) and encourage temporal and spatial separations of working mothers and children, in that "transnational mothers" work in the United States to support their children back home in Mexico or Central America, creating new meanings and practices of motherhood among these women. Nicky Gregson and Michelle Lowe (1994) similarly underscore middle-class women's disengagement from childcare and housework in contemporary England. They argue that middle-class women's full participation in the labor force in dual-career households with no fundamental reorganization of the gender division of labor at home have again made domestic labor class specific. "In certain middle-class households," they write, "cleaning is no longer being seen as a suitable use of middle-class women's time-space" (110). The heaviest, most repetitive and unpleasant domestic work in middle-class homes has become the work of a new class of women. This middle-class disinvestment from domestic work has far-reaching consequences for both groups of women. Certain aspects of domesticity become less fundamental to the gendered subjectivities of middle-class women, who see and define themselves in terms of nondomestic roles, while the same aspects become fundamental to working-class women's identity. With the middle-class women's disengagement from the physical tasks of the household, social class differences between women are being amplified.

Yet this process of middle-class disengagement is fraught with contradictions and tempered by the gender ideology that intimately links the performance of household work with women's gender identity. Performing domestic work is seen as an essential aspect of womanhood and dealing with dirt is equated with love and feminine caring. Women in Gregson and Lowe's study (1994) purchase domestic help but continue to see the job as "theirs" and evaluate themselves on their performance as wives and mothers as much as on their performance as professionals. Indeed, the traditional equation between femininity and domesticity continues to underpin the general parameters of social relations in domestic service. Both groups of women, domestic workers and women who employ them, in the constitution of social relations of domestic service attempt to equate waged domestic labor with "the work which they do 'for love' in their own homes" (Gregson and Lowe 1994:227). Both groups personalize dirt with the notion that cleaning up the personal dirt of kin is an expression of love. In short, they constitute themselves and are constituted in such ways that they share the assumption that domestic labor is carried out for love not money. And in doing so, they do not permit the establishment of rationalized labor relations between themselves and resist a polarization between them on the basis of dirt and purity, and body of the job and mind of the job.

Unlike the situation in England and the United States, in Turkey the purchase of waged domestic labor is in most cases not a labor-coping strategy (most employers, or 62 percent, are housewives, whereas 38 percent work outside the home). Yet, the changing structure of Turkish society, sketched in Chapter 1, promotes the emergence of polarized identities of womanhood. Changes in the cultural norms of housewifery and motherhood have shifted middle-class women's relationship to the home and domesticity, increasing the importance of women's extrado-mestic activities. These women increasingly invest their labor and time in cleaner areas of domesticity, most significantly in the realms of con-sumption and children's education, leaving the dirt-removing aspect of domesticity to paid workers. However, domestic workers' diverse and often ambivalent responses to such menial labor and their resistance to complete proleterianization undermine some of these polarizing ten-dencies. We see this resistance most clearly in domestic workers' attempt to carve out a third profile, a work identity that allows them to function as housekeepers rather than traditional maids or proletarianized clean-ers. The formation of a different worker identity between two extremes is affected by a host of other forces, especially the husbands' role in choosing employers and the financial and labor needs of the household. These forces establish parameters within which domestic workers make choices about the level of their participation in waged work. What, then, constitutes the ideal work identity? What renders it so desirable?

Zerrin Yasaz, one of those "in-between" workers who works for two employers, visiting each one twice a week, considers her employers her "friends" and claims that working for these two women is pleasurable and less tiring than working at her own home. Her profile is atypical in some respects: both of her employers happen to be housewives with children in college and less-demanding work requirements. Yet, this untypical characteristic provides an insight into the constitutive ele-ments of the "third" profile, one that all domestic workers in this study seem to strive to achieve. When I talked with her one evening after she came home from work, she sketched her workday and her interactions with her employer.

When I arrived the breakfast was already ready. Older brother [*"abi"*—
the employer's husband] leaves early for work. He doesn't eat breakfast.
He just drinks a glass of milk and takes off. . . . She always waits for me
for the breakfast. We had our tea together and enjoyed the sun coming
from the kitchen window and talked for a while. [The narrative continues
with a description of the employer woman's new kitchen window dressing and her promise to get some of the same lace for Zerrin.] You know
she's my friend. She shares everything with me. We have no secrets from
each other. After breakfast I made the beds and straightened and dusted
the bedrooms. I don't touch Güler's [a daughter in college] desk. She has
a computer there. She [the employer] remained in the kitchen and did the
breakfast dishes. Then we watched TV together [soap opera] and had coffee. After that she was in the kitchen again cooking dinner. Older brother
has a big appetite [*boğazına düşkün*] so she always prepares several different dishes. I vacuumed and mopped the floors. Then we had lunch
together and I cleaned up the kitchen afterwards. In the afternoon I did
the ironing, mostly older brother's shirts. I don't like ironing. It's boring.
I like to talk while I am ironing. While she was getting ready for her
neighbors' acceptance day [*kabul günü*], she put away the ironed clothes.
I iron but she puts things away, I don't do the drawers and closets. She
teases me that I undo my ironing by putting wrinkles back in the pressed
shirts while hanging them. She is right. I cleaned the bathroom last. I
always do the bathroom last because afterwards I can wash all the cleaning rags I use by hand and I bathe myself. She gave me a towel set that
her brother-in-law's wife brought her from Bursa [a town in Turkey, center of towel production], which I keep there. I was done by 3:30. We left
at the same time; she went upstairs, I came home.

As Zerrin Yasaz's description of her workday and moments of interaction with her employer suggests for domestic workers in this study,
middle-class homes do not merely represent a space of hard physical
labor. They are also places to retreat from the common drudgery of their
own cluttered homes and escape the unceasing demands of their families for care and attention. Well-furnished, centrally heated, middle-
class apartments and the niceties they contain represent a space of orderliness and serenity, a "domestic haven," that is both admired and envied.
These homes and their interior decorations stand in sharp contrast to
the homes of workers, which lack the comforts of modern household
technology (being able to take a hot bath in the home of employers is
considered a job perk). Furthermore, in middle-class homes, domestic
workers find a domestic interior arranged and run by women who are
regarded as "skilled" in modern housewifery and mothering practices.
Middle-class homes embody many of the constitutive elements and

relationships of modern domestic life. Working in such homes and developing relationships with employers provides domestic workers with an understanding of the habits, practices, and sensibility of modern domesticity and identity. Indeed, domestic workers in Turkey highly value the knowledge acquired by going to work in middle-class homes. Close exposure to middle-class household commodities and consumption forms encourage domestic workers to imitate middle-class modes of housekeeping and decoration (Zerrin Yasaz received lace curtains for her window as she said she would). This space offers possibilities for cross-class friendship on the basis of the shared experience of gender and motherhood as well as womanly support and practical advice. The cultivation of intimacy allows for cross-class identification and provides domestic workers with leverage to negotiate work conditions. Whereas working as a cleaner does not allow for the development of any intimate social interaction with employers and working as a traditional maid confers a menial and subordinated identity on the worker, wholly subsuming her life to that of employer, the third mode of work as "housekeeper" gives workers a sense of autonomy and allows for both intimacy and identification with their employers.

As I document above, autonomy and self-direction are highly valued qualities in work. The statement "I do my job as though I am the master of this home" reflects domestic workers' desire to feel some control over the pace of work and specification of standards and routines. In a sense, by keeping the house as if it were their house, domestic workers can identify with their employers and the house. The multiple weekly visits to the same employer allow them to experience this work as "housekeeping," without their becoming "maids." If the employer is present, periods of sociability with the employer women are accommodated by the more relaxed rhythms of work. The class and rural/urban distinctions between the women can be felt to falter and blur. The distance between the employer and employee can be breached; false kinship relations can be activated. The worker can see herself as a friend and peer of her employer and enjoy middle-class amenities.

In contrast, total "specialization"—laboring in a different home every day of the week, returning to the same workplace only infrequently—allows for greater autonomy, but this is an autonomy by default. The work involves repetitively performing the dirtiest and most physically exhausting labor. The worker's labor is reduced to a single, undesirable dimension of "housekeeping," removing dirt by heavy cleaning. Her labor is masculinized: her body is marked with the signs of peasantry. She suffers from fatigue and poor health. She is detached from the social relations of domestic work, from the people whose mess she cleans up, and from her surroundings. The more employers a domestic worker has and the more infrequently she visits a given employer, the more she becomes a "cleaner" (remover of dirt), a label she and other workers like her refuse to incorporate into their self-images as an important facet of their work identities, regardless of their actual mode of employment. This level of "proletarianization" in domestic service confers a menial identity to the worker and fosters an image of a physically strong and resilient woman—reminiscent of how they were defined as peasant women. In different ways, domestic workers do not wish to embrace this peasant-like proletarianized imagery but with equal force reject a servant imagery associated with being tied to a single employer.

4   Intimate Weapons of the Weak

AT A BUS STOP between a middle-class residential district and a squatter settlement, a group of domestic workers, clutching plastic bags, stand apart from the urban women returning home from work and shopping. Their ill-fitting, ill-matched outfits draw attention to their economic status and their efforts to emulate the middle-class women around them. The plastic bags they carry contain the peasant şalvar—their work clothes—and also may be stuffed with hand-me-down clothes given to them by their employers. Do they carry the change of clothes to conceal their peasant backgrounds?

The contents of the plastic bags and the women's outfits are signs of their identity and reveal their role in the urban environment as well as their peasant roots. The concealed şalvar clearly bespeaks conflicted feelings about their rural identities. The familiar clothes provide comfort but are hidden because they are signs of poverty and backwardness. The hand-me-down commuting outfit is similarly complex, suggesting the women's dependence on and subordination to their employers, as well as their emergent modernity and urbanity. The interpretation of these clothes depends largely on how one understands the relationship between middle-class employers and the migrant women who work for them.

With a few exceptions historical and cross-cultural discussions of the relationship between employers and domestic workers assume that employers define the identity of domestic workers and the nature of that relationship.[1] "What is bought and sold in domestic service," Mary Castro (1989) points out in her study of domestic service in Colombia, "is not simply the labor power of a domestic worker or her productive work and energy; it is her identity as a person. This is the most specific feature of domestic service" (122).

In these accounts the employer woman is seen as an actor and her domestic worker as a passive, subordinated subject. In rare cases, the worker is described as a "resisting" subordinate who deliberately brackets off her degraded work-related identity from her social life. In opposition to these views, I argue that an understanding of this relationship requires that domestic workers be recognized as active subjects despite the fact that they operate within a culturally and economically constituted structural inequality.

Domestic service is a critical arena of intimate social and cultural interaction between two very different types of women inhabiting otherwise discreet worlds. Both women's sense of where they stand in the larger society is developed and reinforced through their interaction. An examination of domestic service allows us to observe the ways women of different classes participate in one another's lives and to examine the effects of class inequalities on the lived experiences of class and gender identities of women. This chapter takes into account the perspectives of two groups of employer women, drawing on data collected through focus group interviews and from participant observation in various settings in the squatter settlement communities.

IDENTITY AND RESISTANCE IN DOMESTIC SERVICE

The recent literature on domestic work emphasizes a sense of inferiority as the effect of daily rituals in the personalized work relations of domestic service. Two contrasting perspectives dominate this discussion. One view, articulated by Judith Rollins (1985), describes black domestic workers' experience as one of *ressentiment*, "a long-term seething, deep-rooted negative feeling toward those whom one feels unjustly have power or an advantage over one's life" (227). However, domestic service does not necessarily undermine the self-esteem and self-image of the workers since they are aware of the subjugating conditions of their work and perceive their status as a role in a game of domination and subordination. "The presence of such *ressentiment* attests to domestics' lack of belief in their own inferiority, their sense of injustice about their treatment and position, and their rejection of the legitimacy of their subordination" (231). She concludes by saying that "domestics' ways of coping with employers' degrading treatment have been effective, then, in protecting them from the psychological damage risked by accepting employers' belief system but have not been effective in changing the behaviors themselves" (231–32).

A second view, articulated by Thornton Dill (1988) and Jacklyn Cock (1980), focuses on resistance strategies that involve internally effective modes of preserving one's dignity against oppression. For example, Dill opposes Rollins's representation of black domestic workers as victims of domination and suggests that we should look at resistance strategies as attempts to alter power relations. According to Dill's analysis, one resistance strategy employed by domestic workers is to demarcate their "own life" from their work thus transcending the limitations of their work-defined identities.

Rollins sees domestic workers as entirely passive individuals who feel they have to endure their deeply felt subordination, even though they are able to maintain a sense of their dignity and self-worth. They are powerless to change their conditions of work, because "if domestics do not pretend to be unintelligent, subservient, and content with their positions, they know the position could be lost" (Rollins 1985:227). In the second view, however, resistance is the act of constituting and defending one's self-worth (Dill 1988:37). In Dill's study, resistance takes the form of overt and covert acts: confrontation, chicanery, or cajolery. Through these strategies, she argues, the domestic workers she studied distanced themselves and their sense of self from the job and the identity associated with it. In so doing, they refuse to " 'own' the job or to be owned by it" (39). She concludes that stories of resistance are "therefore assertions of self-respect" (43). Similarly, Jacklyn Cock (1980) describes South African domestic workers' assuming of subservient masks and engaging in acts of mockery and ridicule as coping mechanisms, what she calls "muted rituals of rebellion," which, she argues, are an effective means of protecting one's integrity and personality.

Mary Romero (1992), critical of what she calls social psychological approaches to domestic service, suggests shifting the focus of analysis from the social psychological aspects of personalism, which limit the discussion to the individualized coping and resistance mechanisms of domestic workers. Instead, she examines the labor process itself by employing a structuralist analysis. Working from a Marxist-feminist framework, she argues in her study of Chicana domestic workers in the United States that "within the structure of advanced capitalism, racism and sexism can not be considered personal relationships but are part of the structure of exploitation" (142). She conceptualizes these employer-worker relations as instances of class struggle in which conflicts between employers and workers involve themes identical to the larger class conflicts under capitalism, such as control over the labor process and wages. Romero's argument that the substance of interpersonal exchanges between employer and employee should be examined as part of the labor process is certainly an important analytical move. Yet her analysis has some fundamental problems. Most notably, the application of Marxist analysis to domestic service fails to specify the structural conditions of domestic service. Even if it is essentially contractual, domestic service is structured in ways that diverge crucially from rationally organized industrial workplaces where workers and employers rarely meet in person, where job requirements are well defined, and where compliance with job requirements is achieved through a technical division of tasks and through disciplinary practices. In Romero's account, domestic service is distinguished only by "emotional labor" (see Hochschild 1983), which is the core of its exploitation. She constructs an argument consistent with her Marxist understanding of exploitation to reconcile the "personalism" of this class relation and class struggle by conceptualizing emotional labor as a commodity. It is a commodity most wanted but unpaid by employer women. She presumes a universal need for employer women to extract emotional labor (nurturing, caring, and enhancing the employer's status) from domestic workers and an equally universal need for domestic workers to avoid giving or selling this labor. Thus within this framework, "doing" emotional labor is treated as exclusively belonging to the "employee."

My interpretation departs from these approaches, each of which is limited in not allowing for a relationally, contextually constructed understanding of identity and of power. First, I suggest that identities should not be seen as automatically emerging from unequal structural positions of the actors within domestic service. They can better be conceptualized as contextually constructed and relationally defined. Leonore Davidoff (1974) specifies: "How far the subordinate identifies with the goals of the system and/or the personal superiors, and by so doing accepts his or her inferior place within it, partly depends on the rewards—both psychic and material—he receives but also partly on how easy it is for him to find compensatory definitions of self-worth" (414).

I argue that the existence of certain powerful alternative definitions of identity for the domestic worker makes it difficult to attribute inferiority as a trait that characterizes her very inner being (or her self-worth). Only by examining alternative contexts and bases of identity can we fully understand the dynamics of power and the role of resistance as part of the work interaction in the domestic worker-employer relationship.

The domestic workers I studied do not passively accept the subordinate or inferior identities associated with work in domestic service but have their own resources and strategies to systematically and constantly negotiate imposed and disempowering identifications. For a full account of domestic workers' self-identifications, we must look beyond their locus of work and try to understand how their other social relationships affect the structure of their work and relations within it. Conversely, such a perspective also allows us to capture how workers' personal relationships are affected by their experiences in domestic service.

Second, I argue that this negotiation is often not a question of "resisting" a dominant mistress. I question the usefulness of the concept of resistance to understand and analyze power relations in the context of domestic service from an actor-oriented perspective. The intimate relationship between the worker and the employer is one that is constructed reciprocally. The management of the relationship between the employer woman and the domestic worker is a product of their joint interaction, and this interaction takes place against a highly structured background of community, patriarchy, the experience of gender identity, urban-rural distinction, and social class.

The dominant analytical approaches employed in studying domestic service view power as a repressive force that structures the hierarchical relationship of employer and worker. They begin with a rather simplified commonsense notion of power as oppression, the exercise of which engenders and shapes resistance on the part of the oppressed. Because of the structural inequalities dictating the capacities of domestic worker and employer woman to exercise control in their interaction, the employer is often assumed to be the active agent, possessing effective means of eliciting compliance with her commands. According to these approaches, "the difference results from the participants' unequal power, which enables the employer to issue commands more often than the servant can choose not to obey" (Hansen 1989:11). One need not deny this overall imbalance to argue that it fails to fully explain the complex interpersonal processes by which relations of work and class are produced.

Rather than neatly reflecting the overall balance of power, conditions of domestic work are structured by the daily interaction of women of different classes who strive to define the employment relationship and who work to their own advantage. These interactions are continually concerned with negotiating conflicting interests, which fall into five areas: (1) the domestic worker wishes to spend fewer hours on the job while the employer wants to keep the domestic worker longer; (2) the domestic worker wants to perform her tasks unsupervised so that she can control her own pace and exercise discretion about how thoroughly a particular task is to be done, whereas the employer wants to oversee work and dictate speed and thoroughness; (3) the domestic worker wants to prompt raises, whereas the employer wants to delay them; (4) the domestic worker wants to use the class perks of the employer woman to her own advantage rather than contest them; and (5) the domestic worker wants to make sure that special work requests do not become a routine part of her job and employers want to expand worker's responsibilities and work load. In pursuit of their respective self-interests, domestic workers and employers engage in social interaction that is informed by opposed self-interest and involves acts of manipulation, compliance, maneuvering, and mutual accommodation.

The point I am making here is that actions taken to produce the desired consequences (the realization of these self-interests) do not constitute "resistance" strategies on the part of employee and "oppression" strategies (applications of power) on the part of employer. We are talking about power practices or forms of resistance that are not "dramatic" in the way they are practiced and in their intended as well as unintended consequences. In this sense, "resistance" may not be the most useful term for describing and analyzing the interaction of two classes of women in domestic service. The actions taken to produce the desired outcomes are permanent, routine features of class interactions in domestic service and do not aim at altering the structure of inequality that supports domestic service. If one is compelled to give these actions a name, they can best be described with James Scott's phrase (1985) "routine resistances," which he uses in reference to peasant resistances.

> Very little of this activity . . . poses a fundamental threat to the basic structure of agrarian inequalities, either materially or symbolically. What it does represent, however, is a constant process of testing and renegotiation of relations between classes. On both sides—landlord-tenant, farmer-wage laborer—there is a never-ending attempt to seize each small advantage and press it home, to probe the limits of the existing relationships, to see precisely what can be gotten away with at the margin, and to include this margin as a part of an accepted, or at least tolerated, territorial claim. (Scott 1985:255)

By emphasizing the joint structuring of labor relations in domestic service, we can move beyond the static approaches in studies of power and resistance to a more dynamic, contextual understanding of how power relations are constructed and maintained. This perspective reveals the ways in which domestic workers are agents acting in pursuit of their own interests rather than passive objects of their employers' power strategies. It is crucial, therefore, to understand the ways in which the self-interests of employers and workers are expressed, negotiated, and contested in the home workplace. What kinds of symbols and idioms are created, invoked, and manipulated in the pursuit of self-interest? What kinds of skills and resources do the actors employ in their production of work relations as they conduct their mundane interactions? These are the questions I attempt to answer in my examination of Turkish domestic workers and their employers.

KIN AND WORK COMMUNITIES INTERTWINED: INFORMAL NETWORKS AND WORK CULTURE

Domestic service does not easily lend itself to collective forms of organization and activism. Domestic work takes place outside of any institutional context that might establish prescribed rights and labor practices. Working separately in isolated households, domestic workers seem excluded from any collective identity that would increase their power in relation to their employers. However, as we see in Chapter 3, domestic workers make approximately three times the official monthly minimum wage and these wages are adjusted periodically without collective bargaining. Domestic workers have contractually determined reasonable work hours that rarely exceed the eight-hour legal limit to the workday. Furthermore, they have unwritten yet widely observed job descriptions. Tasks that are not covered by agreement are subject to separate negotiation.

These are all indicators of formally organized labor. As described in Chapter 3, one factor that explains the existence of these characteristics in this informal area is the supply and demand imbalance. The considerable power of self-determination held by workers is also rooted in the informal networks of domestic workers that are embedded in the migrant communities. Far from being isolated and without resources, these women rely on ties of kinship, friendship, and neighborliness, which effectively counterbalance the negative organizational consequences of isolated workplaces.

The clustering by town of origin and kinship ties that is found among migrants in the squatter settlements and among doorkeeper families in urban neighborhoods is also clearly reflected in the greater proportion of domestic workers (79 percent) who have either female relatives or fellow migrants from the same town of origin living and working as domestic workers in the immediate neighborhood. The residential proximity of domestic workers, along with kinship and ethnicity connections, helps to create network links among domestic workers. These informal networks are part of a larger community where connections with others are rooted in reciprocal kinship rights and responsibilities by which migrants share their symbolic and material resources and exchange labor.[2]

Residential networks play a crucial role for domestic workers in establishing informal social networks that control recruitment patterns for their employment. This is where domestic workers develop, maintain, and enforce a work culture. Thus, what might appear to be a haphazard domestic service market is highly structured and predominantly controlled by domestic workers themselves.

As I show in Chapter 2, while wives of doorkeepers enter domestic work through their husbands or sometimes in an unmediated fashion, squatter settlement workers invariably enter into domestic work through informal residential networks.[3] In the squatter settlement sample, with the exception of former doorkeepers' wives, all workers found their initial jobs through friends (neighbors) and relatives who were working as domestic workers themselves. They used an elaborate personal referral system whereby workers recruit others to work for associates of their employers. This recruitment system involves the juxtaposition of the domestic workers' and the employers' networks. An employer woman seeking a new domestic worker relies on her own network of friends and relatives, who ask their own domestic workers to suggest someone among their friends.

This recruitment process may be more complicated than it appears and is itself regulated by a complex set of norms. Although it is difficult to detect the operating norms in such an informal recruitment process, we can understand their existence and importance when they are violated. The following episode illustrates a shared norm that became visible when a conflict arose.

In one of the informal social gatherings of domestic workers (in which I was a participant), two domestic workers who were not on speaking terms with each other found themselves in shared company. While others tried to persuade them to make up, I pieced together the cause of the dispute. One of the women had started to work for an employer without obtaining the consent of the previous worker, who had quit because she did not get along well with the employer. Throughout the intense discussion of who was right and who was wrong, they consistently invoked one of the subtle rules of conducting business: only with the knowledge and consent of the previously employed worker, can the new worker work for the same employer. The former worker has a legitimate "veto power" over the subsequent worker.

The power of the networks was manifested in a somewhat different fashion in the case of a worker who had been out of work for several months and very much needed to work. She was excluded from the recruitment channels of the network and that exclusion effectively prevented her finding new employers. The reason for the exclusion, I was told by other women, who previously connected her with employers, was that she is "incompetent" and that "she can't keep up with the work." This situation illustrates how the network serves to maintain occupational standards and enforce unwritten work codes. Only by living up to the responsibilities of the ethic of conduct dictated by the network group can one earn the respect and the potential support of other workers.

More than a recruitment channel, this is a true social network that maintains and enforces social and occupational norms. In their interrelation with one another, workers develop a specific work culture in which moral and professional codes of domestic work are established and maintained by community sanctions. On another occasion, a group of domestic workers harshly criticized a fellow worker, who had asked for and received an astonishingly high wage for occasional work for two prostitutes. The main point of the criticism was that "a fair day's pay is for a fair day's work" and that one should "not exploit others on the basis of their moral inferiority," because, as one domestic worker put it, "their selling their cunts is just for the purpose of making a living."

Normative action is also oriented toward maintaining standards and rules of conduct in relation to the employers. The network provides domestic workers with strategies they can employ in interactions with their employers. Within the network, experiences (as well as tricks of the trade) are shared and generalized. Sharing of information about employer practices provides each worker with community standards that can be invoked to refuse excessive, unreasonable demands. When they exchange information regarding employer women's goodness or badness, they describe examples of just treatment as well as mistreatment. "Appropriate" and "inappropriate" tasks are clearly distinguished and defined. Newcomers to the occupation learn from other workers that they need not clean the toilet bowl by hand and that their employers should provide the necessary equipment for such dirty tasks. Cleaning the walls of a room with wallpaper, for example, is not part of the normal duties and should be negotiated separately. In general, they learn the practice and norm that those tasks not originally included in the "job definition" are subject to extra payment.

We must recognize the importance of domestic workers' work culture for generating symbolic and material resources as well as developing standards that are central to domestic workers' ability to challenge and contest employer women's evaluations of their worth and their discretionary power in controlling the terms of interaction. Although these relations are a source of support and solidarity among domestic workers and involve social practices that produce and reproduce what is accomplished more formally in other labor markets, they are hierarchical and characterized by tensions and contradictions. It would be erroneous to portray these networks as ideal kinship-based communities that entail no conflict, hierarchy, or exploitation. For example, recruitment practices are a realm of contention that provides the most strikingly visible source of tension. Through these more transparent relations, it becomes possible to understand that the network does not function equitably, distributing equal shares to every member. "Desirable" employers (those who live at a reasonable commuting distance, those who have better prospects for patronage benefits, those who demand less work, and those who also match the criterion of "desirable" to husbands) are the most important cause of competition among domestic workers. The worker who is in a position to offer such a "desirable" employer exercises considerable discretion about whom she will favor, what reciprocal favor she will expect, and what jealousies and animosities she will create in her circle of fellow workers during the process.

An example will help to illustrate the complicated and tension-laden interactions entailed by employer referral. Aliye Ali, whose conflict between motherhood and work is described in Chapter 2, works only three days a week because of childcare problems, despite her need to increase her workdays. She let everyone in her community know that she had been searching for work taking care of children in the afternoons after school. Such a rare arrangement would permit her to leave the responsibility of taking care of her own three-and-a-half-year-old daughter to her eleven-year-old daughter when she came home from school. One day Aliye heard that although such a position had recently become available, she had not been informed. The domestic worker who had been contacted for recruitment, it turned out, was her sister-in-law. According to Aliye, her sister-in-law chose not to let her know about the job because of a past unpleasant incident between them. Aliye explained that she had once unwittingly prevented her sister-in-law from taking a client's order for lace making. When confronted by Aliye, the sister-in-law denied having acted in revenge and told Aliye that she was not aware that such a position would interest her. As this episode illustrates, work-related engagements intertwine with and sometimes strain other relationships. Kinship animosities get played out in these job referral incidents. Yet kinship ties are also often overridden. There are no formal lines of demarcation that define a separate work-related network free from other social relationships. Relations within these networks are inextricable from other ties of kinship and neighborliness from which they are constituted.

PATRON-CLIENT RELATIONSHIPS AMONG WOMEN

The concept of patronage[4] appropriately characterizes certain significant aspects of the interaction between the employer and the domestic worker, even though the patron-client relationship is not central to the domestic workers who are situated as proletarianized cleaners within the repertoire of work identities. What I discuss under the rubric of the "patron-client" relationship has been generally understood and analyzed as an integral part of "paternalism" or its modern variant "benevolent maternalism" in other studies of domestic service (e.g., Rollins 1985). The patron-client relationship has been linked to the most demeaning aspects of the experience of domestic workers. Therefore, it is important to clarify the often fuzzy boundaries between "patronage" and "paternalism."

Nicholas Abercrombie and Stephen Hill (1976) provide an analytically comprehensive definition of patronage, clearly distinguishing it from paternalism. They argue that in patronage the asymmetry clearly favors the subordinate party, who receives tangible benefits, "while the patron's rewards are more difficult to detect" (423). In marked contrast are paternalistic arrangements, where the patron's benefits extend even beyond receiving such intangibles as honor, deference, and a good reputation. Furthermore, patronage, unlike paternalism, does not assume dominance in the client's life and is temporary: it "may cease once a particular exchange has taken place" (Abercrombie and Hill 1976:423).

Although this rigid distinction may not readily allow for analysis of less clearly marked situations where paternalism mixes with patronage, it is clearly applicable to the Turkish case, where the relationship between employers (patrons) and domestic workers (clients) is essentially contractual, and the organization of domestic service in the form of day work for multiple employers does not allow for diffuse relations. In other words, it is an organization in which domestic workers have the significant option of navigating in the job market to pick the best "patrons" for themselves, although their husbands can impose limits on the exercise of this option.

In almost one-half (47 percent) of the squatter group and about one-third (34 percent) of the doorkeeper group, relations with employers entail some degree of patronage. Patronage varied by the kinds of benefits (or favors) received, including assistance in placing family members and significant others in urban jobs (26 percent in the squatter group and 9 percent in the doorkeeper group), interest-free loans in the form of advances (19 percent in the squatter group and 31 percent in the doorkeeper group), and access to medical care (4 percent in the squatter group and 23 percent in the doorkeeper group). Also, in the squatter group, 7 percent reported receiving patronage in the form of aid in securing their children's education. Because patronage is a process and workers receive patronage benefits sometimes from single and sometimes from multiple sources, it is not possible to quantify this relation. Furthermore, although each type of patronage is covered by the idiomatic expression of help or assistance (*yardım*)[5], these benefits are situationally relative and their importance to the participants varies considerably.[6] For example, other means of assistance are less substantial and more diffuse (but for that reason more ubiquitous) forms of

patronage, including gifts of new items and cash received on the occasion of religious holidays, as well as more routinely received hand-me-
down clothes, discarded household-items, food, and school supplies
for children. Being taught how to read and write in one case and being
taken on a summer vacation with children in another case constituted
yet other forms of patronage.

Many discussions of domestic service have explored whether domestic workers achieve status or prestige in their own community and in
the hierarchy of a servant class in direct relationship to the power, privilege, and wealth of their employers. David Katzman (1978b) and Thornton Dill (1988), point out, for example, that domestic workers seek high-
status or upper-class employers not because of the symbolic status
gained from associating themselves with prestigious employers but
because these employers are the ones who are better able to pay high
salaries and provide more generous fringe benefits and better treatment.
Katzman argues that "there is nothing to support the assumption that
within their own community black domestics attained high prestige by
virtue of the social standing of their employing family" (1978b:247). In
the Turkish case, the employer's social position is important for yet
another reason. Domestic workers prefer and actively seek employers
who have privileged positions or who are likely to have contacts who
will provide jobs for members of their family (adult children and husband) or provide free professional services. The desire for access to
scarce resources, especially jobs at times of high unemployment, moti-
vates workers to seek out a well-connected and powerful patron. Rural
migrants who have minimal resources and means of establishing institutional contacts are most desirous of finding a patron. In fact, one of
the most common expressions among the less privileged segments of
Turkish society is, "To find a job you must find a patron."[7]

Beyond obtaining jobs, patrons can provide interest-free loans that
are crucial to the domestic worker's ability to build a house or make purchases requiring large sums of cash. For example, a domestic worker
might request a sizeable sum of money for her son's or daughter's university preparation classes as an advance payment on her future labor.
Similarly, if a worker is working for a doctor, or the wife of a doctor, she
and her family are likely to have quick, free, and otherwise more con-
venient access to medical facilities. Patronage can also give workers
valuable access to other professional services.

In one particularly pronounced example of patronage, a domestic worker was able to secure a stable job for her husband, one neighbor, and two relatives, in addition to a scholarship for her son. She expressed her sentiments toward her patrons by saying, "I can't leave them [the employer families]. I'll work for these families until I die." Her statement is a strong expression of her loyalty, commitment, and gratitude and provides a textbook case of patronage. Although one might conclude from this woman's story that her relationship with her employers became one of dependency, such a conclusion would be misleading. Even in this extreme case, the interaction does not necessarily cultivate vulnerability and dependency. Her ties with these employers continued not only because she is loyal but, more important, because she genuinely benefited from this relationship. What makes these ties enduring is the fact that she and others like her continue to get their raises regularly, to get paid when the employers go on vacation, and to receive other benefits. If not for these material benefits and the good relations, their "loyalties" would not endure.

As suggested by the scene with which this chapter opens, the most routine and apparently universal form of patronage in domestic service is the giving of old clothes, discarded household items, and furniture. Drawing on the pioneering work of Marcel Mauss (1954), scholars in the social sciences have widely explored the social meaning of gift giving and receiving between individuals and social groups. Mauss conceived of unreciprocated gift giving as constitutive of inequality that establishes or reaffirms one's superiority. "To give," he says, "is to show one's superiority, to show that one is something more and higher.... To accept without returning or repaying more is to face subordination to become a client and subservient" (Mauss 1954:72). Studies have documented that power differentials between domestic workers and employers find their most potent expression and daily confirmation in gift giving. For example, the domestic workers Rollins (1985) studied accepted the gifts but only to throw them away or sell them to thrift stores because unwillingness to accept gifts would constitute a threat to the power differential that gift givers strive to achieve. But gift giving in some domestic service arrangements is also understood as payment in kind. Since this payment in kind, unlike wages, is subject to the discretion of the employer, using it enables them to manipulate service and loyalty in more excessive and subtle ways than formal contracts. Thus "gifts" in domestic service have the double function of discouraging workers from negotiating for wage increases and of underlining the inferior position of the domestic worker who cannot and should not reciprocate.

Unlike most cases discussed in the literature, my data suggest that unreciprocated gift receiving is relatively undemeaning.[8] Turkish domestic workers do not perceive these gifts as demeaning for two reasons. First, domestic workers actively seek these "gifts" as part of what I call their class guilt-inflicting strategy. In another context, E. P. Thompson puts it another way: "What is (from above) an 'act of giving' is (from below) an 'act of getting'" (quoted in Scott 1985:309). Second, domestic workers can redistribute some of these gifts, thus taking on the role of patron themselves. They can translate the gifts into items of prestige in their own community by distributing them to others in need. This redistributive mechanism may even extend to include friends and relatives of the domestic worker in her original rural community.[9]

To fully understand the significance of patronage, one must look beyond the relationship between the domestic worker and the employer. Patronage crucially impacts the domestic worker's status in the family and among other kin and in the community. Patronage is a powerful resource that workers use to gain status, respect, and good reputations within their community. Although domestic work is seen to lower a woman's status, her ability to find jobs for others enhances her status. She becomes the linking agent that gives the community access to an otherwise inaccessible resource. She adopts the role of patron toward others in the community, who pay loyalty and gratitude to her.

Yet this conclusion does not apply to domestic workers from the doorkeeper group. These women cannot "carry" the gifts with prestige, for they inhabit the same neighborhood as their patrons. Indeed, such gifts are among the mechanisms that stigmatize doorkeeper families and differentiate them from their employers. Patronage often includes the family as a whole, because husband and wife may be clients of the same patron. For that reason, the domestic workers in the doorkeeper group are not the sole controllers of the use and redistribution of the gifts they accrue. Finally, the doorkeeper wives' network, unlike networks within squatter settlements, is not particularly conducive to a redistribution of patronage goods, because their immediate subcultural community consists of other migrants (doorkeepers or domestic workers) who are clients of similar if not identical patrons.

What do employers get in return for "gifts," if not enduring ties, unfailing loyalty, or cheaper labor? It was clear from domestic workers' accounts that some practices of gift giving occur around religious holidays, a time when the well-off are supposed to be more (and visibly) charitable. By giving gifts to their workers, they discharge their charitable obligations. But as I show in the next section, more routine and ubiquitous forms of gift giving are used to overcome "class guilt" inflicted by domestic workers. Through their role as patrons, employers also seek more tangible benefits in return and use their gifts to create a sense of gratitude and thereby to obligate domestic workers to return their favors.

We must keep in mind, however, that well over half of the employers (62 percent) are housewives. Therefore, a greater proportion of employers are not in a position to directly take the role of a patron of employment; they can serve as patrons only through their husbands. Such employer women are themselves clients to their husbands. Indeed, we often see multi-level patron-client relations that involve husbands playing the role of patron toward their wives, who in turn serve as patrons to domestic workers, who become patrons for their husbands and a multitude of others. Against this background, we can now look more closely at the interaction between the two women in the "workplace."

INTIMACY AND CLASS "WORK"

Interactions between employers and workers are organized and practiced as ways of dealing with potential conflicts and anxieties arising from the structure of domestic service. The sources of tension and conflict are many: How are boundaries between the roles of employer and employee defined in the private sphere? How are conflicts arising from the blatant disparities of material conditions of life (registered in such visible signs as clothing and furniture) foreseen and managed? How are the more universal conflicts that arise from the visible class relationship of buyer and seller of labor managed in the context of the household? These problems are resolved by a few typical strategies. I call such strategies "work" to register the fact that there is more work entailed by domestic service than cleaning and other contracted tasks. The term "work" also underscores the fact that the interaction between these two categories of women is not limited to supervision of work by a nonworking supervisor. Both the employer and the domestic worker practice work strategies. These can be conceptualized as strategies of management that involve presenting an image of oneself with the expectation of training the other party into a certain behavioral interaction (Goffmann 1959). When these strategies are successful the job gets done better, and potential identity problems are avoided or resolved. However, the very strategies used to manage the domestic service are likely to create their own tensions for the participants in the interaction.

Intimacy "Work"

The rules and norms of domestic service are structured by the values and practices associated with family life wherein the home, as opposed to the "workplace," is an arena for personal and private relationships. Thus, "family" is the metaphor by which the labor relations are lived. Defining the workplace in the terms of the private sphere makes it difficult to demarcate the roles of "employer" and "employee." This difficulty is exacerbated in cases where housewives are employers who find themselves shifting uneasily between their two roles. There is no language in which the actors can articulate conflicts of interest or conceptualize their relations as purely those of buyers and sellers of labor. The use of the familial-kinship idiom, however, gives an immediate identity to a stranger. Intimacy starts with the form of address when the employer, regardless of her age, becomes *"abla"* (older sister) and the domestic worker automatically becomes *"kardeş"* (younger sister) and is addressed by her first name.

Both workers and employers perceive the creation of intimacy as very important. Receiving good treatment for domestic workers is not limited to the quest "to be treated as a person" and "not to be looked down on." For domestic workers, good treatment includes "social closeness" *(yakın olmak)* and connectedness, a realization of the "older sister/younger sister" metaphor in practice. Intimacy also insures better "patronage" benefits for the domestic worker. For the employer, a desirable degree of "intimacy" guarantees better work results because she gets work done as prescribed, she gets tasks done that were not originally negotiated as part of the job description, and she receives emergency help during holidays and other special occasions when she wants to change the work schedule on short notice at the expense of the worker's other employers. For the domestic worker, intimacy insures better "patronage" benefits.

This worker-employer intimacy is always strategic. By "strategic" I want to suggest that such intimacy is a means of pursuing opposed interests rather than an emotional relationship. Intimacy is generally defined as substantial empathy for each other's joys, concerns, and problems. It requires that two actors share more or less similar values and that they have sufficient common experiences to be able to understand each other's perspectives. Thus, by definition, intimacy entails some denial of difference. In domestic service it functions as a strategic device for covering up and making manageable some of the differences in status and class that structure the relationship.

Although domestic workers and employers otherwise belong to radically different worlds, they draw upon their common, gender-based qualities and skills as wives and mothers (as culturally recognized intimacy makers) and use patriarchal gender beliefs in their interaction as they negotiate the terms and conditions of the work arrangement. They use those aspects of women's experience that reflect their shared accommodation to the power of husbands. Although it is exclusively a woman's job to find, screen, recruit, and manage a domestic worker, husbands, as the embodiment of patriarchal power, are invisible yet important actors in domestic work relations. While the two women do not necessarily share the same understanding of the patriarchal norm of female subordination and experience them differently in various spheres of their lives, both parties allow, if not actively seek, mediation of supposedly shared patriarchal assumptions about women's subordinate position in the family and status in society in their interaction. This shared understanding and vocabulary, while playing an important role in reducing the sense of difference between the two groups of women and creating a sense of intimacy and even solidarity, nevertheless reinforces patriarchal definitions of women's identity. For example, when the domestic workers want to set a particular schedule (leaving early or coming late) or when they want to quit, they routinely invoke their husband's authority. This may or may not be a legitimate excuse, because husbands do have control over their work conditions. The point of exaggerating or making up the excuse of a husband's prohibition is to challenge or negotiate work arrangements. In so doing, however, they inevitably tie themselves more closely to their status as socially inferior to their men. Autonomy from patronage at work is thus gained at the price of naturalizing patriarchal control by reaffirming it as an instrument of negotiation.

Employers may use the same tactic. They introduce their husbands into the relationship to avoid a prompt raise ("I can't ask him now; he's crabby these days.... Let's wait until next month"), to get more work done, to get unscheduled help, to set extra visits during holiday periods, to set certain restrictions over the kinds of amenities the domestic worker is allowed to use (such as the telephone), and to excuse themselves from helping out. A young housewife who has two children and whose husband is an executive in a big company reported the following conversation she had with her worker to excuse herself from not giving her a hand: "I told her that when I complain about how I'm exhausted and tired when he comes home, he says, 'Then don't hire a domestic worker. What's the use of her?' and gets upset." Her domestic worker's response was, "Yes, my older brother ["*abi*"—referring to the employer's husband] is right, you mustn't be doing anything."

The structures underlying these episodes perhaps represent a more general set of mechanisms whereby subordinates reproduce their own subordinate status while appearing to assert their discontent with their superiors. Both women refer to an immediately appreciated, pre-established, and unquestionable pecking order in exchanges that can be summarized as follows: I would like to do what you ask (because we have a close relationship; we are sisters), but this man, who regrettably has the ultimate say in my doings, does not let me. The employer women and the domestic workers collectively presume and invoke hierarchical circumstances in which both legitimately present themselves as lacking ultimate authority and being subject to the same type of patriarchal control.

Husbands, however, are not introduced only "symbolically." In some cases, patriarchal control has a more direct presence in the relationship. Some domestic workers' husbands actually oversee their wives' work arrangements and appropriate their incomes. Against such husbands, the employer and the worker consider themselves natural allies and try to reduce the possibility of the appropriation of the worker's earnings. Employers sometimes do this by keeping a portion of the worker's wages in a savings account or by buying gold and keeping it for her. Sometimes, they pay extra money unbeknownst to the worker's husband. It is important to note, however, that such extras are not regarded as a bonus but part of the legitimate pay.

Inflicting Class Guilt and Mending Class Wounds

How are class inequalities between domestic workers and employers perceived and dealt with in their daily interactions? Domestic workers have direct knowledge and experience of their employer's social lives and consumption patterns. Employers, rightly, believe that domestic workers are well placed to observe the enormous differences between their life-styles and those of their employers. They think that the domestic worker's observation of this disparity gives rise to class envy—by creating material and emotional resentment. In response, employers perform what I call "class" work: the mending of what they perceive as class wounds. Feelings of "class guilt" are, to a large degree, shrewdly elicited and sustained by domestic workers. A series of examples involving the consumption of meat, which is an important cultural class marker, imbued with religious and folk significance, illustrates how this "class work" is performed.

An employer reported the following incident: One day she had *börek* (pie) with ground beef for lunch, and her worker made an appreciative remark. The employer offered her the recipe and told her how easy it is to make it. Her worker responded by saying, "I couldn't make it because we can't buy meat." The employer woman encouraged her to use spinach or lentils instead of meat. Since the employer believed that domestic workers can learn only by example, two weeks later, despite her personal distaste for spinach, she made a *börek* with spinach to show her maid how it could be made as delicious without meat.

Another employer described a practice that she said she uses frequently. While she eats leftover food she cooks a fresh meal, preferably with meat or chicken, for the worker to show that she is being treated well. The purpose of doing this, she explained, is to show that "we also eat leftovers." Another employer said that after repeatedly hearing her domestic worker complain that she could not buy meat for her children, the employer told her: "Look at us. We all have high cholesterol. Meat is not good for your health."

Employers believe that such strategies make their workers' lives more pleasant, reduce the contradictions that they believe their workers experience, and make them content with their lives. This sentiment, often expressed among housewife employers, indicates that the domestic workers are quite successful in eliciting class guilt. One employer described how she sees the domestic workers' situation: "They are caught between two worlds. They can't be in either of them." Employers feel it is their responsibility to bridge this gap, or at least the perception of it. Employers thus perform valuable class work by teaching the poor to live within their wages, restricting the scope of their demands (or "complaints") and narrowing their aspirations. One question here is whether this "work" is really meant to benefit the worker or to protect the employer. These tactics primarily seem to benefit the employers by reducing the intensity of what they perceive as the emotional exploitation inflicted by the workers. When domestic workers say, "I can't buy meat for my children," "School started but my kid goes in shoes with holes," or "This meal is delicious but my children are eating bread and cheese now," employers might be right in their sense that they are being emotionally manipulated. Workers use such guilt-inducing statements to reassert their difference and distance from their employers. Along with sympathy, workers hope to receive better work conditions, more generous favors, and better pay.

Friendship networks among employers provide workers the means of manipulating employers' charitable behavior. An important tactic domestic workers use is to create competition among employers by talking to one employer about the favors bestowed by another. A worker might report to one employer, for example, that another employer contributed toward her family's purchase of coal for the winter or bought school supplies for her children.

I was present during a conversation in which one domestic worker told another that she had been taking off one of her six golden bracelets before she went to work because she was planning to ask for some advance payment. That sixth bracelet was new and she thought that her employer might notice the addition and be reluctant to give her the money. She asks the favor not as one who is dependent on her employer's whimsical benevolence but more as a savvy worker who accomplishes her ends by strategically managing the way she is perceived.

Among employers, working women and housewives differ in how they interact with their employees and how class relations in those interactions are played out. Professional employers' absence from home gives workers, by default, an autonomy over the labor process while also making this group of employers less subject to what housewife employers call "emotional exploitation." However, this distance does not create a merely instrumental, businesslike relationship. Instead, these employers develop a pervasive sense of distrust, making the familiar assumption that those who have uncontrollable freedom and liberty at their disposal exercise it by transgressing rules and restrictions. A recurrent and underlying thread of their accounts was the suspicion that domestic workers abuse their autonomy, that they "cut corners" to shorten the workday, make long-distance telephone calls at the employer's expense, spend hours in front of the television, liberally use their employer's expensive cosmetics (creams and perfumes), and engage in petty theft of such items as "Nescafe." The following employer's account is typical.

> She was working here yesterday. I called her around noon to tell her that there was a variety of fruits in the refrigerator, such as apples and plums, that she should help herself to. She said, "I have already eaten, *abla*. I ate the cherries in the fridge." She had eaten a full bowl containing about a kilogram of cherries. You know how expensive cherries are at this time of the year. . . . They are about 7,000 TL a kilogram [the equivalent of one third of domestic worker's daily salary]. She can't afford it herself. Even we can barely afford it. She is inconsiderate. They envy us; they are doing all this on purpose.
>
> She emptied a bottle of my expensive night cream, even though I provide Vaseline for her hands. I also realized that she was using my perfume instead of the lemon cologne I had offered her. I told her that it wasn't a perfume but a cleanser I use to take off my make-up [a ruse to keep her from using the expensive perfume]. She said, "Oh, I thought it was cologne."

In other similar accounts, we see the cherries of the plot above replaced by a full bag of fresh hazelnuts or a pot of fresh beans. Professional employers, being away from home, are not subject to emotional exploitation. Instead, domestic workers tend to get what they want by direct action rather than by cajoling the employer to "give" it. In the case of housewife employers, domestic workers articulate and inflict class guilt, and, in return, employers "do" their class work to cope with the guilt. Housewife employers perceive this work as "benevolence" or as a response to emotional exploitation because they directly interact with the worker. Hence, housewife employers are burdened by guilt and blame themselves while working employers tend to blame domestic workers.

It is not surprising to learn that housewife employers are eager to engage one of the newly emerging commercial cleaning services. All the housewives I spoke with reported that their roles in creating intimacy demand constant management of their feelings.[10] They described in great detail how difficult it is to sustain this pretense of closeness under all circumstances. Some of the housewives said that they feel themselves dominated by the worker they employ. They complained, for example, "She twists me around her little finger" or "I became her slave."

Part of the uneasiness of housewives' relationships with their workers is due to the perceived incompatibility of the roles of housewife and employer. Housewives' sense of disempowerment is intensified because they know that the kind of employer most despised by domestic workers is a housewife who does not help. Yet, as I report in Chapter 3, the majority of domestic workers prefer working for housewives because they help them. This apparent contradiction is perceived by both parties and sometimes requires aligning actions or statements on the part of employer.

Since employers believe that their intimacy and class work disempowers them, they use a range of strategies to protect themselves. One wealthy housewife, for example, reduced her domestic worker's schedule from three days a week to once a week. A feminist professional (an academic) said she scheduled her domestic worker for a day when she is out; others simply try to be away from home when their workers are there. In fact, all the women said they hire workers for much less time than they actually need to avoid the demands of intimacy work. A wealthy housewife's statement about why she does not want to employ a domestic worker every day typifies such evasiveness. Referring to her routine way of avoiding intimacy work, she said, "I can't pretend that I'm sick everyday."

Domestic workers' daily experience of class inequality nurtures attitudes among them that result in an affirmation of the traditional feminine roles. Numerous times during my interviews and conversations with domestic workers they portrayed and judged middle-class employers by recounting episodes that demonstrated their own acute awareness of class injustice and the implications of the income gap between classes. Their narratives repeatedly illustrated ways in which their employers miserably failed to "do" their gender appropriately. In domestic workers' accounts, employers' class privilege is conflated with a failure to properly perform the responsibilities of their gender as women. The following fragments from interviews with different domestic workers illustrate this articulation of class inequality with gender.

I know how much she spends on a bottle of nail polish. It's worth my salary for a whole day.

Well—I don't know if you call this woman, a woman. Can you call her a woman if she cannot wash her own underwear and lets a stranger do it for her?

They are so lazy. The other day, one of them was going away. She made me prepare her suitcase. She cannot even pack.

They are so lax with their children. . . . They don't teach their kids the value of money. They buy expensive stuff for the kids and the kids abuse it. She bought an expensive pair of sneakers for her son the other day, and the next day the kid comes home with a torn sneaker. She says nothing and doesn't punish the kid. The sneaker gets thrown away without a word.

She does not even cook a simple lunch. She orders "kebabs." You know how costly they are—sometimes more than what she pays me for a day's work.

Although domestic workers emulate the styles and tastes of middle-class women in their daily child-rearing and homemaking practices, it would be simplistic to say that their self-definitions as women are modeled entirely on what they see in their urban middle-class employers. On the contrary, articulations of class inequality through the criticism of gender enables the domestic workers to define their own identities against urban middle-class femininity and, in the process, to reaffirm the value of traditional femininity and their own moral superiority as women and mothers.

The contrived nature of the behavior that is designed to overrule the genuine differences and the unequal nature of the domestic service arrangement is best revealed when employers talk with the outside observer (the researcher, who, as a middle-class woman, is considered an "insider") about their true, unbridgeable distance from their domestic workers. They believe that they are functioning as positive modernizing agents for domestic workers. The workers are expected to learn good housekeeping skills and modern values from them. However, when a domestic worker's emulations take the form of asserting her independence from her husband or when she buys pretty houseware or luxury gadgets, such actions are perceived as transgressive. These women are supposed to behave and consume within their means and know their place. The employers firmly believe that domestic workers are ultimately not like them and should not pretend that they are or aspire to be so. Thus, the pretense of a shared womanhood among the women of different classes is confined to the sphere of intimacy that the work relation requires.

David Katzman (1978a), in his influential study of domestic service, makes a statement that has since been echoed many times by students of domestic service: "Some women (like some men) find fulfillment in exercising power over another woman's life. Rather than seeking an intelligent, resourceful, and independent worker, they may want a servant to whom they can feel superior and dominating. Employing a domestic offers them a position of power not otherwise available to housewives" (384).

The image of a domestic worker oppressed by an all-powerful employer underestimates the interactive construction of social situations and workers' agency in this process. In this study, employment of a domestic worker does not automatically offer the perception of a "position of power" to employers. Nor is employment in domestic service experienced as a position of powerlessness by domestic workers. Power is constructed, maintained, and negotiated interactively by and between domestic worker and employer.

Approaches that infer a direct mirroring of power relations between women according to the structural conditions of domestic service are misleading. By focusing on the dynamics of the relationship between the two women we can see that they participate equally in its making. The way these women structure and negotiate their relationship raises questions about the very operation of power and about the utility of "resistance" as an analytical tool when it is automatically assumed to be a response to oppression. Approaches that assume that workers are powerless treat them as passive subjects, capable only of minimizing the damage made to their self-worth by their experience in domestic service, rather than as actors pursuing their own goals. Domestic workers are, however, as much self-interested actors as are their employers, deploying a variety of strategies and resources to pursue their interests.

Are domestic workers and employers acting purely in class terms as suggested by Romero (1992), who introduces gender into her Marxist framework by the concept of emotional labor as a commodity? My analysis suggests that emotional labor is not added on to the labors at hand but rather is coextensive with them and, more important, is performed by both domestic workers and employers.

It might seem plausible to conclude that both women are victims of a patriarchal gender order that implicates both classes of women. Yet, if they are "victims" of this system of domination, they are not passive victims, because women do not simply accept patriarchy—or "fight" against it. Instead, they selectively utilize and negotiate patriarchal gender beliefs in numerous, subtle, and equivocal ways in their day-to-day interactions with each other. Through such experiences and from different positions within a patriarchal gender order, employer women and domestic workers construct a language to discuss and negotiate the labor process and reconcile the diverse experiences of their lives. They connect one to another and seek to assert the differences in their simultaneous efforts to both reinforce and alleviate the consequences of class inequalities and differences in class cultures.

5   The Domestic Work of Maids, Mothers, and Men

IN MIDDLE- and upper-middle-class neighborhoods of Ankara when most men are away at offices playing the role of distant bread-winner fathers, it is not unusual to see other men strolling at an easy pace, holding a toddler's hand. These men are doorkeepers whose wives are out working. These are also men who are thought to constitute the most traditional segment of men in the Turkish society. But inside the home do the same doorkeeper fathers also change diapers, feed small children, cook, and wash the dishes afterward?

Are we really observing profound departures from the gendered division of labor among these working-class families with peasant backgrounds? A great number of studies continue to document extensively that women's taking on paid employment does not alleviate their domestic burden. Employed women continue to perform more work in the household than their husbands. Moreover, a gendered division of tasks continues even when men participate in childcare and household work. Gender-based inequalities in employment limit the development of a more egalitarian division of labor at home, which women's employment would seem to foster, and leaves women effectively working a double load.[1] An unequal division of labor by gender in the household, a common international pattern, remains pervasive in Turkey, especially among working-class families and those middle-class families that cannot afford domestic help.[2]

Studies undertaken in the 1980s indicate that the relationships among income, gender, power, and the division of labor, particularly in the context of intimate familial relations, are complex (Berk 1985; Blumstein and Schwartz 1983; Hochschild 1989). These studies point out the strong link between notions of gender identity and household work, which is more important than the factor of "power resources." For example, men who have the fewest resources (unemployed men) or men who earn less than their wives often do less domestic work than men with more resources (Hochschild 1989; Segal 1990). A relative lack of power resources does not automatically lead to increased sharing of household responsibilities by men.[3] There is thus a need to account for the ideological and psychological dimensions of gender inequality in the household division of labor.

The general pattern of an absence of male domesticity is contradicted, however, by several other studies. Pierrette Hondagneu-Sotelo's *Gendered Transitions: Mexican Experiences of Immigration* (1994a) and Matthew C. Gutmann's *The Meanings of Macho: Being a Man in Mexico City* (1996), for example, illustrate significant modifications in the male role among working-class families. Both authors conclude that material conditions of life rather than exposure to and embracement of feminist beliefs generated alterations in the realm of gender-role identities in the families they studied. Hondagneu-Sotelo's cohort analysis of Mexican immigration to the United States demonstrates that earlier cohorts of male immigrants who migrated alone and found no community of women to perform domestic tasks for them started fending for themselves and eventually mastered domestic skills, including making tortillas from scratch. These men continued to exhibit the same domesticity even after women joined them in the United States some years later. Gutmann describes transformations in gender roles in urban Mexico as a process of "degendering." He argues that many activities and behaviors traditionally associated with either gender are becoming gender neutral (fathers are changing diapers, women are drinking publicly). He explains that the active role of women in autonomous, community-based movements to obtain jobs, housing, and many social services in working-class communities of Mexico City, together with international migration and other social and demographic changes during the 1970s and 1980s, challenged dominant gender practices. Men and women creatively responded to such changing circumstances by experimenting with new and unorthodox roles.

As I show in Chapter 2, the majority of domestic workers with young children are able to work full-time schedules because their husbands are available to meet the demands of young children. Data, especially on the doorkeeper group, offer intriguing insights into the changeability of the traditional gender division of labor with women's employment and allow us to explore some of the questions addressed in the literature. Differences between the employment situations of husbands in the doorkeeper and squatter settlement groups and differences in their household composition (the squatter settlement households contain kin as coresidents) allow us to make comparative points. In this chapter I explore the following questions: Do the employment structures of men and women have more effect on altering the traditional roles of husbands and wives than a conscious commitment to gender equality? To what extent does the doorkeeper husband's home-centered occupation create the possibility of new divisions of domestic labor? How do women feel about the distribution of housework and childcare in their families? Do they think that the distribution is fair? How do different social and geographic spaces they inhabit inform doorkeeper wives' and squatter settlement women's experiences of housework and childcare? How does the stigma attached to the doorkeeper families by their urban middle-class employers, through the link established between children and uncleanliness, affect the organization and distribution of household chores and childcare?

SPACES, TECHNOLOGIES, AND SOCIAL RELATIONS OF UNPAID LABOR

Some of the questions on household division of labor in this study were answered in the form of observed behavior even before they were posed to the respondents. To accommodate heavy paid-work schedules, we held interviews with domestic workers after they came home from work to begin their "second shift" (Hochschild 1989). Thus we caught most of them "backstage" (Berk and Berheide 1977) with their household work. Some answered our questions while fixing dinner or cleaning up lunch dishes or doing laundry while simultaneously trying to attend to their children's needs that had accumulated during the day.

Families in this study experience housework and childcare in ways shaped by their subordinate class status, their sociogeographic location in the city, and the community relations that are founded on reciprocity and obligation. The material conditions of the residence and the possessions owned by these families determine the scope and nature of domestic work. The availability of tools (vacuum cleaners, washing machines) and technological resources (running water, electricity) dictate the nature of work and time required to perform it.

Heterogeneity in terms of economic standing is well reflected in the wide range of housing conditions that exist within a given squatter settlement neighborhood. Housing varies widely, from Gülgitmez

Hasankayalı's four spacious rooms with a sunny kitchen full of large cupboards and a bathroom equipped with a modern hot water heater to Zelzen Simalı's little two-room house with a kitchen that doubles as a make-shift bathroom and an outdoor toilet in the courtyard that is shared with the next-door dwelling. Between these two extreme cases lies a wide range of housing conditions that can be classified according to size of the dwelling, number of rooms, bathroom facilities, outdoor space, distance to a paved road, and distance to public transportation.

Distance of a house from a paved road determines how much dirt and mud household members bring inside and, accordingly, how much cleaning work needs to be done. Some houses are connected to one another by paved roads but most are cut off from public transportation (in one neighborhood, for example, the nearest public transportation is about a ninety-minute walk away). Most houses are located on unpaved roads, rendering dirt control extremely difficult during any season.

The squatter settlement sample in this study is almost equally divided between owners and renters, or 52 percent and 48 percent, respectively. Homeowners have larger and better-kept houses than renters, who often have dilapidated properties. Owners improve both the exteriors and interiors of their houses on a piecemeal but regular basis. Although both men and women participate equally in the improvement work of exteriors, women usually do a springtime painting of the interior walls. These differences in housing conditions in the squatter settlements produce differences in the processes of housework between those who perform housework under more "decent" conditions and those who do not. Yet despite this residential diversity, women confront collectively the same structural inadequacies that define squatter settlement living. In Turkey, the past four decades have witnessed, as in Latin America, various mobilizations of squatter settlement dwellers demanding roads, electricity, and water and sewage systems. Because of these movements, these settlements now have running water and indoor plumbing.

Squatter households lack central heating. A single room at the center of the house is heated with a stove that requires coal or wood for fuel and is sometimes also used to heat water and even to cook food. Women in the squatter settlements do the seasonal heavy work of carrying coal and wood. Women are usually the ones who store coal and wood delivered to the door or the nearest paved road and carry heavy buckets from the storage place several times a day.

Even though residential water shortages are a fixture of urban life in Turkey, they affect squatter settlement residents more severely than apartment building dwellers, who can rely on accumulated water in storage tanks. Periodic water shortages require squatter women to collect and save water in buckets, pots, and bottles. Under these circumstances the management and conservation of water becomes an important household chore for women and makes every task requiring water more difficult and time-consuming. In these households, bathing children is more difficult because water must be heated on the stove.

Houses are not connected to gas mains but use butane gas sold in individual steel containers. Every household has a gas range (the kind without an oven), but some poorer households own the simplest kind with a single burner, making it difficult to carry on several different cooking operations simultaneously and increasing the overall time women spend cooking.

Although squatter settlement dwellers live in houses that are not spacious, they usually equip them with many modern conveniences, such as washing machines, refrigerators, and small kitchen appliances, such as mixers and electric toasters. Most families have old-fashioned washing machines, usually bought or "inherited" from employers, which require wringing and hanging of wash. Small homes are modestly decorated with *sedirs* (sturdy steel bed-frame-and-mattress combinations) in the living room, which double as beds for children and kin and may contain a small table or side tables. Larger homes, owned by the better-off squatter settlers, are often decorated with matching furniture: sofas, chairs, and a dining table. Many households included in my study continue the practice of having meals on the floor. Even owners of the large dining sets do not eat at the table. Some households also continue the practice of having meals out of one large communal dish rather than on individual plates. This practice saves women in large households the task of heavy dishwashing. Indispensable to virtually every home is a display cabinet (*vitrinli dolap*) where the family can show off through the glass doors such status-bearing consumer durables as sets of cups, porcelain figurines, and other ornamental objects. Women's handwork (lace or embroidered runners) beautifies the crowded spaces of these working-class homes.

The absence of cabinets and work surfaces in some kitchens makes cooking and washing dishes difficult in the small, cluttered spaces. During summer women happily work outside in courtyards and on front steps, where they clean vegetables, bathe small children, hand wash laundry, and prepare laborious meals. These semipublic spaces are an important social locus for women, allowing them to share and exchange homemaking skills, and chat and pursue "leisure" activities, such as sewing, knitting, crocheting, and mending clothes. Women, especially young wives, who do not perform such "leisure" chores are condemned with the phrase "She sits with her hand upon her hand and with her hand upon her cunt" (*El eli üstünde, el amı üstünde oturuyor*).[4] Some families also raise chickens and tend a garden.

One marked quality of squatter communities is the easy permeability of household boundaries and the informality of social interaction among women who are neighbors. The concept of neighborliness is very important in daily life and governs the moral economy of these communities. Neighborliness is created and maintained by close interaction, mutual sharing, and generosity between women. In a study of a Turkish village community, Carol Delaney (1991) observes: "The boundaries between women who are close neighbors are fluid; the gates, doors, thresholds are open . . . [and] close neighbors are enclosed in an open world by proximity" (188; also see A. Ayata 1989). Women enter one another's home without knocking, to chat, to borrow things, and to help with laborious tasks. Keeping the inside of the home a private place for the family threatens these reciprocal relations in fundamental ways. Reciprocal aid in the form of exchanges of household technology and amenities such as hot water, irons, and small electrical stoves, and exchange of labor is quite common and forms an integral part of the moral economy of these communities. For example, one of my main respondents did not own a refrigerator but routinely "borrowed" a space in her next-door neighbor's refrigerator to keep milk for her small children. However, she had a thermosyphon and her neighbor with the refrigerator often borrowed buckets of hot water from her.[5] In times of need neighbors frequently turn to each other because goods and services cannot be readily bought. If someone runs out of butane gas in the middle of cooking a meal or discovers that she is short of a main ingredient, she finishes cooking at a neighbor's or borrows what she needs.

Women in the squatter settlement group shop daily. Although they tend to stock up on staples such as sugar and flour and shop once a week for vegetables and fruits at the *pazar* (open market), they typically spend daily cash wages on their way home from work. Inadequate storage space and a shortage of cash discourage women from purchasing in large quantities. The physical strain of getting it all home, waiting in long lines for buses and vans, makes shopping notably heavy work. Children are usually sent to purchase small items such as bread, milk, or eggs in neighborhood grocery stores.

Although some structural features of apartment house living such as central heating systems and running hot water simplifies the housework and childcare activities of women in the doorkeeper group, these women also share some of the problems encountered by women in the squatter settlements. The most important of these problems is the absence of kitchen cabinets, counter tops, shower areas, and other built-in facilities and the cramped spaces, which make housework difficult. The sample of the doorkeeper group was drawn equally from middle- and upper-middle-class districts of Ankara. Serving these two different classes might be expected to create different housing conditions and thus a hierarchy within the doorkeeper household group. Surprisingly, I found no correspondence between the doorkeeper apartments in luxury apartment houses and those in more modest buildings. Substandard housing conditions are the norm for doorkeepers, regardless of the class location of the apartment building.

Doorkeepers' quarters are underground (in the basement) and mostly consist of airless and damp rooms with inadequate windows. The majority (70 percent) of doorkeepers' dwellings have only two rooms with a half kitchen and inadequate bathing facilities. About 18 percent live in apartments with a single room; 11 percent live in apartments that have more than two rooms. The absence of sociospatial boundaries for eating, sleeping, socializing, and bathing create and perpetuate their sense of living in an alien space, which they often describe as a prison. These conditions, however, are also instrumental in making women strive even more energetically to fix an irregular domestic space through their housework. Doorkeepers' basement apartments are often filled with various types of discarded furniture and other household items given to them by the tenants.

Although some doorkeepers' quarters have access to small backyards or the gardens of their apartment building, the doorkeeper families do not use these outdoor spaces in the same ways that the residents of squatter settlements use their outdoor space. The spaces outside apartment buildings do not become extensions of the doorkeeper families' homes, where some of the housework and socializing can take place. Although doorkeeper families visit one another frequently and informality dominates their interaction, these visits are usually family visits and take place in the evenings. The rhythm of work of doorkeepers and of their wives, combined with the absence of clear boundaries between work and home, do not permit the same type of informality and reciprocal exchanges observed in the squatter settlements. Their locations in apartment buildings erects boundaries between doorkeeper households in such a way that the spontaneity and fluidity of material and symbolic exchanges that characterize daily interaction between women neighbors in the squatter settlement is impossible. The absence of resource sharing in the form of an easy exchange of labor and goods leads to a measure of privatization and isolation of the labor of housework and childcare in doorkeeper families.

DISTRIBUTION OF HOUSEHOLD WORK AND CHILDCARE

Women do a vastly greater share of household and childcare tasks than do men in both doorkeeper and squatter settlement households (see Table 5). For example, with the exception of caring for infants and older children and doing grocery-store shopping and the weekly *pazar* shopping, the wife in the doorkeeper group performs exclusively more than 50 percent of all tasks. In the squatter settlement group, the wife performs close to 50 percent or more of all tasks (i.e., including the tasks that are not performed exclusively by doorkeeper wives). With the exception of grocery-store and *pazar* shopping and the care of older children, the remaining portion of all other tasks are done primarily by daughters or daughters-in-law. However, doorkeeper wives rely more on husbands for a limited range of tasks, including outside activities and childcare, than do squatter settlement wives, while squatter settlement wives are able to muster more help from female kin than are doorkeeper wives. Although, compared with doorkeeper wives, the squatter women perform a relatively *lower percentage of tasks* "exclusively," they perform *a higher number of tasks* exclusively. These additional tasks are those that are executed outside the household—such as food shopping. Another salient difference between the two groups of women is that squatter settlement women's participation in routine household chores, such as

TABLE 5. Distribution of Household Tasks and Childcare Contribution of Household Members in the Doorkeeper Group (DG) and the Squatter Group (SG)

Household Members Who Do the Work	Doing the Dishes		Cleaning Up		Cooking Breakfast		Cooking Lunch		Cooking Dinner		Doing Laundry		Ironing		Doing Pazar Shopping		Doing Grocery Shopping		Caring for an Infant		Caring for Older Children	
	DG	SG	DG	SG	DG	SG	DG	SG	DG	SG	DG	SG	DG	SG	DG	SG	DG	SG	DG	SG	DG	SG
N	103	53	103	53	103	52	103	53	103	53	103	53	98	53	103	49	103	53	61	23	62	35
Wife																						
Exclusively	62.1	47.1	68.9	50.9	71.8	48.0	50.5	58.4	86.4	64.1	88.3	66.0	73.4	56.6	16.5	48.9	10.7	43.3	26.2	52.1	40.3	51.4
With help from female kin	17.5	13.2	18.4	13.2	8.7	5.7	6.8	7.5	9.7	7.5	9.7	9.4	9.1	1.8	1.0	4.0	2.9	3.7	1.0	13.0	0.0	5.7
With help from husband	13.6	5.6	8.7	0.0	4.9	7.6	14.6	0.0	1.9	1.8	0.0	1.8	5.1	0.0	4.9	4.0	5.8	5.6	34.4	4.3	16.1	2.8
Wife and husband																						
Equally or jointly shared	0.0	0.0	1.0	1.8	3.9	0.0	4.9	0.0	1.0	0.0	0.0	0.0	4.0	0.0	30.1	18.3	20.4	13.2	13.1	13.0	25.8	28.5
Husband																						
Exclusively	0.0	0.0	0.0	0.0	5.8	5.7	13.6	3.7	0.0	0.0	0.0	0.0	0.0	0.0	37.9	14.2	44.7	22.6	4.9	4.3	6.4	5.7
With help from wife	0.0	0.0	0.0	0.0	2.9	0.0	1.9	0.0	0.0	1.8	0.0	0.0	1.0	1.8	8.7	4.0	15.5	5.6	13.1	0.0	9.6	5.7
Daughter or female kin																						
Exclusively	6.8	30.1	2.9	28.3	1.9	26.9	6.8	26.7	1.0	20.7	1.9	18.8	7.1	33.9	1.0	2.0	1.0	2.0	6.5	13.0	1.0	0.0
With help from wife	0.0	1.8	0.0	3.7	0.0	3.8	0.0	1.8	0.0	1.8	0.0	1.8	0.0	3.7	0.0	4.0	0.0	0.0	0.0	0.0	0.0	0.0
Equally shared by kin and wife	0.0	0.0	0.0	1.8	0.0	1.9	0.0	1.8	0.0	1.8	0.0	1.8	0.0	1.8	0.0	0.0	0.0	0.0	0.0	0.0	0.0	0.0

Notes: Sample sizes vary for certain tasks because not all tasks are carried out in all households. The categories of household members who do the work include all the contributors mentioned by the respondents.

cooking, laundry, cleaning, and ironing is lessened by the greater amount of sharing among female members of the squatter household, chiefly between mothers and adolescent daughters.

In both groups of households, however, the gender segregation of tasks is a defining element of the household division of labor. The husband's contribution in both groups is concentrated in the area of food shopping—though squatter settlement husbands' relative contribution is markedly lower than doorkeeper husbands'. Shopping and childcare constitute the activities performed jointly by wife and husband.

Doorkeeper husbands also contribute significantly to childcare—31 percent of these men are involved in taking care of infants, compared with 17 percent of squatter husbands. Doorkeepers do more than squatter settlement men, largely because shopping is also part of the doorkeeper's professional duties. Husbands in squatter settlements typically contribute nothing to the work of household activities carried out inside the household.

Help from other female household members in squatter settlement households accounts for the differences in the household-labor efforts of the two groups of wives. The relationship between the kinship and employment status of female household members age 14 and over indicates that the proportion of eligible females for housework and childcare is greater among squatter households than among doorkeeper households, reflecting the larger size of the average household in the squatter group (5.3 persons per household, compared with 4.3 in the doorkeeper group). Daughters constitute 67 and 80 percent, respectively, of these women. Thus, when domestic workers draw on family members for help with household and childcare chores, they primarily draw on their daughters, many of whom are also enrolled as students or are employed and are not available full-time.

In this study, the "homebound" nature of doorkeeper's work was expected to produce an objective condition for a redistribution of household and childcare work. While this objective condition appears to have affected the gender division of labor in the area of childcare, there is no sign of a fundamental change in other areas of household work. In fact, even this "change" is somewhat superficial. Husbands' involvement in childcare is directly related to the unavailability of the wife. Husbands do what they absolutely have to do in the absence of their wives. In practice, their participation does not extend beyond keeping an eye on the children. Answers to questions such as, "Who gives children their lunch?" "Who cooks the lunch?" and "Who does the dishes?" provide us with insights into what doorkeeper fathers actually do in the home, when they engage in childcare, and whether their "daytime" childcare activities expand to include some of the surrounding household work typically done by mothers. Husbands feed the children, but their contribution to the lunch primarily consists of heating up the food that their wives prepared the night before and putting the dishes in the sink, thus leaving the routine household work to wives.

To ascertain how doorkeepers' wives measure their husbands' contribution against what they take to be the existing societal average, the wives were asked whether they agree or disagree with the following observation: "Husbands who are employed as doorkeepers seem to participate in household labor and childcare at higher levels than husbands in different employment circumstances." Of those who expressed an opinion (N = 83), 60.2 percent said that they agreed with the statement and the remaining (39.7 percent) said that they did not. Had the question treated *childcare* as conceptually distinct from *household work*, it would have confirmed the distinction that had been found through other relevant questions.[6]

Although we have a clear picture of the amount of childcare and housework doorkeepers do, we do not know whether their practical childcare work produces changes in their attitudes toward childcare or their experiences of fatherhood. To what extent and under what personal and social conditions these men embrace this new role and the work of fatherhood and construct different relationships with their children are important questions to be investigated in future research. For example, in a small number of cases, domestic workers indicated that as a result of their husbands' giving primary care to their children, the children now relate better to their fathers. One domestic worker, the wife of a former doorkeeper from the squatter settlement group, volunteered a concrete example: "My middle daughter [11 years old], for example, still calls her father, not me, when she wakes up at night to ask for a drink of water."

Hours in Waged Work and Housework

When examining the relationship between how much work domestic workers do at home and their weekly paid-work schedules, we find, among the squatter group, a strong inverse relation between the hours domestic workers devote to household and childcare work and the hours they devote to paid work. The relationship is more clearly reflected in a comparison of part-time and full-time workers than in comparisons of semi-full-time and full-time workers. In the doorkeeper group, hours devoted to housework are more or less uniform regardless of the paid-work schedules for the 70 percent of women who claim to devote between twenty-one and forty hours a week to housework.

On the average, domestic workers in both groups with part-time schedules spend a greater amount of time on household work and childcare than the ones with semi-full-time or full-time work schedules. Domestic workers in the doorkeeper group devote more hours overall to housework and childcare than do their counterparts in the squatter group. However, the larger load of housework reported by doorkeeper wives may be attributed to their performance of work in the apartment building. While such work is officially the husband's job, it can get fused with women's own housework, an issue I discuss below. Domestic workers from the squatter settlement group who work five to seven days a week report doing the least amount of housework and childcare. Half of this group devotes less than twenty hours to housework and childcare a week. In contrast, 70 percent of doorkeeper wives with full-time work schedules spent between twenty-one and forty hours on housework and childcare a week. This striking difference results from the longer workdays of squatter women, who have long commutes, and the type and life cycle of the households to which they belong. While the doorkeeper households are younger and the wives have little help from others, the squatter settlement women can draw on the support of adolescent daughters, daughters-in-law, and other adult women. It is not surprising, for example, to find that among the domestic workers who spend zero hours on housework, all (5) belong to the households with nonworking and homebound daughters-in-law or adult daughters who take over all of the work of the household.

DOORKEEPERS' WIVES' UNPAID LABOR

Doorkeeping is, in many ways, an occupation that resists definition along the axes of the informal/formal, premodern/modern, and servitude/service polarities commonly used in conceptualizing the social-cultural aspects of work and the identity of the worker. Doorkeeping is fraught with anomalies. What makes doorkeeping especially problematic is that it borders on servitude and involves multiple masters (each doorkeeper serves an average of fourteen masters). Furthermore, the doorkeeper is not implicated alone. The social identity of his wife and children are defined by his occupation as well. The common, unmarked urban phase "doorkeeper's family"—also used by the doorkeeper's wives in reference to their own families ("We are doorkeepers") suggests the extent to which doorkeeping defines the entire family, in a circumstance reminiscent of serfdom. Finally, doorkeeping is organized by the state and defined as a service occupation. Labor legislation and condominium ownership laws gave the doorkeepers formal worker status in 1970.[7] Like other workers in the formal sector, they are covered and protected by the labor regulations of the state through pension, paid holidays, severance pay, health and safety regulations, and disability and medical coverage. A doorkeeper's spouse and children are also automatically covered by free health insurance. Apartment house tenants pay doorkeepers an official monthly minimum wage.[8]

The bounded nature of the occupation is also legally sanctioned. According to the labor legislation regulating the doorkeepers' work conditions,[9] a doorkeeper must supply a laborer to work in his absence, whether he leaves his post because of an emergency or for a vacation. This substitute can be his wife, his child, a nephew, or even a friend. More often than not the substitute is a member of the doorkeeper's family. The use of unwaged family labor plays an important role in defining the servitude aspect of the occupation.

The fact that doorkeepers live in the same place that they work makes the doorkeeper's and his family's time available to his masters-employers at all hours. He and his family are kept on call all day and night for "emergencies." What constitutes an emergency is quite subjective. For example, apartment number 2 unexpectedly receives a guest and needs some pastry to go with tea; apartment number 5 remembers she is out of milk while preparing her toddler's lunch; number 10's son returns from school sick and needs cough medicine; number 15 is off to Istanbul and needs the doorkeeper to carry down his luggage; a stranger wants to know whether Mr. X lives in this building. The doorkeeper may choose how to respond to such requests. The more he guards his and his family's time, the more he confirms the stereotype the dissatisfied tenants have always known that doorkeepers are lazy good-for-nothing persons.

The following schedule for a doorkeeper, which was framed and hung on the wall of the entrance in one of the apartment houses we visited, is a striking illustration of why stabilizing of work hours and establishing a locus of work are impossible. While one might argue that a schedule like this formalizes and depersonalizes the doorkeeper's routine, countering the servitude aspect of the occupation, I argue that this type of scheduling actually strengthens the stereotype of doorkeepers and requires the unpaid labor of the doorkeepers wives.

5:30–6:30 a.m.	Starting the central heating furnace
6:30–7:30 a.m.	Bread and newspaper service
7:30–10:00 a.m.	Rest
10:00–11:00 a.m.	Shopping services
11:00–12:30 a.m.	Rest
12:30–2:00 p.m.	Noon shopping services
2:00–4:00 p.m.	Cleaning
4:00–6:30 p.m.	Rest
6:30–8:00 p.m.	Trash collection

Notes:

1. Sundays are the doorkeeper's day off.
2. The doorkeeper cannot leave the apartment house within his work hours, even if he completes his duties.

The scheduled periods of rest seem to allow no opportunity for service requests. Tenants do, however, have "emergencies." And since the relationship between tenant and doorkeeper is highly personal, in the absence of a schedule, tenants tend to request special, off-duty favors. These favors are granted at the discretion of the doorkeeper, fueling the judgments about perceived misbehavior. The formal specification of several long "rest" periods or "forced leisure time"[10] further legitimates the existing perceptions of laziness. The schedule literally mocks itself by its very statement. Notice the paradoxical postscript. Who operates the heating system on Sundays, if Sunday is the doorkeeper's day off? How can the doorkeeper perform his shopping duties without leaving the building?[11]

The location of the doorkeeper's apartment in the building and the conventional means of accessing the doorkeeper undermine the efforts of doorkeepers' wives and children to distance themselves from the image and identity of the "doorkeeper family" and from the tasks of the apartment building. The boundary between work and home is routinely breached by the interruptions of tenants calling loudly from the stairway of the building or sounding the buzzer inside the doorkeeper's living quarters. These buzzers, one might think, are remnants of an order that would have disappeared with the formalization of the occupation. Instead, however, they are an increasingly common fixture of apartment houses as more and more luxury buildings are equipped with intercom systems. The existence of buzzers and intercoms not only undermines the well-defined schedule but involves the doorkeeper's wife and children in his work. The doorkeeper is conventionally obliged to respond whenever a resident buzzes with a request for service. Since most doorkeeping tasks require no special knowledge and skill, the doorkeeper's wife or his children can perform the obligation.

Only a small percentage of the wives never get involved with their husbands' work. There is no correlation between their own work loads and their lack of involvement with the apartment house work. Of the sixty-six wives (71 percent of the total) who regularly or occasionally help out their husbands, close to one-half perform tasks in three areas of work (42 percent). A substantial proportion of women with their own heavy work schedules (the "five-to-seven-day" category) still perform multiple tasks associated with doorkeeping, although fewer than their counterparts with light weekly work loads (54 percent). Although some wives are spared doorkeeping work by their own heavy work schedules, their work is not wholly effective in exempting them from "unpaid family labor."

There is a significant difference between tasks carried out predominantly by the doorkeeper and his children and those carried out by the wife. The doorkeeping task most frequently performed by wives is periodic apartment house cleaning, a physically laborious task often requiring the joint labor of both husband and wife. Starting the central heating furnace is the second task women perform most often. This is the only doorkeeping task that requires formal training (a three-week course) and certification. Although doorkeepers would like to define their occupational identity with this task, it requires getting up early and is often delegated to the wife. Wives are less involved in the outdoor activities of the doorkeeping.

In this study, among those who have eligible children, about one-third reported that the doorkeeper received help from his children. However, only 5 percent "regularly," and 22 percent "occasionally" received it. Children were involved mostly in shopping (14 percent), followed by collecting trash (7 percent). It should not be assumed that doorkeepers happily appropriate their children's labor. They harbor hopes of generational mobility and therefore try to protect their children from the stigma of their occupation. The low percentage of doorkeepers receiving help from their children suggests an active resistance to the use of children's labor. There are even a couple of examples of doorkeepers leaving employment because of the mistreatment of their children by tenants—"tenants who burden them with assignments."

Despite its formalization as a service occupation, doorkeeping does not allow the doorkeeper to become an individualized wage laborer. On the contrary, it reconstitutes the migrant family as a laboring unit with a male head of household who continues to act as the head of the "enterprise" and to direct its combined labor processes. Doorkeeping gives the husband great discretion to organize work and allocate his own and his family's labor power. In the process, the wives partially retain their former "unpaid family worker" status along with their identities as independent earners. The system is based on the exploitation of family labor, building on and reinforcing the gender and age-based hierarchies within the family. As one woman ironically remarked, "You become the daughter in-law of all the tenants of the apartment house." Her comment suggests that the doorkeeper institution reconstituted her role as a hard-working new wife at the service of her status superiors in the domestic hierarchy of the patrilocal extended households of her early marital years in the village. An apartment house recruits an individual laborer but always presupposes the recruitment of the whole family. This presupposition is not necessarily "imposed" from above but is typically shared by doorkeeper wives themselves. When probed about why they take part in their husbands' work, the majority of women were baffled by the question because the circumstance strikes them as only natural. Only in rare instances did women offer an explanation for their performance of doorkeeper work. Some of those instances involve husbands who are defined as "lazy" and "irresponsible" by their wives, who fear that these men jeopardize their jobs. In other cases, the doorkeeper has "too much work" because of moonlighting or because the apartment house has too many units for one man to serve. The doorkeeping job emphasizes work commitment and cooperation among family members and reinforces their interdependence. Women resent having to work for the apartment house but see it as a necessity. Because they belong to a "doorkeeper's family," they must do the doorkeeping tasks. The doorkeeper husband benefits from the structure of the occupation in two ways: he has the autonomy and authority to organize the labor process and he has more leisure (or more correctly, idle) time than his wife.

DOORKEEPERS' GENDER ANXIETY

While the "homebound" nature of doorkeeping produces an "objective" condition for a redistribution of household and childcare work, this "objective" condition is not effective in breaking the strong link between doing household work and gender-role identity. In fact, I argue that this link becomes even stronger in this case because the doorkeeper's very occupational role is likely to generate a gender anxiety, which is easily and typically managed by avoiding "female" chores. Within the normative structure of patriarchal gender order, the private (inside) is associated with the feminine, and the public (outside) is associated with the masculine. "A husband's place is not in the home," as Ann Oakley (1974:153) parodistically puts it. These spaces not only symbolize gender roles but also reinforce them. Manliness is performed and cultivated through activities, work roles, and social practices that take place in the extra-domestic realm. Those men who spend a great deal of time within the home are considered less masculine (one of the domestic workers expressed the idle and captive condition of her husband by pointing out her husband and saying, "Look, he sits around the house all day, like a woman"), while women who frequently inhabit external space risk social disapproval for their transgressing in male realms.

The doorkeeper's locus of work and his occupational role do not conform to socially defined notions of the masculine: he is placed in a position in which he must be on call, dependent, subordinate, nonassertive, and attentive to the needs of his social superiors. He must learn the skills necessary to cope with a subordinate status. These characteristics are traditionally associated with the female role in Turkish society.

Everyday conversations and observations reveal that both door-keepers and their wives are acutely sensitive to how they are perceived, especially by their fellow migrants, the squatter settlement dwellers. They often talk about how their fellow migrants are critical of their servitude and feminization, how they ridicule doorkeepers by making fun of the basket in which he carries bread to distribute to the tenants and his deferential behavior—servant to his social superiors. On the other hand, the doorkeepers criticize the squatter group for letting their children grow up in a disorderly environment with bad influences. Also, wives of the former doorkeepers, who are in a position to express the intensity of the degradation they experienced, cited the required servitude as the reason their husbands switched jobs. They said that their husbands could not bear to be doorkeepers.

The doorkeeper is often represented in Turkish popular culture as a peasant in the process of modernization, still wearing his cap (kasket)—a palpable symbol of peasantry—yet ready to adapt to urban ways. In a sit-com on public television that chronicles the daily lives of tenant families and their relationships in an apartment building, a young doorkeeper is one of the main characters. This character embodies the popular percep-tions of doorkeepers and their occupation. His portrayal reflects an image of the doorkeeper as slow, lazy, backward, uneducated, and coarse but also cunning, opportunistic, connivingly tactful, and nosy. He tries to get ahead by "kissing-up" to those who are above him. While juggling often contradictory demands of the tenants, he successfully avoids finicky res-idents but drops everything to cater to the demands of others who are good tippers. He hears and sees a lot of things about the personal lives of his tenants but knows how much and with whom he should strategi-cally share his information. He strongly resents being in the position of an order-taker but pretends to passively accept his position.

In fact, his occupational role resembles the role of a traditional housewife in many respects. His relationship to the apartment house is similar to that of a housewife to her home. The structural absence of any direct supervision and the erratic patterns of work and leisure, as well as the absence of a coherent job structure, are all similar to the housewife's role. The doorkeeper's occupation entails obvious servitude, yet, it has, at the same time, many structured possibilities for strategically undermining its negative effects. Many of the tasks and roles assigned to doorkeepers are carried out outside the "work place" (apartment building). Getting out to buy bread, newspapers, and groceries for tenants and going to the bank to make payments for the building's utilities mean that the doorkeepers often operate without any supervision.[12] This gives him the opportunity to organize his own rhythm of work. All tenants are the doorkeeper's "masters," yet they give orders without having much effective power over his labor process. It is service to an imprecise lord. The erratic condition of work and leisure leads people to regard doorkeeping as an easy occupation, despite the long hours on call. The doorkeeper finds himself, like the housewives studied by Oakley (1974:104), defending himself against the allegation that he does nothing at all. Ironically, but quite understandably, some of the doorkeepers' wives expressed the same sentiment when they complained that the work is not challenging enough to fully occupy their husbands, thereby leaving them idle and leading them into bad habits, such as going to coffeehouses. When I asked the women what their husbands do in their spare or leisure time, many women responded with the figurative saying, "All of his time is leisure time." Women who take this view are not compelled to demand more of their husbands' help with the routine household work. Such work would confine these men to the home more firmly and degender them as "househusbands." These women's quest for an egalitarian division of labor remains mostly at the abstract level. Instead, like women in Hochschild's study (1989), they engage in a "gender balancing act" to help their husbands manage and diminish their gender anxiety in a variety of ways.

In addition to avoiding feminine household chores, doorkeepers have ample structural opportunities to reinscribe their manliness or masculinity in a range of strategic ways. The preference for the unused title of "licensed heating-system operator" in place of "doorkeeper," for example, suggests how they attempt to remove themselves from the negative (servitude and feminine) associations of the occupation and to masculinize the occupation. They frequent male-only spaces of sociability, such as coffeehouses, excessively and play cards in the service of their masculinity. They leave the most feminine janitorial tasks to their wives. They control and manage the household money. The overwhelming majority of women are the main sources of household income, but they rarely deal with money after handing over their wages. Men's homebound and shopping-centered occupation creates a potent mechanism that affects and directs the internal structure of the household economy, constraining women's control over their own earnings, as I illustrate in Chapter 6.

Doorkeepers effectively subvert the stigmas associated with their work and confer honor upon themselves in the very process of doing their work. Modes of dignifying an otherwise degrading or "dirty" job have been analyzed in many studies since Everett Hughes's famous injunction (1958) to students of work and occupations to study "arrangements and devices by which men make their work tolerable, or even glorious to themselves and others" (342). As many studies show, the source of "dishonor," "indignity," and "degradation" of an occupational group is not the "dirt" they must handle and deal with. It is, instead, the "outsiders" who interfere in the relationship between the worker and his or her object of work (see Dill 1988; Hood 1988; Meara 1974; Romero 1988).

The doorkeeper finds honor in those aspects of his work that offer him a sense of self-worth and indispensability—a sense of honor that is independent of stigma, prestige, and social ranking in the larger society. He represents the apartment building to the outside world. His daily work helps to define the status of the apartment building and a clean, well-maintained building confers status on him (a status often achieved by the appropriation of his wife's labor). His work allows him to identify with his place of work ("my apartment house") and take pride in the status of the building in relation to other buildings in the neighborhood. In a very real sense, he becomes the master of the building.[13] He deals with strangers (salespersons, beggars) and protects the building and the tenants from potentially disturbing and threatening elements. He provides order. His relationship to the apartment building is in this sense also similar to that between a housewife and her home, especially when considered in terms of the effects of their daily work. Both the doorkeeper and the housewife strive to establish and maintain order by removing disturbing, unpleasant, and threatening elements from their respective spheres to protect their superiors (husband and tenants, respectively).[14] Furthermore, in both cases, a domestic worker, which, for the doorkeeper, is his wife, aids their status enhancement by removing dirt.

DOING GENDER AND MAKING A SPOUSE

As the analysis in this and the preceding chapters reveals, household tasks are performed solely by women in both samples. Doorkeeper husbands do only "nondeferrable chores," to borrow Rae Lesser Blumberg's phrase (1991). And there is no relationship between the relative resources of husbands and wives and their status in the household division of labor. The work each performs is independent of the variations between wives and husbands in terms of the one main "resource," time. Theoretically speaking, this means that the perspectives of "family-power"/resource and Marxist-feminist approaches cannot satisfactorily explain the relationship between work (household and childcare work and paid work) and gender experiences of women and men in the families I studied.[15] As Sarah Fenstermaker Berk (1985) notes, each of these approaches focuses on the abstracted consequences of household and childcare work rather than actual mechanisms and aspects of the work itself and the gender arrangements surrounding them. By so doing, they overlook women's and men's different relationships to housework and childcare and underestimate gender normative constraints on both women and men (Berk 1985). What is needed is an analytical framework that would allow for a direct understanding of the complicated and mutually informing relations between gender identity and the performance of household work.

Conceiving of gender as an ongoing accomplishment poses the question of what is produced through household work and childcare (Berk 1985; West and Zimmerman 1987). Berk's view (1985) is helpful in uncovering the reasons for individual men's and women's resistance to changing the traditional division of labor—despite the expressed wish to change it. "At least metaphorically," she writes, "the division of household labor facilitates two production processes: the production of goods and services and what we might call the production of gender. Simultaneously, household members 'do' gender, as they 'do' housework and childcare" (199). Accomplishing gender refers to the "ongoing task of rendering oneself accountably masculine or feminine. . . . The task of measuring up to one's gender is faced again and again in different situations with respect to different particulars of conduct" (Fenstermaker, West, and Zimmerman 1991:294–95). Household labor and childcare are among the primary practices through which gender is done. Women make themselves accountably feminine by doing house-work and men make themselves accountably masculine by avoiding it. Together they produce enactments of wifely and husbandly existence. These tasks are done with the feeling that they are consistent with one's internalized normative beliefs, rather than as a burden imposed from without. However, "doing gender" does not always entail preserving the gender status quo. When the squatter settlement women do the food shopping (a traditionally male job) on their way back home from work and act as the main "providers" for their families, they are also doing gender, but in a way that enlarges the legitimate territory of woman's gender practice and femininity.

Is this distribution of labor perceived to be unfair by women? Do women imagine or normatively endorse an alternative scenario for the reallocation of household tasks? Or do they accept their position because they see it as appropriate or natural? Do they accept it as an integral part of their womanly existence or does this inequality constitute a source of marital conflict and tension?

As it turns out, the vast majority of women would prefer an equal sharing of household work. When asked, "Should both husband and wife divide evenly the household tasks of washing dishes, preparing meals, and doing the laundry or is it better if only women do all of them?" 75 percent of the women in the doorkeeper group and over 80 percent of women in the squatter settlement group expressed a prefer-ence for an equal division of labor, whereas only about 20 percent in both groups endorsed the idea of a rigid gender division of labor at home. This latter, "gender conservative" 20 percent of domestic workers consider household tasks unmanly. Men are seen as lacking the special abilities that are required to do housework. Housework does not befit a man and his manly identity. Bodily metaphors (references to hands, especially) and proverbs, such as "Men's hands don't fit this type of work," "Men cannot do women's work," "Men are entirely incompetent when it comes to such work," and "Men and women gotta do their own things each" emphasize the undesirability and unnaturalness of men's performing "women's" work. Men's doing housework is perceived as a transgres-sion of the boundary between the womanly and wifely and the manly and husbandly. For this minority of women, gender principles are intran-sitive: while they may allow themselves to engage in wage-earning activ-ities and thus move into a sphere of activity defined as "manly" (their employment in domestic service, of course, renders the move less transgressive), they still express intolerance for the possibility of men moving into a "womanly" sphere.

In marked contrast to the gender conservatives, the majority of domestic workers desire a household arrangement in which husband wife share family work—and, in the same way, wage-earning work—equally. Common expressions reflect the principles informing this normative egalitarian preference and are consistent with these women's general commitment to wage work: "Life is shared" (*Hayat müşterektir*) and "The worth of his life-force and mine are equal" (*Onunki de benimki de can*).[16] In the absence of a popularly articulated feminist discourse, these Turkish cultural clichés, or their symbolic resource, serve as a justification in the quest for an egalitarian division of household labor. The harsh conditions of daily life and the experience of backbreaking paid work cause the domestic workers to question the "naturalness" of a gender-based division of labor, not an abstract notion of gender equality.

This pragmatic quest for equality, however, does not result in significant negotiation over reallocation of household tasks. A sizeable minority of women report conflicts over housework and childcare. Twenty-eight percent of the doorkeeper group and 30 percent of squatter group report conflicts over housework, and 20 percent of the doorkeeper group and 28 percent of squatter group report conflicts over childcare. Attempts to redefine duties and responsibilities between the wife and husband in childcare and household work are always initiated by women.

A closer look at the most recurrent theme of conflict illustrates the stakes entailed in these negotiations. Doorkeeper wives and squatter settlement wives negotiate different things, reflecting their own and their husbands' differing positions in the gender division of labor, as well as different social and geographic spaces they inhabit. Doorkeeper wives object to their husbands' "sending small children outside to play in cold weather without putting on coats," "letting school-age children go outside to play rather than overseeing their homework," "being too soft [or too harsh] toward children," "failing to change a baby's diapers frequently enough," and "sending children to school without combing their hair." Women expect the husbands to do more than just "keep an eye on children." They want their husbands' involvement in the routine, worklike, less pleasant aspects of bringing up children. They also aim to make their project of family modernization a shared one by developing their husband's parenting skills in accordance with modern child-rearing practices. This concern is closely related to the need to alleviate the stigma associated with doorkeepers' children (see Chapter 1). Indeed, these women attach a great deal of importance to their children's public appearance, grooming, and behavior. The following comments typify the doorkeeper wives' strong emotional and practical investment in their children's tidiness, cleanliness, and overall appearance. As one subject, Yasemin Coşan, observed, "Regardless of how well you dress and groom your kids, they are still identified as the doorkeeper's kids. [The tenants' kids] still don't play with our kids." She further explained her frustration by referring to her 12-year-old son's persistent but unanswered question, "Mother, why did my father have to become a doorkeeper? Were there no other jobs for him?" In contrast, Gülten Yazmaz proudly reported, "Tenants never treat my children like doorkeeper's children," and, she added, "If you dress your children clean and then send them among other kids, they do not segregate your children as doorkeeper's children." Here, she does not reject the tenants' stereotype of doorkeepers "uncleanliness" but takes pride in her exception from it. Both cases clearly illustrate the importance attached to producing and presenting middle-class-looking children, and it is not surprising to find that these women's negotiations with their husbands mainly center on the issue of stigma removal.

Among the squatter group, conflict about the household division of labor occurs only in relatively young households that do not contain other women to substitute for or help the wife. In general, these women run their households single-handedly day-in and day-out, shopping on their way back home from work, carrying their purchases for hours, and then cooking and cleaning up. They take children to the hospital when they get sick and go to their schools when they have a problem. They arrange childcare for the times when they are out at work. They manage all the budgeting, buy and store coal, and set up the heating stove for winter and dismantle it in spring. They send their husbands to work with clean shirts and ironed trousers. In contrast to the doorkeeper wives, who have more specific demands, these women seem to have mainly unspecific or "symbolic" stakes in the conflicts over the division of household labor. What they are trying to accomplish is not so much a reallocation of tasks as an acknowledgment and appreciation of their hard work. This demand for recognition is sometimes met with resist-

ance by husbands who retaliate against their wives' quest for appreciation with the threat of withholding their consent for paid work: "If you
cannot manage both [home and work] do not work then." It is important, in this context, to recall that cooking dinner is the only task rarely
performed by others. Women seem to delegate domestic tasks other
than cooking with fewer repercussions. Relaxing standards of housekeeping in order to accommodate paid work can go unnoticed by the
husbands but compromising cooking by either delegating it to others
or taking shortcuts and relaxing the timing is seen as a sign of women's
inability to successfully combine paid work with home responsibilities.
In the Turkish culture, food preparation and serving are quintessential
women's tasks, central to women's identity.[17] Food preparation sym-
bolizes the material nurturance of motherhood (Delaney 1991), and
motherhood defines a woman's identity. Thus, women are reluctant to
relinquish the work that symbolically defines them as mothers and
women.

Squatter wives' desire for recognition and respect and doorkeeper
wives' demand that their husbands participate more fully in childcare
suggest a desire on the part of these women to emulate an imagined, and
sometimes witnessed, middle-class marital ideal of spousehood. Unlike
the peasant relationship of husband and wife, spousehood entails mutual
understanding, companionship (*hayat arkadaşlığı*), and appreciation of
each other's labor. It is telling that these women would never use the
word "spouse" in their own daily conversations. "Spouse" (*eş*) is part of
a more polite and formal vernacular that does not have a place even in
day-to-day middle-class conversation. Yet, many of our respondents
"corrected" the interviewer who asked the question with the term "husband" by replacing it with "spouse." Indeed, theirs is a quest for making a "spouse" out of an "un-understanding peasant husband."

6   Earning Power and Women's Prerogative

"WE WORKED but never saw the face of money." So women in this study described their lives as peasant women. This sentence expresses a powerful awareness of, and sometimes ambivalence toward, changing experiences and life conditions. With these words the women characterized an important part of their life as they recalled the transition they made from unpaid family workers to urban, "individualized" wage earners. Holding, managing, and spending money is a concept alien to the identity of the peasant woman and antithetical to the precise definition of peasant womanhood in social scientific descriptions. Urban domestic workers now have access to money and wages and participate in consumption decisions from which they formerly were excluded. What do women do with the money at their disposal? In this chapter I explore the impact of women's wages on practices of household gender hierarchy, the relations of subordination-domination, and women's self-conceptions. Are women able to translate economic agency into decision-making authority? If so, how and in what areas of life? Does earning power superior to that of their husbands entail an unproblematic disposal right? How do women feel about earning wages? What role, if any, does earning wages play in the alteration of their subjectivities? Does earning wages put them in circumstances to challenge patriarchal authority?

To answer such complex questions, I sorted out and analyzed quantitative data all dealing with money. To organize the rather "messy" data, I constructed indexes, developed categories for comparisons and for decision-making profiles, and made some tables for illustrations. In the following pages, I present some conclusions based on this analysis and in the context of debates on the relationship between gender and money. But first, to set the stage, I recount an event that one of the women in this study, Demet Kibar, described to me. Although recounted matter-of-factly, this event dramatically expresses a critical moment in women's attempts to change the dynamics of their marriages with regard to money and represents a common understanding of economic empowerment.

177

Demet Kibar described a Sunday afternoon when she and her husband took their two children, an 8-year-old girl and a 10-year-old boy, to an amusement park (*gençlik parkı*). At the beginning of this outing, the boy misbehaved, and what he did made his sister cry. The father decided to punish the boy on the spot: first, he lightly smacked him and then declared that the boy would not get the ice cream he had been promised and was eagerly anticipating. Demet intervened, turning to her husband and saying, "The boy is going to get his ice cream. I'll pay for it. In fact, my money is paying for this whole outing." A marital argument ensued and continued at home; the husband accused her of using her money to undermine his authority. "Who do you think you are?" he asked. The boy did not get his ice cream because Demet could not act in direct defiance of her husband's wishes. Her defiance of his will was limited to the mere assertion of a disposal right. Going further than that by actually buying the ice cream would have been costly to the relationship.

Demet's experience is representative of the possibilities that earning and claiming money introduces to women's subjectivities and the salience of self-invention through economic agency. It is important to ask why women like Demet do not attempt to exercise such disposal rights more actively. I explore this question in depth in the last section of this chapter, proposing some conclusions based on the interpretation of quantitative data dealing with comparative profiles for decision making.

As many studies show, for many different reasons, women's earning power neither inevitably translates into their exercise of independent control over their money nor automatically increases their decision-making authority in the household (Blumberg 1991; Blumstein and Schwartz 1991; Safilios-Rothschild 1990; Standing 1985). Gender and family ideologies naturalize and legitimize gendered relationships to money and authority. The structure of women's employment and the relative size of women's monetary contribution to the household economy also condition the impact. Researchers have placed special emphasis on two factors of women's earning power in the third world: the difficulty of women's retaining control over their earned income and the channeling of women's earnings into the collective well-being of the family rather than into personal expenditures.

Recent research has shown that women's intra-household status is affected not only by their access to income through employment but also, and more important, by their ability to control the earned income. Rae

Lesser Blumberg's cross-cultural studies (1991) show that wives' incomes affect their power only to the extent that they retain control over that income. Similarly, Sherri Grasmuck's extensive review of the literature on this topic (1991) leads her to conclude that "cash must not merely cross over a woman's palm; her fingers must close around it, her hand must enter her pocket and stay there before we can expect to see her declare interests that are distinct from those of her husband and father" (10).

The Turkish case provides a critical context for an examination of the relationship between gender and money, especially the dynamics involved in women's ability to control their income and to translate income into decision-making influence. First, domestic workers' earnings are often much higher than their husbands': a full two-thirds of the domestic workers are either equal or primary contributors to the total household income. This nationally and cross-culturally uncommon pattern enables us to rethink the assumption that their inferior earnings are the basis of women's subordinated position in the realm of decision-making authority.[1] Second, the different situations of domestic workers in the doorkeeper and the squatter settlement groups provide a vantage point for delineating the conditions under which women are able to retain control over their earnings. Both groups of women have undergone a radical transition from unpaid family laborers (as peasant women) to individual wage earners (as domestic workers). The basic patriarchal organization of the Turkish peasant family and its economic and social life allows women no direct control over money when women do not receive individual wages. In this system women's access to consumable goods is limited by the nature of the peasant market and the mediation of men who always control spending. Women's independent-earner status as domestic workers entails changes in the nature of the distribution and consumption relations within the household. This transformation may be seen as more incomplete in the case of domestic workers in the doorkeeper group, not because of an ideological or cultural atavism, but because the institution of doorkeeping, by sheltering the tradition, perpetuates the familiar patriarchal structures, albeit in modified forms. The doorkeeper's job structurally lends itself to, or reinstates, some of the terms of the peasant conjugal contract. This reinstatement is especially manifest when delayed payment occurs: as I show in Chapter 3, cash wages owed to domestic workers are occasionally paid to husbands (just as they used to be in the village). Thus, in these cases, cash does not even cross over the woman's palms, let alone enter her pocket.

"THE MONEY THAT COMES IN DAILY GOES OUT DAILY": ALLOCATION OF WOMEN'S INCOME

Emphasis on the family as a unit has been the hallmark of the classical theory of the family (Parsons 1970) as well as a diverse range of theories from the New Home Economics to Marxist economic and development theories. These theories identify the household as an undifferentiated whole, without considering the relations of power that structure it. The concept of the moral economy of the household, common to these views, assumes that the internal economy of the household is governed by principles of reciprocity, consensus, solidarity, and altruism among members (see Berk 1985; Folbre 1988; Harris 1981; and Wolf 1992 for criticism of the New Home Economics and Marxist models). According to this model, adaptive household strategies are "objectively" beneficial for all members of the domestic group, regardless of gender and age, united by common interests. This consensus model of the family, however, ignores differences of gender and age in family experiences and underestimates conflict and adversarial negotiations concerning money or distributional practices within the household.

Feminist scholarship denaturalizes this model of the household as a sharing and pooling unit and points out the need to view the family and household as a divided and potentially conflictual unit (cf. Dwyer and Bruce 1988; Harris 1981; Hartmann 1981a; Hondagneu-Sotelo 1994a; Thorne and Yalom 1982). A growing body of research focuses on the actual family interactions and intra-household dynamics of income and power to understand the role women's employment plays in reducing or eliminating their subordination.

Research also shows that resources, such as food, education, and health care, are distributed in households unequally by gender and age (Charles and Kerr 1987; Fapohunda 1988; Hoodfar 1988; Maher 1988; Mencher, 1988; Whitehead 1988). Income and other financial resources are not always pooled and reallocated according to the family's collective well-being. There are important differences in the ways men and women spend household earnings under their control. Women devote more of their incomes than do men to subsistence and nutrition, while men withhold their earnings for individual spending.

What happens to domestic workers' income? Is it pooled, partially pooled, or earmarked for certain expenditures? Can women act independently of their husbands in the disposal of their wages? How do domestic workers' earnings assert the workers' status within their families?

In the Turkish case a pattern of gender-specific purchasing is observable, where husband's and wife's incomes are channeled into different spending categories. Nearly 40 percent of the women in the doorkeeper sample reported that their earnings go toward specific expenditures, primarily for food but also clothing, household durable goods, children's education, and their daughters' trousseaux. In the squatter settlement group, a much higher percentage of women (78 percent) reported that their income pays for subsistence and nutrition, primarily for kitchen expenses.

Meanings attached to husbands' and wives' financial contributions and the devotion of their incomes to specific expenditures are related to differences in the ways in which husbands' and wives' earnings enter the household, reflecting differences in the frequency of payment for women and men. In these households, except for "single-employer workers" (N = 15), women bring home cash wages daily, whereas men bring them home monthly. Thus there is a built-in tendency to spend women's wages on food and other daily expenditures and men's wages on fixed expenditures that require monthly payments, such as rent, utilities, telephone, and installments for consumer goods. Many women pointed out, "The money that comes in daily goes out daily." But this expression is more readily translated into practice for women in the squatter settlement group who, on the way home from work, spend a great proportion of their daily wages on food. Differences in the mode of wage payment determine whose money is directed toward what expenditures as well as other aspects of financial control, allocation, and savings.

Yet this clear-cut channeling of women's earnings into gender-specific spending areas does not always mean that women control spending in those areas. Even when women's earnings are earmarked for particular kinds of expenditures, they are consolidated in a "common pot," or fund. This common pot is often the husband's pocket and he controls it. With the exception of a small number of cases (N = 8) in the squatter settlement group where only "abstract" pooling is present, *as far as the members of the nuclear family are concerned,* all households in this study pool their income, their (physical and emotional) labor, and their other financial resources.[2] More important, even if they do not literally pool their income, as in the eight aforementioned cases, expenditures and accumulation strategies are still "planned" under the presumption that a household member will dispense his or her income in relation to others' labor or cash contributions. As discussed in Chapter 2, for example, fluctuations in the financial needs of the household or of its members are reflected in the changing work loads of domestic workers. Hence, the presence of pooling does not mean that decisions about the allocation of household income are made equally or cooperatively by members of the family. The control of money, rather than the presence of pooling, is a crucial factor that allows us to assess the relations between power and income for women.

WOMEN'S LEVEL OF CONTRIBUTION AND CONTROL OF MONEY

To compare the control women have over the disposal and distribution of their incomes at different contribution levels, I subdivided the sample into three groups according to the relative size of women's contribution to household income.[3] Women whose contribution is equal to or higher than 60 percent of the total household income are classified as "major" contributors; those who contribute 40 to 60 percent are classified as "equal"; and those who make up less than 40 percent of the total income are categorized as "minor."

In the doorkeeper group, the overwhelming majority of women are the main source of household income. The proportions of women who are major, equal, and minor contributors are 44.1 percent, 38.2 percent, and 17.6 percent, respectively (see Table 6). In the squatter group, 13.7 percent of women are major contributors, 49.0 percent are equal contributors, and 37.3 percent are minor contributors.

Do the proportions of women's contributions to family income correspond to their perceptions of the significance of their contribution? Are the status and value of women's and men's earnings in domestic workers' households equal? Do different proportions of male and female contributions produce differences in control and redistribution within the household?

TABLE 6.   Women's Level of Contribution to the Household Income

	Doorkeeper		Squatter	
	%	N	%	N
Major contributor	44.1	45	13.7	7
Equal contributor	38.2	39	49.0	25
Minor contributor	17.6	18	37.3	19
Total	99.9	102	100.0	51

Control signifies a capacity to enforce direction and disposal of money against competing claims. Control over money is a difficult concept to measure, because the important distinction between "execution of money" (management) and "control" often gets blurred and these two sometimes overlap. Jan Pahl (1983) usefully distinguishes between "control" that concerns major intra-household decisions of a "policy-making" kind and "management" that puts policy decisions into action. "Budgeting," concerned with manipulating available resources to comply with predetermined expenditure decisions, is a subset of "management." The concept of control as I use it here covers both "policy making" and "management."

To measure control over money, I used two items from the survey instrument that produced a four-way categorization. The following variables were used in assigning each woman to a specific control category: (1) who physically holds the household money—the wife, the husband, or neither (neither holds it but they have a designated place where money is kept), and (2) who manages the household money. The four categories developed from these two variables are "male control," "female control," "shared control," and "separate control" (see Table 7). In the majority of doorkeeper households (61.8 percent) money is under male control. In the squatter settlement group, male and female control are equally distributed (37.3 percent for each category). "Money under separate control" is found only in the squatter households (15.7 percent). "Shared control" is the second most prevalent mode among the doorkeeper households (20.6 percent) but the least in the squatter group (9.8 percent).

Male Control

Under this system labeled "male control," the husband holds and administers the household money. The system takes two basic forms.

TABLE 7.   Control of Money

	Doorkeeper		Squatter	
	%	N	%	N
Male control	61.8	63	37.3	19
Female control	17.6	18	37.3	19
Shared control	20.6	21	9.8	5
Separate control	—		15.7	8
Total	100.0	102	100.0	51

In the first the husband holds and manages the money, and the wife rarely deals with money after handing over her wages. In the second, the husband controls the money but delegates the daily management of a portion of it to the wife in the form of "partial housekeeping allowance."

A typical case of the *male-control* system is the household of İncigül Osman.

İncigül has been an earner for fifteen years. The mother of two adolescent children (a daughter and son, both in school), she currently makes twice as much as her husband. Yet her superior earnings entail no control of money. Unlike in many other households in this group, the common pot is not the husband's pocket but an actual pot. But she does not have direct access to this pot—"I cannot take a cent out of that pot without my husband's permission." Although her husband makes all routine household spending decisions and carries out all monetary transactions, she has her say in decisions regarding major expenses. She resents handing her money over to her husband and then having to ask for it. She says these exchanges often result in fights because she has to justify her spending. She says, "I don't want to be accountable for my own money" (*Hesap vermek zorunda olmak istemiyorum, kendi param için*). She would like to have separate purses. Keeping a separate purse, as she explains, would permit her to define the amount of her contribution to the common pot and what her contribution should cover. Without telling her husband, she regularly holds back money from her wages to buy gold coins as security for herself.

We found the second variant of the male-control system, the partial housekeeping allowance system, only among minor contributors. In these households the husband is considered the main provider and the wife earns considerably less than he does. The husband holds and controls money but leaves daily budgeting to the wife, who gets a weekly or daily allowance for housekeeping. A case in point is Nermin Köksal from the squatter group, a young mother of four.

> Nermin's is one of the poorest households in the group and the only household that does not have running water inside the house. Nermin's husband, a waiter, pays fixed expenditures—rent and electricity—then gives her a daily allowance to cover food-related expenses. But since this allowance is too low to meet the basic needs, she buys food on credit. With the money she earns (which is not much since she works only two days a week), she buys small household items, such as pots, sheets, towels, and clothes for children, and also pays some portion of the expenses for the food she buys on credit in the neighborhood grocery. Nermin's contribution to the household budget is less than one-third of her husband's contribution—calculated on the basis of what she guessed as her husband's income. She suspected that he could be making more and spending a disproportionate amount of his income on his gambling habit. Scarcity of money and his refusal to give her an extended (monthly) allowance are the main recurring themes of their daily quarrels. When asked who makes decisions about purchasing household durables, she responded, "There has been no such decision, since we did not acquire anything during our fourteen years of marriage. . . . We couldn't add anything to the refrigerator and a black-and-white TV set we purchased when we first married. But I guess my husband would decide in such a situation since he is the one who would pay for them."

Some women in the doorkeeper group interpret their limited relationship with money in terms of a traditional conjugal contract that defines men as leaders of the household and the absolute money holders. In the modern form of this traditional idea, they believe that the husband's *job* places him in an objectively privileged position to decide what is needed in the household and how it can be obtained. These husbands are characterized as good with money, skillful shoppers, and more knowledgeable about money management than their wives. Other women, while committed to sharing and the well-being of the family, would prefer separate purses and control of their earnings. Regardless of whether they are happy with male control, some of them, like İncigül Osman, adopt the age-old strategy of secretly diverting a portion of their earnings for discretionary spending.

Female Control

If the husband's and wife's earnings are combined and she manages the money, which is either held by her or kept in a place where she has exclusive access, it is defined as money under female control. This system, to repeat, is more prevalent in the squatter settlement households. The following case illustrates the conditions that stimulate and sustain the female control system in the doorkeeper households. It shows both the anomalous nature of the female control system in the doorkeeper household and the natural affinity between the doorkeeper's job structure and the prevalence of the male control system in these households.

> Thirty-five-year-old Fatoş Ak, who has six years' work experience, controls and manages the common fund even though she contributes only half as much as her husband. Her husband's regular second job as a driver for a bakery makes her the de facto money manager. Not only does she manage the money but she also performs many of his doorkeeping tasks with the help of her 13-year-old son, who does most of the shopping for the apartment house. She manages money without consulting her husband. "After paying off the color TV's monthly installment and keeping some pocket money for cigarettes and tea, he gives me the rest of his salary. He asks me when he needs money." She earmarks 50,000 TL every month for emergency or contingency expenses (mostly for unexpected company from the village or treatment for sickness). The family owns a house in a squatter settlement that they rent out. Although the rent money becomes part of the common fund that she controls, she resents the fact that the house, even though they purchased it together, is in his name.

The main reason a female-controlled system develops in a doorkeeper household is that the husband is distant from the doorkeeping post. If the wife assumes the doorkeeping responsibilities in the husband's absence, female control becomes necessary. In fact, the next system of control, shared control, could develop for the same reason. Female or shared control occurs for reasons ranging from the husband's extreme laziness (as in the following case) to the husband's having either a second job (which may be another doorkeeping post) or other informal work that separates him from the routines of doorkeeping.

Shared Control

Shared control presents a pattern of joint conjugal financial control and management where the money is either held by the woman or is kept in a designated place to which both the husband and the wife have access.

> Aliye Tar is 29 years old and has three children. She attributes her involvement in the management of the household money to her husband's laziness: "My husband is so lazy that he thinks if he works a little harder he would age quickly. He takes care of himself well. . . . He does not drink and smoke." Although she works seven days a week, her husband's responsibility of cleaning the apartment building also falls on her shoulders; she assumes this responsibility out of fear that her husband will lose his job if the cleaning goes undone. Her earnings are not earmarked. They keep their combined money in a pot to which both have equal claim. Neither withholds money for personal spending. Sharing in this case means that both take responsibility for shopping and managing money. She believes this system works well because her husband has no bad habits: "He behaves responsibly. He does not gamble or otherwise spend any money on bad habits."

Separate Control

Under the fourth pattern of financial control, which occurs only in squatter settlement households, each spouse holds and manages his or her own money. Physical pooling does not take place. A gender-specific division of responsibilities for expenditures constitutes one of the bases for the separately controlled system. While women's and men's incomes are allocated to gender-specific expenditures across the sample, within the separate control system women and men assume control of gender-specific spending. Pahl (1983) calls this the "independent management system." Spouses contribute their income to the household's collective maintenance through separate allocative responsibilities. The division of responsibilities is well defined. The more secure, stable, and monthly income (usually the husband's) is devoted to fixed commitments, such as rent and utilities, monthly credit payments for consumer durables, and investment payments (such as house and land). The less secure, variable, daily income (usually the wife's) is used for kitchen expenses. In principle, money and responsibilities are not transferred except in times of crisis or other unexpected circumstances. The case of Hafiza Yersiz illustrates the operation of this system of financial control.

Hafiza's is an extended household that includes her widowed mother-in-law and her unmarried sister-in-law. While Hafiza and her husband hold, control, and manage their respective earnings, Hafiza's sister-in-law does not contribute to this "abstract" pooling. The husband makes 500,000 TL a month as a clerk in the police force, exactly the amount Hafiza makes. Her husband also moonlights as a truck driver some weekends, making between 30,000 TL and 40,000 TL for each job. More than half of his salary (300,000 TL) is allocated to monthly payments on an expensive furniture set (a wall unit with a bookcase extension, a matching dining set, a sofa, and velvet upholstered armchairs). He is also responsible for the water, electric, and telephone bills. Last year he paid for a video-camcorder they bought to tape their 11-year-old son's circumcision festivities. Hafiza spends her earnings on kitchen and other daily expenses. She is extremely pleased with this arrangement, explaining, "I wouldn't like to hand over my earnings to him and then have to ask him for money. I would find it humiliating. Two years ago when I had a kidney operation and couldn't work for three months I had to ask him for money for daily expenses, but I felt so humiliated." Her unmarried sister-in-law, who spends her salary on preparation of her trousseau and clothes, is considered a "free-loader." Her failure to help with housework and her secrecy about how much she makes as a secretary intensify Hafiza's resentment of her sister-in-law. Hafiza's widowed mother-in-law knits for neighbors to earn petty cash, which she spends on bus fare and small gifts when she visits her village. Their well-kept house is owned in the husband's name, a situation that makes Hafiza insecure: "The house belongs to my husband. . . . If, one day, he throws me out, I have nothing to rely on." This concern must have prompted her, with the aid of one of her employers, to open a savings account she hides from her husband. She deposits close to one-fifth of her monthly earnings but occasionally allocates the money for buying nice clothes for her children. She does not know exactly how much he keeps for himself.

How does women's level of monetary contribution to the household economy correlate with each control type? Other things being equal, one would expect women who are major contributors to the total household income to maintain control of financial resources. That is, major contributors would be the least represented under the male-controlled money system. This expectation is confirmed in the case of the squatter group, in which 57 percent of households where women are major contributors are female controlled. As the women's contribution increases, the proportion of squatter settlement households with money under male control decreases and the proportion under female control increases. However, in the case of the doorkeeper group, no *linear* relationship is apparent between who controls the money and the level of women's contribution. Instead, the relationship appears to be hyperbolic. While nearly three-quarters of the minor contributors are under male control, a much smaller proportion of major or equal contributors are under male control. Yet, the proportion of *equal* contributors under male control is smaller (54 percent) than that of the *major* contributors (64 percent) under the same type of control.

The overall proportion of doorkeeper households under female control is not very large either. While 82 percent of doorkeeper wives are either major or equal contributors, only 15 percent of these households are under female control. Indeed, incidence of female control is relatively uniform despite differences in contribution levels.

In the doorkeeper group, then, the type of control and the size of contribution are relatively independent factors, while the two are closely correlated in the squatter group. This striking difference results from the doorkeeper husband's job, which allows him to exert substantial control over household money. His homebound and shopping-centered work informs the internal structure of the household economy, constraining women's control over their own earnings.

Comparable "Worth" of Women's and Men's Personal Spending

As the cases above illustrate, some women hold on to a portion of their earnings to spend or save at their discretion. The degree to which women can claim any part of their earnings for themselves or for discretionary purposes varies. Three groups emerged: "non-claimers," "known-claimers," and "clandestine claimers." A great majority of both doorkeeper and squatter women openly claim parts of their earnings for themselves or for purposes that they specify.

Thirty percent of the doorkeeper wives and 57 percent of the squatter women set aside some portion of their income as money under their exclusive control. The frequency at which money is set aside and the amount set aside vary considerably in both groups. Some regularly reserve a portion of their daily wages, while others withhold money as they need it. About one-quarter of the women in the doorkeeper group and one-third in the squatter settlement group are "clandestine claimers" who set aside money without the knowledge of their husbands.

In both the doorkeeper and squatter groups, a strong relationship exists between male control of household money and women setting aside money for discretionary use. There is, however, a difference in the relation between control type and clandestine withholding in the two groups. In the doorkeeper group eight of the nine clandestine claimers are in the "money under male control" group. In the squatter group, clandestine claimers are evenly distributed across types of control.

Men also claim personal spending money, with nearly 20 percent of doorkeeper husbands and 52 percent of squatter settlement men withholding some portion of their income. A larger percentage of doorkeeper husbands do not hold back money for two reasons. First, the majority of these husbands have exclusive access to the household money. When asked whether their husbands set aside money for their personal use, these wives said, "All money is his money." When money is under his control, the doorkeeper, as well as the squatter settlement husband, can spend it for personal use without designating it as "his set-aside money." The same explanation may apply to women whose set-aside money becomes more visible when men control all household money. Second, since the doorkeeper works inside the apartment and its vicinity, he has fewer work-related expenses requiring personal spending money. In contrast, among the squatter group, where men work away from the home, a much higher proportion keep personal spending money regardless of the type of control in the household. Both groups' percentages of set-aside money still fall below the percentages of women's set-aside money.

Men's personal money is spent on cigarettes, work-related expenses, such as transportation, and routine socializing activities, such as trips to coffeehouses, the most popular "recreational" activity among lower-class Turkish men. Men's personal spending patterns occasion no conflict unless they are markedly irresponsible (with gambling or drinking problems). Indeed, women believe a man should not go around without any cash in his pocket, for, as I discuss below, day-to-day male-gendered routines require more visible personal cash.

Women's "personal" spending money is usually channeled into collective and nonpersonal expenditures. A great proportion of women spend their discretionary funds on children's education and clothing (61 percent in the doorkeeper and 34 percent in the squatter group). Such expenses might include sending children to *kurs* (private courses outside the school system) or to extra-curricular courses (for example, a mother from the doorkeeper group sends her artistically gifted 11-year-old daughter to an art class) and providing children their daily allowance for school.

Many women also spend discretionary money on gold bracelets and gold coins. Although they use the bangles as ornaments to display wealth and self-worth,[4] they buy gold primarily as an investment for the well-being and security of the family. The jewelry is converted into money when an urgent need arises, most typically when a big sum of cash is needed for a property investment, to purchase a house or land, or when the family marries off a son. The gold bracelets and coins also frequently function as currency in an informal banking and loan system in the women's community, where women borrow and pay back gold rather than cash. In these cases, the lender does not charge interest but does not lose money either because of Turkey's high inflation rate and the perception that gold continually increases in value.

Women open credit accounts in neighborhood stores to buy items to beautify their homes such as drapes, towels, blankets, tablecloths, expensive steel pot sets, and fancy teapots and sets of coffee cups to be displayed in their glass cabinets. Husbands commonly think of these purchases as frivolous and unnecessary. Women also spend discretionary money on sheets, comforters, and other bedding items as well as on material to make embroidered household items for a daughter's trousseau.

These patterns of discretionary spending are fully consistent with other cross-cultural findings. Scholarly studies consistently document that men distinguish between spending on one's self and spending for the collective family, whereas women tend to merge these two by closely identifying their spending interests with those of the family and children (Delphy 1979; Dwyer and Bruce 1988; Kıray 1985; Maher 1988; Pahl 1980; Whitehead 1988; Wilson 1987). On the basis of her in-depth study of forty-one İstanbul working-class households, Hale Bolak (1995) reports that husbands do not cooperate with their wives for the collective well-being of the household but instead engage in what she calls ostentatious and self-indulgent spending in the "service of their masculinity." From such observations, it is often inferred that women's inability or unwillingness to distinguish between "self" and "others" (what Ann Whitehead [1988] calls "maternal altruism") benefits families and children at the expense of their own autonomy and empowerment.

It is further argued that women's empowerment is especially limited in low-income households where women, even when they have full control over money, cannot translate their income into increased power for themselves because subsistence incomes allow for little discretionary spending. Or, in Blumberg's terse formulation (1991), "the degree of control over surplus allocation is more important for relative male/female economic power than is the degree of control over resources needed for bare subsistence" (100).

Both of these explanations of gendered patterns of spending and their implications for gender stratification within households need to be qualified. First, subsistence and surplus-level spending are neither empirically tangible givens nor universally applicable categories. It is important to recognize "subsistence" and "surplus" as variables whose definitions are context dependent. An abstract "subsistence/surplus" theory would tend to evaluate women's food expenditures as mere "subsistence" spending that presumably does not enhance women's status. For example, stews—which can be made with or without meat— are an important part of the Turkish diet. Some women interviewed felt they had provided something out of the ordinary for their children when they were able to add meat to such dishes. Clearly, in these women's lives, adding meat is a "surplus" level act. These women rarely worry about their ability to feed hungry children, wonder whether they can bring them bananas (the most expensive fruit in Turkey), buy their family kabob from the corner kabob shop, or serve their guests pastry from the bakery rather than homemade cookies.

Second, it is incorrect to assume that "maternal altruism" necessarily entails negative consequences for women. One should, instead, empirically demonstrate the actual meanings and consequences of maternally altruistic practices of women. Accepting the proposition that women do not benefit from their earnings *because* of their maternal altruism risks ignoring cultural meanings of such spending and the ways it defines identity. Even though domestic workers, like other women in similar contexts, channel their earnings into home- and children-centered spending categories, they often cherish independent access to and control of money, even for apparently "subsistence" level spending, because it allows them to exercise consumption and disposal rights. Women's independent access to money undermines one of the most visible mechanisms of male control, which these women feel to be particularly pernicious and demeaning: the need to ask their husbands for money for even small expenditures.

Let us closely examine the assumption that women do not gain power from discretionary spending unless, like men, they spend on themselves. This conceptual framework is workable only in circumstances where men and women participate in the *same sphere of activities* (especially leisure consumption). Such circumstances, however, are unusual. We must therefore qualify the assumption to express cultural contexts where women's social identity depends upon their role in the family and where there is generalized gender segregation. A simple example suffices to illustrate this point. In a context where it is illegitimate for a woman to go out and drink beer, we cannot infer that her income has not increased her autonomy and control because she spends on her children while her husband spends in pubs.[5]

A "fair" gender comparison can be made only in the rare circumstance where equal gender spheres can be presupposed. What happens when the activities that women and men engage in and the possible terrains of sociability are gender segregated? Under conditions of gender segregation, the comparability issue should be examined from another perspective. By borrowing the notion of "comparable worth" from the wage-equity movement (Steinberg and Haignere 1991), we can assume a comparable worth of women's and men's personal expenditures even when women do not spend their "personal money" on items and leisure activities that are deemed to be personal. Accordingly, gender-based spheres of activity do not necessarily or by definition entail a hierarchy.

What I am suggesting is that the "worth" of a wife's entertaining her friends by baking chocolate cake (plain cake has a rural, unprestigious identity), serving instant coffee (a prestige item in the Turkish context) rather than cheaper traditional coffee, or sending her daughter to an art class are comparable in status value to her husband's treating his friends to coffee in the coffeehouse or smoking high-priced imported Marlboros rather than Turkish cigarettes. Although men and women operate within partially divergent gender domains with distinct conceptions of value and prestige, they may perceive themselves as gaining comparable degrees of status and self-esteem from different forms of spending.

Moreover, intra-gender competition is not an exclusively male phenomenon. Women compete among themselves for recognition and identity within their gender sphere—and, in financial terms, such competition can be just as costly as men's, if not more so. Women are judged, gain worth, judge themselves, and find fulfillment according to culturally established standards of womanhood. Maternal altruism is not necessarily "altruistic" in its overall effects: it may, instead, be a highly feasible form of investment in a cultural sphere with good returns of fulfillment and social recognition. Given their gender-segregated world, these women, quite rationally, devote their "personal" money to home- and children-centered spending categories to enhance their status as wives and their reputations as good mothers. If one can speak of winners and losers in these competitions, the woman with chocolate cake and a college-educated son wins.

Social standing and reputation derived from family-oriented consumption are central to women's identities and sense of self-worth. The predicament of Zekiye Güzel, one of the veteran domestic workers from the doorkeeper group, dramatizes this observation, albeit in a convoluted fashion. I had long conversations with Zekiye and spent a considerable amount of time at her home, socializing and having meals with her, her husband, and her new daughter-in-law. At the time of my visits, the possible purchase of a television dominated family conversations. Zekiye's family was relatively well-to-do as a result of her earnings from six days of work a week and savings accumulated when her husband worked in Saudi Arabia. Zekiye and her two sons took over the doorkeeping responsibilities while he was away. They were, however, strained for cash at the time when I met her. All of their savings, she proudly explained, had gone to marrying the older son, who was making a good career for himself as a carpenter. Their younger son was about to enter the army for his mandatory service, throughout which the family would need to support him. The newly married couple uneasily shared the small two-room doorkeeper's apartment consisting of a living room, which doubled as the older couple's and younger son's bedroom, and a small bedroom given to the newly married couple. I was quite baffled by this arrangement. Doorkeeper families are usually nuclear in structure and do not extend in this fashion. The arrangement appeared even stranger once I learned that the newlyweds had a nicely furnished apartment of their own (owned by Zekiye and her husband) in a low-income neighborhood near the son's workplace. All major appliances and furniture sets were paid for. The couple had even purchased and stored coal for the winter. Why, then, were they still living with their parents in such crammed conditions? One significant item was missing from the newlyweds' home: a color television; hence, the concern with different brands and sizes of televisions and the constant comparisons of different installment plans. The daughter-in-law, for example, pointed out to me that the large-screen television set that her in-laws owned was a Sony brand and she wondered whether it would be possible to exchange it for two less-expensive sets. I resisted the temptation to suggest that she could sell a couple of the eleven thick gold bracelets she wore. It was obvious that the newlyweds would not be moving to their own apartment until they owned a television set. In one of my subsequent visits, Zekiye was home alone and our conversation again turned to the matter of purchasing a television for the newlyweds. In the course of that conversation, she finally expressed her real concern: "Look—If I allow them to move to their own apartment without owning a TV, people are going to start gossiping because they will go to visit their neighbors and relatives [their apartment was located in a community where their relatives also lived] every night to watch TV. They are young. They can't resist." The issue was not the lack of a television but the implication that they could not afford one. A television set stood between status honor and ill reputation. Zekiye wasn't going to let the lack of a television ruin the prestige gained by marrying her son glamorously and starting a new household without debt. Of course, converting those nice gold bracelets was not a viable option either since converting gold this early in the marriage would equally tarnish her reputation.

Thus, in the context of the Turkish case, I am arguing that we should not assess women's autonomy and agency pertaining to income control by focusing only on where or for whom the woman spends her money. As this example suggests, seemingly private, altruistic spending can be experienced as enhancing the status and self-image of the spender.[6] To deny the benefits derived from "altruism" spending disregards women's agency and empowerment and belies their own perceptions of their lives and decisions.

Women's Influence in Household Decision-Making

To understand women's agency in doorkeeper and squatter settlement families we must examine the relationship between women's earning power and the extent to which this power is translated into women's claiming influence in household decision-making and the relationship between women's feelings about earning wages and their sense of the impact these wages have on their marriage. As noted by many family sociologists, measuring decision-making power in families by asking the question "Who makes the final decision?" involves many theoretical problems, since decision making entails a multilayered process of interaction and exchanges between husbands and wives.[7] In my research I made no attempt to study these underlying mechanisms and processes of decision making quantitatively except by probing into these questions during the in-depth interviews. What follows is an examination of women's perceptions of decision making within the household. The computed figures should be considered rough measures of some aspects of the intra-household power and influence these women experience.

The survey instrument contained questions about spending decisions in five areas: the purchase of food, the purchase of household electronics, the purchase of household durables, the purchase of clothes for special holidays, and expenses for children's education. It also included one question about how saved money is spent and one question about the raising of their children. In addition, three questions explored decisions about both self and social life that involve birth control and sex. The survey concluded with a question about who has the "last word" in important family matters and its normative counterpart: Who should have the last word? For each decision, the respondent was asked to state which of the following choices best describes the household arrangement: (1) "I have all"; (2) "I have more than he"; (3) "Equal"; (4) "He has more than I"; and (5) "He has all." A summary ratio index was developed to quantify the claimed relative weight of women's decisions compared with men's in such matters. A score of 1.00 indicates that, according to the women's perception, the men and women have "equal influence" in decision making; scores of less than 1.00 indicate that the women have less influence than the men, and scores of more than 1.00 indicate that the women have more influence than the men (see Table 8). Women in both doorkeeper and squatter households

TABLE 8.   Women's Perceptions of Their Influence in Decision Making

	Doorkeeper			Squatter		
	Influence	N	%	Influence	N	%
Consumption and saving decisions						
Food	0.64	81	79.41	0.82	30	58.82
Household electronics	0.45	102	100.00	0.65	43	84.31
Household durables	0.74	102	100.00	0.87	44	86.27
Clothing	1.36	99	97.06	1.59	44	86.27
Children's education	0.67	76	74.51	1.08	26	50.98
Savings and investment	0.45	95	93.14	0.61	45	88.24
Marital and self-related decisions						
How to bring up children	0.86	96	94.12	1.15	44	86.27
Birth control	1.97	46	45.10	6.20	18	35.29
Woman's association	1.46	102	100.00	1.45	49	96.08
When to have sex	0.20	97	95.10	0.16	39	76.47
Who has the last word on important family matters	0.13	102	100.00	0.13	49	96.08
Who should have it	0.55	102	100.00	0.44	49	96.08

Notes: N = number of applicable responses to the item; % = the proportion of applicable responses to the item in the total number of cases.

claim to have a pronounced influence on purchasing and savings decisions.[8] Although most figures are below 1.00, indicating that in more households the woman has less influence than the man, the results for certain items in this survey are striking, for they suggest a level of women's influence that is markedly different from the levels found in other decision-making profiles of Turkish families.[9] It is also important to emphasize that the wife's increased participation in decision making is really an index of shared decision making rather than evidence of autonomous decision making.

Women generally claim to have more influence in purchases that benefit them directly, including items related to household technology that would reduce their work load, than they do in purchases related to electronic gadgets, a male domain. Women have less say in deciding how much to spend on food than do men, even though a greater proportion of women's earnings go toward food-related expenses. This finding is not unexpected in the context of the income-control patterns of these households but it does deviate from the more general cross-cultural pattern found in similar contexts where women have predominant or exclusive influence. The score on this item for the doorkeeper group is smaller than that of the squatter group, indicating the significant role of the doorkeeper husbands as agents of food-related purchases.

Besides purchasing decisions, women in the doorkeeper group also have markedly less influence than men in decisions concerning expenses associated with children's education and how to bring them up (0.67 and 0.86, respectively). A substantial difference in this area of influence between women in the doorkeeper and in the squatter households is also evident. Squatter settlement women claim to have more influence than their husbands in making decisions concerning children (1.08 for education and 1.15 for expenses associated with upbringing), further evidence that doorkeeper husbands share childcare responsibilities, whereas squatter settlement husbands take virtually no such responsibility, as analyzed in Chapters 2 and 5.

In both groups, husbands have considerable influence over whom their wives associate with. Although the score that reflects women's influence on choice of associates is very high for both groups, the size of the score for this item should not be considered comparable in size to the scores of any other decision-making items. In the doorkeeper group, for example, 50 percent of the women report having the say on this matter, 19 percent report having equal say with the husbands, and 31 percent report that the husband decides with whom she may associate. Corresponding percentages for the squatter group are 57, 4, and 39, respectively. The fact that husbands are involved at all (as "equal" or "more" influential) in such directly personal decisions at such high proportions is indicative of the extent of patriarchal control of women's social interactions in these families.

Birth control is the only area of decision making in which husbands do not have any predominant or exclusive influence. Questions pertaining to birth control were asked only of those respondents who reported practicing birth control in response to a previous question; therefore, these scores apply to a subset of a sample and should be interpreted with caution. If and when a "decision" about the birth control is present, women are the predominant decision makers (1.97 for the doorkeeper group and 6.20 for the squatter settlement group). In the doorkeeper group, thirty-one of the forty-six women who use birth control (mean age 30.3) reported that using it was a joint decision, whereas fifteen women (mean age 31.1) stated that it was exclusively their decision. In contrast, thirteen women (mean age 35.1) out of eighteen (those who use birth control) in the squatter settlement group reported that using birth control was their own decision, and five women (mean age 33.4) said that this decision was made jointly with the husband. Women seem to have less influence on the decision of when and how frequently to have sex. The ratios are almost identical for both groups (0.20 for the doorkeeper group and 0.16 for the squatter group).

The ratios on overall decision-making, identical for the two groups (0.13, the lowest ratio), indicate that the "last word" in both groups belongs to the husband and are consistent with my analysis of men's influence on "woman's association." This unspecific item contrasts well with a question that frames the same issue with a normative orientation, "Who do you think should have the final say about important decisions affecting the family?" While only 22 percent of the wives of doorkeepers and 12 percent of the women in the squatter group report having equal or more influence on important matters that affect the family, 65 percent and 55 percent of the women uphold the normative view that women ought to have equal or more influence. I return to a discussion of these two items at the end of the present section.

On the whole, doorkeeper wives seem to have a more limited influence on household spending decisions in all categories than the wives in the squatter settlement group, a discrepancy reflecting their different positions in the money-control systems discussed in the previous section. Yet their decision-making profiles are almost identical in the areas of decisions concerning self, sex, and overall decision-making.

Do Women's Higher Earnings Translate into Greater Power? Or, Is It Who Controls the Money That Matters?

How do women's earnings and control of money affect decision making for the doorkeeper and the squatter groups? In the doorkeeper households, a positive relationship exists between the level of women's contribution to the household income and their influence in decision making in the spending areas, indicating that major and equal contributors have more influence than minor contributors (see Table 9). But this difference is more clearly manifested in decisions about how to bring up children (1.15 for majors, 0.75 for equals and 0.55 for minors), decisions about savings (0.51, 0.61 and 0.13), decisions about clothing purchases (1.67, 1.39, 0.80), and, finally, decisions regarding self (2.00, 1.36, 0.80). Across the board, major and equal contributors have more influence than minor contributors, except in the case of household electronics. The most notable observation, however, is one marked difference between "major" and "equal" contributors in an unexpected direction. Being a major contributor does not immediately entail having more influence than an "equal" contributor. In fact, in all but one of the items, major contributors have less influence than equal contributors.

In the squatter settlement households, major contributors tend to participate in purchasing decisions to a greater extent than minor contributors. Since the number of cases is too small to obtain meaningful index figures for the major group, a comparison between equal and minor contributors is more pertinent. With the exception of decisions concerning food and savings, equal contributors have more say than minors. The difference is especially marked in the area of sex, self, children's education, and clothing purchases. Bringing up children is the only area in which there is a reverse relationship between the level of contribution and decision making.

In the doorkeeper group, control of money is closely related to decision-making power and, generally speaking, women who belong to

TABLE 9. Women's Influence in Decision Making by the Proportion of Female Monetary Contribution to the Household in the Doorkeeper Group

	Major			Equal			Minor		
	Influence	N	%	Influence	N	%	Influence	N	%
Consumption and saving decisions									
Food	0.63	31	68.89	0.83	33	84.62	0.36	17	94.44
Household electronics	0.38	45	100.00	0.56	39	100.00	0.38	18	100.00
Household durables	0.70	45	100.00	1.00	39	100.00	0.44	18	100.00
Clothing	1.67	44	97.78	1.39	37	94.87	0.80	18	100.00
Children's education	0.68	32	71.11	0.75	28	71.79	0.52	16	88.89
Savings and investment	0.51	40	88.89	0.61	37	94.87	0.13	18	100.00
Marital and self-related decisions									
How to bring up children	1.15	44	97.78	0.75	35	89.74	0.55	17	94.44
Birth control	1.94	25	55.56	2.09	17	43.59	1.67	4	22.22
Woman's association	2.00	45	100.00	1.36	39	100.00	0.80	18	100.00
When to have sex	0.28	41	91.11	0.16	39	100.00	0.13	17	94.44
Who has the last word on important family matters	0.15	45	100.00	0.15	39	100.00	0.06	18	100.00
Who should have it	0.53	45	100.00	0.63	39	100.00	0.44	18	100.00

Notes: N = number of applicable responses to the item; % = the proportion of applicable responses to the item in the total number of cases.

households where money is under their control have a greater influence in all decision-making areas than women who are in households where money is under male control (see Table 10). This difference is especially pronounced in decisions concerning food and children. Parallel observations can be also made in the case of the squatter settlement group, where a strong association exists between women's greater control of money and their greater influence in decision making in all areas. Because of the small number of cases in some groups, a meaningful comparison across all the allocation of groups (especially in the case of shared and separate categories) is not possible.

"Money Counts, Up to a Point"

The preceding observations suggest that women's agency as decision makers is based on their control and disposal of their earnings. Comparing higher contributors with minor contributors, we clearly see the influence of earning power on decision making. However, this relationship does not seem linear: major contributors (i.e., those who contribute over 60 percent of total household income) have less, not more, influence than equal contributors (i.e., those who contribute between 40 percent and 60 percent of total household income). This finding, too, is consistent with the nonlinearity of the relationship between contribution level and male or female control of money. Just as the size of women's contributions does not ensure them control over money, contribution size does not automatically translate into a proportionately increased influence in household and self-related decisions. Does this mean that the key to power is not in the size of the earning? Does male control of money override the effect of women's higher earnings in relation to men's?

The major contributors who are under either female or shared control are clearly more influential in most decision areas than the corresponding groups among the "equal" contributors. The intriguing fact is that the women who make a major contribution but whose money is controlled by men are worse off than the corresponding group of women who make only an "equal" contribution.

How then do we explain the predominance of male-control arrangements under conditions where women are the major contributors? It is possible to conclude that wives' earnings generate increased decision-making influence as long as those earnings are subordinate or equal to

TABLE 10. Women's Influence in Decision Making by "Control of Money" in the Doorkeeper Group

	Men			Women			Shared		
	Influence	N	%	Influence	N	%	Influence	N	%
Consumption and saving decisions									
Food	0.42	47	74.60	2.09	17	94.44	0.55	17	80.95
Household electronics	0.34	63	100.00	0.64	18	100.00	0.68	21	100.00
Household durables	0.70	63	100.00	0.57	18	100.00	1.10	21	100.00
Clothing	1.26	60	95.24	1.77	18	100.00	1.33	21	100.00
Children's education	0.58	49	77.78	0.86	13	72.22	0.87	14	66.67
Savings and investment	0.39	59	93.65	0.68	16	88.89	0.48	20	95.24
Marital and self-related decisions									
How to raise children	0.64	60	95.24	1.62	17	94.44	1.24	19	90.48
Birth control	1.84	27	42.86	3.00	6	33.33	1.89	13	61.90
Woman's association	1.47	63	100.00	2.00	18	100.00	1.10	21	100.00
When to have sex	0.14	58	92.06	0.38	18	100.00	0.27	21	100.00
Who has the last word on important family matters	0.09	63	100.00	0.29	18	100.00	0.17	21	100.00
Who should have it	0.47	63	100.00	0.71	18	100.00	0.68	21	100.00

Notes: N = number of applicable responses to the item; % = the proportion of applicable responses to the item in the total number of cases.

husbands' earnings.[10] When women's earnings surpass those of their husbands, men appear to exercise increased control in decision making. The threat entailed by women's economic power is countered by an increased exercise of patriarchal prerogative. Given the increased stakes involved in who controls money, under these conditions men tend to enforce their existing power more stringently by insisting on having exclusive control over money.

Conversely, women under such conditions do not seem to try to increase their influence commensurate with their earnings, perhaps because continued gains involve different kinds of costs for women and result in increasing marital conflicts. Women, therefore, may be more likely to avoid using their superior earning power as leverage for intra-household bargaining once they clearly become the dominant income providers. There seems to be a threshold, a saturation point, beyond which women cannot—or imagine they cannot—proceed.

This study's data do not allow for a more nuanced understanding of this saturation point on the threshold of female power. The data, however, clearly underscore the extent to which men reassert male control of female income once that income clearly surpasses their own.

When asked, "Who has the ultimate say in important family matters?" women, departing from previous responses pertaining to specific consumption decisions, indicate that the husband has the final word. Over three-fourths of the women, regardless of their level of contribution to household income, said that the ultimate word is their husbands'. It is possible that women achieve "equal participation" in a range of specific household decisions while traditional male domination is maintained at structural levels. The overall decision-making score is not therefore a summary of other item-specific scores but is instead a measure of " idealized authority" reflecting the husband's traditional institutionalized role. These husbands' traditional authority does not derive from their roles as providers (i.e., the resources they are capable of bringing in), but rather it emanates from their position in the traditional patriarchal family.

Women in this study, however, are markedly critical of their husband's patriarchal authority: only about one-third of the women think "husbands should have the ultimate say." Women feel that familial authority should be based on the resources one contributes to the household rather than on gender. They cannot, however, directly demand more power or authority.

Women are able to offset the ultimate authority of the husband only to the extent that they have control over the resources they bring in. Women who control the household budget are, on the average, 25 percent to 15 percent more likely to claim that it is *not* the husband who has the last word in their homes. In fact, these women are decidedly more opposed to arbitrary male authority: only 19.0 percent of women in "shared control" households and 27.8 percent of women in "female controlled" households hold the normative view that the husband should have the ultimate say, as opposed to 42.9 percent of women in "male controlled" households.[11]

Women's desire for egalitarian power in the household is rooted in the fact that women necessarily become decision- making partners with their husbands, even when their own earnings are at their husbands' disposal. I suggest that consumption decisions in these families cannot be made without women's cooperation. In these families' lives, decisions concerning consumer durables have substantial importance, entailing the allocation of an entire salary to installment payments. Such important decisions cannot be made without women's consent because prolonged installments require women's continuing commitment to wage earning. More important, these decisions entail investment and debt spending in articles that are closely associated with these women's aspirations for urbanity and modernity.

The relationship between autonomy and income control should also be analyzed in the light of women's relationship not only to their earnings but also to other forms of property, such as land, housing, and nonmonetary savings. A relatively high level of home and land (urban) ownership among domestic workers' households points out the need to look at this issue. Homeownership is an important means by which migrant families anchor themselves in the city. While both husbands and wives share this aspiration, women are largely responsible for its realization.

The cost of building a house in a squatter settlement is enormous and takes years of commitment. First, prospective homeowners buy a plot of land on an installment plan and begin gradually to accumulate construction materials. They must pay taxes and expenses related to water and electric connections. Finally, they must pay for construction and furnishing. Purchasing an apartment in a low-income neighborhood also entails a long-term commitment to large monthly installments.

Women's savings, in the form of gold coins and bracelets, as well as advance payment from employers, account in large part for the relatively high level of home-ownership among these low-income families. Despite women's continuous commitment to earning wages, men almost exclusively own property. In the doorkeeper sample only three women are the sole owners of a house or a plot of land, and only one woman is a co-owner with her husband. Thirty husbands own such property. Figures for women in the squatter settlement group are similar: only two wives are property owners in thirty-one families. Women's power to claim the fruits of their labor seems weakest in this area. Many women said, "I built it, but I let him put his name on it." To avoid marital conflict and the disruption of a traditionally gendered power structure, women engage in "power balancing" (Hochschild 1989). Their lack of property ownership is indeed an underlying source of women's resentment but not a cause of marital conflict. Property ownership is an area of women's gender subordination in which a large "ideological discount rate"[12] is applied because of patriarchal ideology on women's economic contribution.

Is Earning Money Good for Women?

The salience of a sense of economic agency in women's understanding of their own identities appeared when they went into debt to purchase a set of steel cookware or to help out adult children with clandestinely saved cash. Throughout this study paid work was found consistently to be significant for women insofar as it relates to their identity as mothers. The experience of working "outside" the home and the income that it brings increases the independence and autonomy available to women in Turkish society, women's sense of status in the family and community, and their relation to patriarchal authority. These women never underestimate the role of their earning power in sustaining the family and improving the life chances of their children. They know that their earnings are crucial for their household's consumption and improvement on their standards of living. This knowledge translates into an enhanced sense of self-worth and feelings of self-sufficiency. These qualitative shifts in women's self-perceptions cannot be quantified easily by statistical description and may not be adequately reflected in decision-making ratios. Their commentaries on the positive or negative consequences of their employment for their marriage and family life also illustrate the value of paid work for these women.

Over 80 percent of the women in the doorkeeper group, and 75 percent in the squatter settlement group, responded affirmatively when asked whether being employed and earning wages has had positive consequences for their marriage and family life. Only a small percentage of women (2 percent of the doorkeeper group and 5 percent of the squatter settlement group) claimed that working has negatively affected their marriages.[13] The open-ended probing of this question also revealed that there is little variation in how women feel about working and earning wages.

Instead, I found three consistently repeated themes in the women's responses: the understanding that economic security is the basis of domestic harmony, the understanding that wage earning is the foundation of equality between husbands and wives, and the appeal of self-sufficiency derived from financial autonomy in marriage. These themes, often interrelated, were emphasized with various degrees. The following comments by six women illustrate the ways that wage earning was positively characterized.

> I am supporting my husband both materially and morally. I am now able to buy what I want to. When you have money in your hand, you can spend it more freely. Otherwise, even if he gives you money one day, another day he may not. You are in his hand.

> We bought furniture and household appliances for the home. Because of my earnings, we moved up from not being able to even replace the broken tube of the old black-and-white TV set to buying a brand new color TV.

> When he was the only money-maker in the family, he was reckoning himself superior, privileged, but now I am in the same position as him. I see myself as equal to him. I have more power to speak.

> Economic ease solves many problems. Absence of money causes disagreement and disharmony, even when you aren't aware of it. . . . Being able to contribute something to your home is wonderful. Being able to say "I bought this" feels wonderful.

> If I had not worked, I would have to look at [my husband's] hands. When I have money I have no need of him. I can go out and get whatever I need.

> When you earn money, you are not in need of your husband. I live by my labor. I'm self-sufficient and do not depend on my husband. I felt better about myself when I earned money.

In many accounts, the most readily invoked theme was that of financial autonomy within the marriage. It was expressed often through the popular idiom of "not having to look to the husband's hand" (*koca eline bakmamak*) a circumstance that attributes value and dignity to financial autonomy in the marriage. For most adult women in Turkey, especially women of peasant origins and of the lower social classes, there is little, if any, question of life outside marriage. Turkey's very low divorce rate, despite permissive divorce laws, suggests that divorce is not a viable alternative. Thus, these women's perceptions of increased autonomy within the confines of marriage are extremely important.

7   Conclusion

THIS STUDY is about women and men who left their peasant communities to find better lives for themselves in the urban center of Ankara, where their work and lives became closely involved with the urban middle class who employed them. While the data I collected as an interviewer and participant observer provides the foundation of this study, my own relationship with these people as an urban middle-class woman informs it also. In the following pages I glance at a few of my experiences while highlighting the theoretical and empirical conclusions of this study.

I was born and grew up in Ankara in a modest middle-class family with three sisters, all close in age, and one youngest brother. Although we were not wealthy, my parents enjoyed high social status and a sense of prestige as a part of the bureaucratic and professional class of the new nation-state. Urban and staunchly secular, my parents belonged to the first generation of sons and daughters of the new Republic who undertook the project of modernity, conceived of as the creation of a secular, Western-looking, industrialized nation-state. The traditional peasant population was to be converted to a modern citizenry through the exercise of an authoritarian, paternalistic, and secular state. During my childhood years in the sixties, my parents and their friends shared a way of life defined partly by a strong attachment and deep commitment to this modernizing project and a high regard for education while also deriving prestige and a sense of self-importance from their "civilizing" mission.

My father, who never touched a dirty dish or a soiled piece of clothing in his life, was a distant breadwinner. And since his job required him to be away from home for long stretches of time, he was also spared the manly chores of parenting and household work, such as repairs, money management, and the parent-teacher conferences that were expected of men of his generation. My mother, who never had a paying job in her life, was a de facto single mother—a concept alien to Turkish culture. She was quite aware of her anomalous position among her peers, saying often, "I am both the woman and the man of the house" (*Bu evin hem kadınıyım hem erkeğiyim).* She did everything without shifting her burden to us, her daughters, in any significant way. She never hired regular domestic help. She was an undesirable employer who hired domestic workers only when she was seriously sick or when the house really needed cleaning after a painting job.

However, my mother used the doorkeeper's services extensively. In fact, doorkeepers figured significantly in the routines of my mother and her peers' everyday lives. The intimacy between these urban middle-class women and the peasant man was strange. The doorkeeper was the only man, besides their husbands, who saw these women in every mood and state. The doorkeeper saw them early in the morning when they were still in their robes with tangled hair and when they were dressed up to go out in the evening. The doorkeeper knew what they cooked every day, who visited them, with whom they visited, whose husband came home drunk, and who failed to pay the electrical bill. He fixed their leaky faucets and helped them move heavy furniture. He kept an eye on children when they played outside. As a collectively shared servant and handyman, he freed these women's husbands from their already limited domestic responsibilities while protecting the women from "the defiling, sordid elements of life," to recall Leonore Davidoff's phrase (1974:412). Their position also gave these women a sense of power over men, albeit a different class of men.

When I was in primary school during the mid-sixties, my father's uncle's family, who lived in our apartment building, hired the doorkeeper's wife as a full-time maid. This doorkeeper and his wife, Veli and Ilimon, provided my first glimpse into the world of the doorkeeper and domestic. To my childish eyes, Veli, the doorkeeper, stood apart from all those stern-looking adult men (most of them bureaucrats with important positions in the civil service) who went to work, dressed in the bureaucratic uniform of the young Republic—coat, tie, and the ubiquitous hat. Compared with these powerful-looking men, Veli looked docile and powerless. Ilimon, with her headscarf and *şalvar* and her clumsy walk, also stood apart from the modern women of the Republic in their homemade two-piece suits (*tayyör*), modern sheer stockings, high heels, and permed hair. For us children, Veli and Ilimon's appearances, names, home, and possessions were objects of keen curiosity. I remember the utter fascination with which we would peek through their window (their quarter was not at the basement but located in a separate unit that housed coal for the tenants) at their barely furnished apartment. When I was 9 or 10 years old, this young couple had their first baby. I was shocked to learn that she was not taken to the hospital to give birth. I heard adult women saying, with a chill in their voices, that the husband cut the umbilical cord with a rusty razor. The day after Ilimon gave birth, my sisters and I went to see the new baby, but to our surprise the new mother was not home—she was working in my grand uncle's home. I asked why she was not in bed, resting, and nurturing the baby. My mother said, "She is a peasant woman. They are strong. In the village they give birth in the field and continue to work." She went on to describe how peasant women tie their babies on their backs and plow fields.

A couple of years later when I started middle school, we moved to a modest apartment-building in a posh neighborhood. My best friend, Azat, from a wealthy family, and I befriended another girl in our class. The three of us lived close together on Kennedy Caddesi (named after the U.S. president Kennedy). We walked home together every day. Our new friend would disappear into the handsomest building on the street, one I assumed sheltered fabulous lives. The next arrival was at Azat's well-to-do building. My building was the last and most modest on the street. Although Azat and I frequently visited each other to play and do homework together, our new friend never visited us or invited us to her home. One spring day our friend did not show up for school. Azat and I decided to swing by her house and give her the homework she missed. We went to the building that she entered every day and diligently studied the apartment directory, but her last name was not listed. With wicked unspoken consensus, we proceeded to the back of the building, where we figured we would find the doorkeeper's quarters. There she was in the backyard, helping her mother collect clothes from the clothesline. I forgot (or repressed) her name a long time ago but still remember the frozen look of shame on her face. Nor can I forget my own shame at revealing her masquerade. My friend and I immediately left the scene, without passing on the homework, and never talked about what we had seen or how we felt.

Years later, when I established my own household in my early twenties, I naively attempted to interact with my doorkeeper, Salim efendi (*efendi* means "master"), according to Marxist principles. To ease his experience of exploitation, I asked Salim efendi not to collect our garbage and told him I would handle it myself. Nonetheless, he unfailingly rang our bell every morning to see whether we had garbage to be disposed of. Nor did he stop deferentially calling me *abla* (older sister) and my husband *abi* (older brother) despite our repeated pleas to call us by our first names. His wife, Taze, was a typical doorkeeper's wife, doing domestic work for the tenants in the building and helping her husband with his doorkeeping tasks. I rarely saw her leave the vicinity of the apartment-building. For about six months, I purchased Taze's labor every other week. I was always at school when she came to clean, but during the evening before, I cooked two dishes for her lunch. I asked her to take her lunch downstairs so that she could share and enjoy it with her husband and son. One day I was home when she came in. I had been up all night trying to meet a deadline for a paper and had not had time to cook a traditional warm Turkish lunch. I fixed what I thought was a nice lunch of expensive cheese and some cold cuts. When we sat down at the table she commented on the inferior quality of the meal, saying, with obvious annoyance, "We eat this for breakfast." I felt betrayed. Here she was treating me as though I were a typical employer woman after all the work I had done to prove otherwise. I had told her that she need not wash windows on cold days—what is the point of it? Nor did she need to do the carpets and doors every time she came. She sent her son up to my apartment every time he needed help with his homework. I served as her scribe, writing her letters to her adult son back in the village.

The view from downstairs voiced in this book suggests that numerous encounters across the rural-urban divide in the politics of daily life are unfolding. And some subjectivities generated by these encounters are more painful than others. The distinction between peasant and urban continues to be central to Turkish society, and the rural-migrants' presence in the urban landscape is still contested by urban others. It is easy to agree with commentators on Turkish culture who emphasize this division. Carol Delaney (1991), who recently studied a village community, reports that her urban acquaintances in the city "displayed horror for the incivility, danger, and filth they believe to exist in the village" (208). David Hotham observes that the divide between peasants and urbanities is "an opposition." "In no country that I have visited do the educated classes speak of the 'ignorance' and 'backwardness' of their own peasants so much as in Turkey" (quoted in Delaney 1991:208).

Indeed, during my fieldwork for this study, I once happened to accompany my mother (at the time 77 years old and in failing health) to the hospital for an examination. As usual, there was a long line and my mother's impatience grew throughout the hours we waited. She finally said, pointing out the peasant women who came in before her, "Look at all these peasant women. They are the ones holding up the line. They come dressed in layers and layers of clothing. They take a lot of time to get undressed to be examined." She could have attributed the wait more plausibly to the fact that there was only one doctor on duty for the entire oncology unit that morning.

As "outsiders within," doorkeepers, literally and symbolically marking the threshold between urban and peasant, modern and traditional, experience this contestation in particularly intimate ways. Among rural migrants with common backgrounds and similar life chances, doorkeeper families constitute a unique group. They have been called "Germanists in Turkey" (*Türkiyedeki Almancılar*), a comparison to Turkish "guest workers" in Germany that conveys doorkeeper families' strong sense of foreignness and alienation in a middle-class urban environment. I explain their predicament as an occupational stigma and argue that in the formulation of that stigma their peasant origins and identity as doorkeepers entail a pool of images and meanings that interact with and operate through structural features of their occupation. Stigma, by structuring the interactions among members of each class, remakes the distance that the physical proximity and lack of ritualized contacts between classes undermines. For doorkeepers and their families, the occupation creates a painful dilemma. While they see living in a better neighborhood among elite classes as a definite advantage for their children's integration into modern society and upward mobility, they and their children nonetheless suffer from the stigmatization. A domestic worker's 12-year-old son persistently asks, "Why did my father have to become a doorkeeper? Were there no other jobs for him?" This question and the shamed masquerade of my school friend voice this painful dilemma.

Since my childhood in the sixties, persistent transformations in rural areas have brought more and more peasants to the city. First- and second-generation rural migrants' children, like those of Veli and Ilimon and Salim and Taze, have had urban childhoods. They have further blurred the rural/urban distinctions. Although few of them became members of professional classes, some have become integrated into the petty bourgeoisie. Most of them, despite their diversity of income and level of integration in modern occupations, have become members of one of the "order-taker, subordinate class" who, through their work as cleaners, janitors, messengers, street peddlers, office "tea makers," small shopkeepers, hospital orderlies, garbage collectors, minivan (*dolmuş*) drivers, and domestic workers, continue to contribute to the social reproduction of salaried bourgeois urban classes in Ankara as a means of establishing themselves in the urban society.

In the process, they have accepted, resisted, reworked, and changed values and practices associated with the modern and urban. They reconstituted their regional communities in the city but claimed an equal share of urban life promised by the city. By their sheer voting power and their resourcefulness in dealing with poverty and exclusion, they disrupted attempts from above to create a homogenized population. They created new modalities of life, sensibilities, styles, habits, taste in work and leisure. In short, they invented new forms of cultural difference in Turkish cities that could no longer be described within the rough oppositional categories of traditional peasant and modern urban.

Only in recent times have social scientists started studying these emerging identities and new modalities of life, not as transitional modes of living, but in their own right. Sencer Ayata's study (1988) of the house interiors of new urbanities (petit bourgeois) reveals the demarcation of modernity and tradition in the spatial arrangement of houses, where commodities, qualities, and styles associated with modernity are displayed in the guest room, and those associated with tradition are "hidden" in the intimate inner space of the house, corresponding to different types of subjectivities and interaction. This contrast forcefully illustrates the way in which the tension between modernity and tradition is understood and experienced. Meral Özbek's study (1997) of arabesk music (music of the squatter settlements) from its origins in the discontents, desires, and expectations of squatter settlement populations in the 1960s to the most prolific form of popular music in the 1980s for millions of people from different classes and backgrounds is another good example of Turkey's ambivalent pursuit of modernization and of the ability of marginalized groups to transform some of the terms of the modernity project. Characterized as the cheap culture of rural migrants—vulgar, tasteless, backward, and fatalistic—this hybrid form of music was prohibited by the modernizing state on state-run radio and television and was never heard on the air until the 1990s when private radio and television companies began broadcasting. Through this popular music, according to Özbek (1997), modernization is "both affirmed and denied and submitted to and resisted" (217). Similarly, the rise of Islamist politics can be seen as an assertion of and investment in traditional values and identities, in opposition to an imposed modernity that has changed the political institutions of the nation-state, the agent of modernization.[1]

The experiences of domestic workers and doorkeepers, who live and work in middle-class domestic environments and are central to the very creation and maintenance of middle-class cultural existence and identity, embody the complex interaction between the traditional and the modern. This interaction of classes informs the everyday lives and subjectivities of the people involved as well as the transformations occurring in Turkey.

This study helps us rethink some of the empirical and theoretical terms of the forces of modernity and tradition in two important ways. First, I agree with those who argue that the tradition/modernity opposition fails to explain adequately the complexity of cultural practices of these groups and cultural change in general. However, building on my findings, I suggest that the centrality of this opposition in the constitution of subjectivities of those people who are at the margins of modernity should not be ignored. The forces of modernity and tradition exercise a special potency in the lives of the people I studied, organizing their experience and consciousness, especially in their encounters with the urban middle classes. These forces also inform their shifting conceptions of gender as well as class. The valuation of modernity and the disparagement of the traditional gives rise to a self-reflexivity in which the conduct and feelings of the self are continuously assessed for their modernity and urbanity. Seemingly trivial aspects of everyday life are invested by this anxiety. Almost every migrant household I visited had a set of cups and saucers for the Nescafe that signifies urban sophistication but is rarely drunk. The women in these households bake chocolate cakes rather than the plain ones that have rural associations. They prize cubed sugar over the less expensive loose sugar because it signifies urban, modern refinement. They adopt the practices of modern middle-class parents, accompanying their children to the university entrance examination and waiting outside for the duration of the test. These are just a few examples of the categorical investment in modernity.

Like commodities and cultural practices, identities and characters are understood and judged in terms of the tradition/modernity opposition. Women attribute men's prohibition of their work as well as other restrictions placed on their physical mobility and social activities to their husband's peasant backwardness, their inability to overcome the constraints of tradition, and their failure to modernize. In these women's discourse, there is no generalized or universal "men" or "husbands." They refer instead to "our men" and "our husbands" conceptualized in opposition to an imagined modern man. The terms in which they evaluate male behavior and conduct when discussing the division of labor at home, marital love, or wife beating reflect this symbolic opposition of peasant and modern masculinity. The centrality of this dualism in people's understanding poses a serious challenge to theoretical attempts to abandon it. Failure to acknowledge the tradition/modernity opposition in interpretation or analysis risks a misconstruing of the terms most central to the self-understanding and worldview of its subjects.

Second, exploring the specificities of tradition and modernity, how they are deployed pragmatically and as ideological values, allows us to see how waged domestic labor has been structured and how the identities of those involved in the domestic labor market have been defined. As discussed in previous chapters, male investment in patriarchal tradition has modernized domestic labor in Ankara.

The interaction of peasant men and elite women demonstrates the power of tradition or, more correctly, the power of the bearers of tradition who are otherwise structurally and economically disempowered. Peasant men's traditional control over their wives' labor has reconfigured their wives' relationship with middle-class urban women. At the macro level, I show that traditional patriarchal controls over migrant women's labor makes their labor expensive and scarce, effectively limiting middle-class women's access to cheap waged domestic labor. This traditional restriction on migrant women's labor paradoxically proves key to the generation of modernized domestic service where the predominant form of employment is day work with multiple employers and work relations are structured contractually. At the micro level I illustrate how both groups of women strategically use their understandings of domination and patriarchal constructions of women's identity in the management of their relationship.

Focusing on the role of doorkeeping as an institution that enables men to maintain their traditional control over women's labor and earnings illustrates the complex ways in which urban institutions inhibit the possibilities of modernization and reimpose traditional forms of class and gender servility upon migrants. Yet, the structure of apartment house doorkeeping undermines the traditional division of household labor by gender.

Doorkeeping can be seen as a labor system based on the exploitation of family labor that both builds on and reinforces gender- and age-based hierarchical relations within the family. The imprecise boundaries between the locus of work and of the home allows for the peripheral involvement of household members other than the official jobholder. In this, it reconstitutes the migrant family as a laboring unit under a male-head household who manages its combined labor. In contrast to squatter settlement women, doorkeeper wives retain the "unpaid family laborer" status that they had in their rural past, despite working as wage earners. It is ironic that urban middle-class existence supports and depends on the continuation of traditional forms of gender authority in doorkeeper families.

Yet the same institution, by tying the husband to the home, changes the traditional division of labor by gender. The husband's home-centered occupation would seem to create the possibility of overcoming the constraints of gender norms regulating the household division of labor. My analysis shows that doorkeeper husbands contribute significantly to childcare and that this contribution is a central factor in releasing domestic workers with young children to work full-time. Yet this "objective" condition does not effectively dissolve the strong link between household work and gender identity. I also argue that I found less domesticity among this group of men as well as less marital conflict over the division of labor than expected. The doorkeeper's femininized and subordinate occupational identity gives rise to defensive strategies, dis-associating them from female household work and heightening assertions of patriarchal authority.

In the squatter settlement households, domestic workers shift part or all of their childcare and household responsibilities to daughters and other live-in kin, who do most of the physical work of cleaning, washing, and childcare in their absence. There were few women who said that they do nothing at all when they go home after work or reported zero hours of household work. These women belong to late-stage households and their complete disengagement from housework, like that of all male household members, is made possible by the presence of other adult women (unmarried daughters or daughters-in-law). Patriarchal kinship ideology, coupled with female socialization into domesticity, gives senior women access to and control over younger women's labor in the female hierarchy of the household. Traditional gender structures are again employed in ways that allow women to assume work identities at odds with traditional gender divisions of labor. This paradoxical relation creates conflicts for the women who rely on their daughters' performance of traditional gender work yet desire and work for modern educational and professional opportunities for their daughters.

In contrast to the doorkeeper families characterized by a great deal of privatization and isolation in their organization of labor for housework and childcare, the squatter settlement community living with easy permeability of household boundaries and the informality of social interaction among women discourages privatization of the family and the emergence of an urban "housewife" role. Traditional ties of kinship and neighborliness with their attendant duties and responsibilities are continually reproduced by women who do not perform their mothering and household work in isolation and within the confines of private family.

Examination of both study groups suggests that partial breaches of the rigid gender division of household labor are possible when there is an absolute logistic need for them. The highest male participation in traditionally female work is in childcare in young doorkeeper households that lack live-in female kin or daughters old enough to substitute for the domestic worker. The labor arrangements in working-class families studied by other social scientists (Benson 1996; Gutmann 1996; Hondagneu-Sotelo 1994a) demonstrate striking similarities with these Turkish families. Like these works, my data dramatizes the primacy of material conditions of life over abstract commitments to egalitarian ideas in changing gendered divisions of labor. The majority of women in this study have a pragmatic quest for equality: they desire a household labor organization in which family work, like wage-earning work, should be shared equally by husband and wife. The harsh conditions of their lives inform this quest and cause them to question the "naturalness" of traditional gender arrangements.

My data on domestic workers' employment patterns offers insights into the gender and class dynamics of domestic service as well as the ways in which domestic workers identify themselves in terms at once traditional and modern. Ninety-one percent of the workers in this study (145 out of 160) worked for multiple employers; only a small number of workers are tied to a single employer. Domestic workers had a total of 691 employers (62 percent housewives and 38 percent employed women). Domestic workers can be defined by their place on a continuum between exclusive "specialists" (proletarianized house cleaners) and exclusive "generalists" (traditional maids), based on days worked, number of employers, and frequency of work for a given week. The majority of domestic workers were situated toward the "specialist" end. Among specialist positions, the most objectively advantageous schedule entailed multiple weekly visits to the same employer, with shorter work hours and volume, a variety of tasks, and better chances for patronage benefits. Complete "specialization," laboring in a different home every day and returning to a given workplace only infrequently, entailed greater autonomy over the labor process but required repetitive performance of the most dirty and physically exhausting labor. Furthermore, this level of "proletarianization" confers a menial identity on the laborer and fosters an image of a physically strong and resilient woman evocative of stereotypes about peasant women. For different reasons, domestic workers reject both the peasant-like proletarianized imagery suggested by specialization and the servant role associated with working full-time for a single employer.

Domestic workers' encounters with middle-class women provide them with an opportunity unavailable elsewhere in Turkish society: to assert their identity as women and their class-specific aspirations and to protest dominant constructions of class and gender and their exclusion from dominant definitions of femininity. In these interactions they express their dissatisfaction with the roles and identities offered them as domestic workers and negotiate symbolic and practical relations that exploit and redress class inequality. A model of power as a dominant repressive force and of resistance as an automatic or mechanical response to oppression, a common analytical assumption in studies of domestic service, fails to account fully for domestic workers' agency in the work and social relations of domestic service. A relational model of power and a more nuanced understanding of resistance allows us to see how domestic workers' negotiations influence the structure of their work and shape the identities of both themselves and their employers.

As I emphasize in previous chapters, the unique constellation of supply-and-demand structures in Ankara's domestic labor market encourages a process of proletarianization that creates a work force of proletarianized house cleaners and thus removes the intimate aspect of domestic service. The effect is that the two classes of women meet in domestic service solely as workers and employers rather than as women and mothers with gender identities. Domestic workers strive to undermine this proletarianization. Their success in rejecting the identity of a domestic proletarian, one that resembles and builds on peasant identity, largely depends on their ability to dictate the terms of their participation in domestic service, including their number of work days and the frequency of visits to the same employer. Within a repertoire of work identities available to them (on a continuum between maids and proletarianized workers), the role of housekeeper defined in opposition to the identity of cleaner is the most desirable because of its shorter hours, varied workload, and better patronage benefits resulting from cultivating relations with middle-class employers as women and mothers. As I show, patronage is a powerful resource for poor women, important not only for the tangible benefits it yields (advance payments, pay while employers are on vacation, and help finding jobs for significant others in the family and community,) but also for the self-esteem derived from the workers' ability to assume the role of patrons themselves. For domestic workers in the squatter settlement group, assuming this work identity depends on two factors. First, they need male cooperation to navigate the market and exert their employer preferences. That is, they need to overcome gender subordination in their own homes with regard to constraints on their spatial and social mobility in order to negotiate class subordination. Second, they must establish and maintain good ties within the recruitment network of the domestic workers' community. In pursuing their various strategies in relations of kinship and neighborliness as aunts, cousins, daughters-in-law, and neighbors they have to simultaneously attend to the needs of their work identities because ties of kinship and neighborliness inform and reinforce the ties of work networks. Through these networks they establish a work ethic and job and wage standards and exchange information on desirable jobs. Also, they exercise power over one another and over employer women. The complexities of these interactions undermine any romanticized notion of sisterly solidarity. Studies of domestic workers elsewhere in Latin America and the United States draw a strong connection between female migration and employment patterns and resulting work identities in domestic service. This empirical reality demands a more comprehensive theoretical approach and research agendas than one narrowly focusing on the dynamics of the relationship between the employee and employer in the locus of work. We need to understand how other social relationships in families and communities in which domestic workers engage affect experiences in the employment of domestic service. In turn, these understandings better illuminate the workings of power, resistance, and identity in domestic service. The Turkish case clearly demonstrates the complex interrelation of kinship, community, and labor relations and the necessity of broadening the scope of inquiry in studies of informally organized labor.

The options of the doorkeepers' wives in picking the best employers are much more limited because they form a captive labor supply for the middle-class women with whom they share the same gate and roof. Doorkeeper's wives have privileged access to a prime demand-pool but lack flexibility in exerting employer preferences and find it difficult to function as housekeepers. When choosing between potential employers, they must give priority to apartment house owners (more permanent residents who have voting power in the management of the building, including the hiring and firing of doorkeepers) and are, to some extent, obliged to work for employers within their own building.

Domestic workers' preferences for certain work options have significant implications for employer women. Domestic workers tend to choose those employers who can afford their labor more frequently and can dispense patronage benefits. Thus, they prefer employers from the upper-middle class to those from the lower echelons of the middle classes. By dissociating engagement with dirt and unclean tasks from other aspects of the housewife's role, domestic service redefines women's relation to domesticity. And by releasing middle-class women for work it allows them better participation in the public sphere. They can perform more modernized roles as consumers, professionals, or mothers and thereby enhance their families' status. This effect is more pronounced for those women who can afford multi-day hiring. There is also the issue of opposing desires of domestic workers and employer women: while domestic workers wish to attain the housekeeping identity, one that allows them to cultivate intimacies with the employer women and force employer women into emotional labor, the employer women, especially housewives, wishing to avoid the emotional labor and what they experience as emotional exploitation, are eager to use newly emerging commercialized cleaning services. In other words, they do not want to deal with their workers as women. For domestic workers, performance of the role of housekeeper—traditional for middle-class women—allows them to avoid the proletarianized work of cleaners that is at once more modern but evocative of the hard labor of peasantry. The role of urban housekeeper also yields the greatest opportunity for economic and social advancement and modernization in their own lives. In contrast, employers preference for proletarian cleaners bespeaks a desire to dissociate themselves from the engagements with peasant women that dramatize their shared gender subordination and are at odds with their desired status as modern consumers, professionals, or mothers. Further exploration of this important issue will require close attention to the differences among various groups of employer women (defined by age, class, generation, and employment and social status).

The Turkish case provides empirical support for the view that the informal sector in third world cities is more than an unstable and chaotic set of economic activities constituting a transitory phase in informal workers' lives and more than a mere survival strategy. It is organized and dynamic. My data suggests that domestic workers' wages, schedules, work histories, and recruitment patterns are characteristics of a "formal" sector marked by regularity, continuity, and stability. The operation of this "informal" labor market is structured and regulated by the traditional relations embedded in family-kinship and neighborhood networks among urban migrant communities.

The contrast between domestic workers and those women who work in other branches of the informal sector enhances our understanding of differences in women's consciousness and subjectivities as wage earners and the way in which a wage-earning identity interacts with women's other identities. Studies of women's participation in the informal sector in particular cultural and national contexts generally documents how women's activities in these spheres—home-based, isolating, and rooted in skills defined as naturally feminine—foster the confluence of women's labor with their social roles as mothers and wives. This confluence of their wage work with traditional gender work prevents them from seeing themselves as working women and denies them a sense of economic agency. Vanessa Maher (1988) best describes this experience in her study of Moroccan women. When she asked women engaged in both income-producing activities and household work to describe their daily activities, she received only puzzled expressions, rather than any definite responses. She writes, "Perhaps the only feasible reply to my question would have been 'I have been being a woman all day'"(122). Researchers conclude that since women do not conceive of a difference between their income-producing labor and household labor, then the income-producing activities do not affect their lives in terms of greater control over resources and decision making. Employment in domestic service, the quintessential women's occupation performed in isolated private workplaces, however, does not permit the conflation of various facets of women's identities. Yet, as this study brings out, a woman's identity as a mother, far from being peripheral or incidental to her identity as a wage earner, is in fact central to her commitment to earning wages. The salience of motherhood as the core of her identity remains unchallenged by her work experience. In other words, domestic workers also define the self in terms of connections and relationships, that is, through the roles of wife and mother. But this does not mean that women ignore the value of their labor in monetary terms or that the ideology of family unity and identity of interests destroys their sense of individuality.

Women's monetary contribution to their households is not directly correlated with independent control over money or with decision-making authority in the household. The wives of doorkeepers are much higher contributors to household income than the domestic workers from squatter settlements, yet they claim less influence in decision making than the squatter women. Money, as this study shows, is almost exclusively under male control in doorkeeper households, illustrating the potency of the doorkeeping institution in perpetuating traditional patriarchal control. Furthermore, wives' earnings generate increased decision-making influence up to a point, as long as those earnings are subordinate or equal to the husbands' earnings. When women pass this point and begin to earn more than their husbands, the latter perceive this as a loss of their patriarchal power in the family and compensate by exerting control over decision making. Yet decision-making profiles of the two groups of women are almost identical in the areas of decisions concerning the self and overall decision making, reflecting that neither the size of the earning power nor the control of it translates into women's autonomy. On the whole, it must be concluded that it is possible for women to achieve "equal participation" in a range of specific household decisions, even when traditional male domination is maintained at deeper, structural levels. Earning money significantly shapes women's self-perceptions. Women in this study gained a strong sense of self-worth by becoming wage earners. Indeed, this effect, along with the fact that their earning power sustained the family and improved the life chances of their children, determined these women's commitment in paid work.

Unprotected labor is a defining aspect of the informal sector. None of the domestic workers in this study had insurance protection (as domestic workers), but the majority of them have developed a strong notion of protection and security as a provision of employment. Domestic workers made very clear that this is one area of need for policy action. However, their conception of labor protection is focused on the ability to earn a retirement pension and to make claims in cases of work-related injury and illness. It is not surprising that a quest for regulations concerning wages and work hours is absent in their definition of protection, for they are satisfactorily managed through the existing informal mechanisms that evolved in Turkey. Expansion of existing social insurance legislation to domestic service should be done in such a way that it would not bring commitment to a single employer but would preserve domestic workers' demonstrated ability to control the supply market. Examined from another angle, their belief in the necessity of an "individualized" form of insurance protection coverage bespeaks their perception of the increasing fragility of the protections entailed by the traditional patriarchal family. Increasingly, they see their work, rather than their husbands and sons, as the source of security and protection. This shift is a testament to these women's strong sense of economic agency. As one of the women in this study put it, "Being able to say 'I bought this' feels wonderful."

Appendix
Sampling Procedures

THIS STUDY required a sample of domestic workers. The sampling frame for the doorkeeper group, however, was a list of buildings prepared by the Construction and Housing division of the Ankara Municipality. Half of these dwellings were sampled from middle-class residential districts and the other half from upper- and upper-middle-class areas in Ankara. I used residential district as a class indicator, because in Turkey the residential areas are relatively homogenous and distinguished according to social class. The primary consideration in the selection of middle- and upper-middle-class neighborhoods was that they be representative of different groups of domestic workers. It was assumed that class differences of employers who live in these neighborhoods would be reflected in the domestic worker's wages and work load and the employer women's attitudes toward the worker. The sampling procedure is summarized in Figure 1.

In 1970 the City Planning Office of Ankara (Ankara Nazım Plan Bürosu), using data from an extensive survey of households, prepared a classification of the neighborhood districts of Ankara by average income level. Based on this information, six income groups defined by average household income were identified covering thirty-two districts (bölgecik). Since the highest income group (upper and upper-middle class) consisted of only one district (Çankaya) covering three neighborhoods (Güven, Aziziye, and Çankaya), all three neighborhoods were sampled from this income level. The second highest income group (middle class) included six districts and required sampling. Thus, the district of Bahçelievler-Emek, which also covers three neighborhoods (Yukarı Bahçeli, Emek, Bahçelievler), was selected by lottery drawing.

After the district selection was made, four adas (an ada [island] is a tract of land bound by three or four blocks and subdivided internally by buildings and nonresidential uses of space) from each neighborhood were randomly selected. Before each selection, however, several exclusions

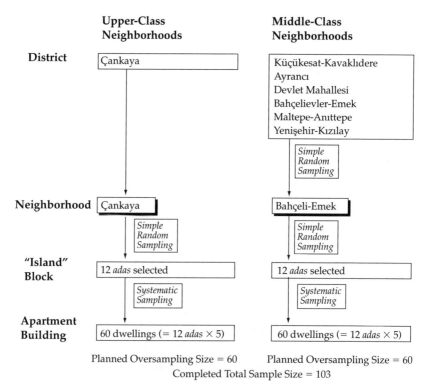

FIGURE 1.   Sampling Procedure for the Doorkeepers Group, Ankara

were made; *adas* vary in the number of buildings they contain, and the ones occupied entirely by parks, schools, embassies, and other public spaces and buildings were left out. Subsequently, a total of twenty-four *adas* were drawn by a simple random sampling method. That is, the number for each *ada* was put in a bag and thoroughly mixed and then twelve *adas* of upper- and upper-middle-class neighborhoods and twelve of middle-class neighborhoods were randomly drawn.

After the *adas* were selected, a systematic sampling strategy was used to select dwellings (apartment buildings) from each *ada*. The first building (designated number 1 "parcel" for each *ada* on the map) was selected, and, thereafter, every third building was selected. In this way, a total of 120 apartment buildings were selected to constitute the sample, 60 from each of the two income categories.

Maps used for this sampling procedure did not include street numbers for apartment buildings. Therefore, the interviewers were instructed first to go to the *adas* with hand-drawn simplified maps to confirm that the maps were correct and to designate the apartment building numbers. We found no inconsistencies in the actual number of buildings per parcel and those indicated by our maps.

In the initial visits, it was found that seventeen of the buildings in the sample were either commercial and business establishments, such as restaurants and banks, or construction sites and empty land. Nineteen of the buildings either had no doorkeeper because the building was too small or had the service of a doorkeeper who was not living on the premises. In addition, the doorkeeper in one of the buildings happened to be single. The three categories of construction site, doorkeeping not on the premises, and apartment building without a doorkeeper were observed mostly in the middle-class Bahçeli-Emek neighborhood. Bahçelievler, which literally means "houses with gardens," is a neighborhood in the process of rebuilding, where high-rise buildings are replacing small villa-style apartment houses. Because of this characteristic of the neighborhood, a high proportion of the dwellings in the initial sample had to be substituted.

After the initial elimination of thirty-seven buildings, it was found that of the remaining eighty-three, all of which had doorkeepers with wives, eighteen of the wives were not working as domestic workers at the time of the survey. The breakdown of this group is as follows: twelve "never worked" as a domestic worker; four have not been working as domestic workers for the past one or two years; and two were employed in other occupations. This small proportion, in fact, confirmed one of the initial hypothesis of the study: the great majority of wives of doorkeepers in Turkey tend to work as domestic workers. Also, three out of those eighty-three wives refused to be interviewed.

Those buildings in the initial sample that were eliminated because of their unsuitable characteristics were replaced by the next building that had a doorkeeper's wife working as a domestic worker. Among the substitutions, five domestic workers refused to be interviewed. The completed sample size of 103 households includes seven domestic workers who were officially employed as doorkeepers in addition to working as domestic workers.

Notes

CHAPTER ONE

1. See Hanson and Pratt 1995 for an excellent feminist study of differences in women's work experiences living in different neighborhoods of Worcester, Massachusetts.

2. The average family income of Ankara's highest income group is 6.5 times greater than that of the lowest income groups found in squatter settlements (Türel 1987:164).

3. The closest North American term for this job is "janitor" or "super," or "concierge" in France, though none of these words fully describes the Turkish doorkeeper's work and occupational identity. For a study of janitors in the United States during the 1950s, see Gold 1952.

4. Bread is the main component of diet in Turkey.

5. I use the term "tenant" in this book for the sake of convenience to refer to middle- and upper-middle-class residents of an apartment house, regardless of their real status as owners or tenants, to whom a doorkeeper provides services. The gender of the "tenant" is female in a double sense: first, women are the chief clients of doorkeepers, from whom doorkeepers take "orders"; and second, women are the employers of doorkeepers' wives as domestic workers.

6. The law was known as the "Flat Law" (Çulpan 1979; Keleş and Danielson 1985).

7. I borrow this notion from Patricia Hill Collins (1991), who uses it to describe the marginal status of black intellectuals in academic settings. She argues that by making creative use of their marginality, these "outsiders within" produce distinctive knowledge.

8. About half of the domestic workers in my squatter settlement sample sought employment as domestic workers while their husbands were employed as doorkeepers. In addition, a representative survey (Çınar 1991) conducted among subcontracted female home workers in the squatter settlement neighborhoods of İstanbul found that the majority of respondents (40 percent) cited employment in domestic service as being not only the most desired job but also the most feasible (45 percent). Yet, the main reason for not working outside the home involved lack of permission from husbands (55 percent).

9. Sencer Ayata (1989) explores the meanings given to living in an apartment house among a group of Ankara residents who recently moved to the apartment houses from squatter settlements. His analysis reveals that these two types of residentiality are defined in opposition to each other by these "new" tenants; while the squatter settlement embodies negative values attached to ruralism and

traditionalism, the apartment house represents modernity and modern values. From the perspective of the doorkeeper families I studied, apartment-house residency is inextricably linked with occupation, and, therefore, the meaning of being a resident in an apartment house is quite different—especially since the definition of "tenant" includes having access to a building doorkeeper.

10. Here I assume that the middle class maintains much greater control or concern than does the upper-middle class over the informal contact between their children and those of doorkeeper families for the reasons mentioned above and because upper-middle-class children rarely cross paths with doorkeeper children. Upper-middle-class children, for example, are more likely to go to private schools and to possess subcultural markers that doorkeeper children cannot afford. Although I do not have distributional data to make this generalization, the inference seems warranted by comments from doorkeepers' wives, such as, "The ones who treat us as their inferiors are the ignorant ones" and "We get this kind of treatment only from those who do not know their place." Another interpretation is equally plausible: perhaps the wife of the doorkeeper receives the same kind of treatment from upper-middle-class tenants as well but she feels more embittered and resentful toward middle-class tenants because the income-status difference between them is less pronounced and therefore she feels that middle-class tenants have less right to treat her and her family as their social inferiors. Yet, no significant differences appear between those who express experience of stigmatization and those do not. This observation further suggests the pervasiveness of the stigma attached to doorkeeper families. Also, see Ayata and Ayata (1996:125), who argue that the desire not to "mix" is stronger among middle classes who achieved this status only recently.

11. We can also talk about a sense of future-oriented fear of "mixing" from the middle-class perspective. It is worth noting that compared with other migrant families who live in squatter settlements, children of doorkeeper families are more likely to achieve intergenerational mobility. Doorkeepers' children have higher educational attainment and lower dropout rates than do children of squatter settlement families.

12. See Davidoff 1974 and 1976 for a thorough analysis of notions of dirt and cleanliness as manifest in the class and gender distinctions of nineteenth-century England.

13. This occupational profile is similar to the one described in Ayata and Ayata 1996:4.

14. See Huntington 1968; Inkeles and Smith 1974; McClelland 1976; Rostow 1960.

15. See Amin 1974, 1977; Cardoso and Faletto 1979; Frank 1972, 1979.

16. For an excellent feminist "rereading" of modernization and dependency theories see Scott 1995. Catherine V. Scott demonstrates that despite the absence of gender category in their analyses, both theoretical approaches are based on very gendered foundations. They share similar masculine notions of what it means to be modern (the figures of rational economic entrepreneur man in modernization theory and of the heroic revolutionary man in Marxist dependency

theory) and are grounded on the "powerfully charged opposition of femininized tradition with masculinized public life" (Scott 1995:20).

17. There is now a mushrooming literature on "globalization" and "transnationalism." See Appadurai 1996; Featherstone; Harvey 1989. For a feminist analysis of globalization, see Sassen 1996.

18. The following works have played an important role in underpinning much scholarly endeavor and empirical research on women in a variety of cultural contexts in third world countries by challenging the very meaning of development and proposing new ways of asking questions about the connections between gender meanings and structures of inequality, immigration, nationalism, and citizenship: Bhabha et al. 1985; Fernandez-Kelly 1983; Jayawardena 1986; Kandiyoti 1988; Mies 1986; Mohanty 1991a; Nash and Fernandez-Kelly 1983; Nash and Safa 1985; Ong 1987; Sassen 1988.

19. The term "critical tale" was coined by John Van Maanen (1988) to define a type of ethnographic analysis that is "strategically situated to shed light on larger social, political, symbolic or economic issues" (127).

20. Carla Freeman's study (2000) of Barbadian female data entry workers reveals that not only do international corporations relocate to high-wage countries, where women do not make cheap workers, but they are not particularly selective about whether to incorporate young single women or mothers into the "open offices" of global factories. Similarly, Helen Safa (1990), in her earlier study of women workers in the Dominican Republic and Puerto Rico, also reports departures from the global pattern, where the majority of women workers are not single young women, but mothers. Sylvia Chant (1991), in her comparative study of three Mexican cities with different local labor demand structures, shows the importance of considering the diversity of household structures in mediating women's labor force participation and, more important, the flexibility of the size and composition of household and gender relations in response to women's participation in formal and informal work. Rosario Espinal and Sherri Grasmuck's survey (1993) of male and female micro entrepreneurs in the Dominican Republic shows that this expanding sector is generally divided by gender according to types of production activities; however, both cater exclusively to the local market and, thus, the common linkages between larger firms and these informal enterprises are missing. Maria Patricia Fernandez-Kelly and Anna M. Garcia's study (1989) of Hispanic home workers in the garment industries of Miami and Los Angeles examines internal variation in this area of the informal sector. The authors demonstrate how the different class origins and immigrant statuses of Cuban and Mexican women are responsible for dissimilar patterns of incorporation into the networks of the informal sector that result in variations in earning differentials and social outcomes. Jean L. Pyle's study (1990) of the Irish shows that export-led development practices did not give rise to increasing female labor force participation, despite a heavy influx of multinational corporations in Ireland that elsewhere hired women. Pyle's careful analysis demonstrates that the operation of patriarchal gender relations at the household level, supported by the state's attitude toward family relations, produced this outcome.

21. For an analytically rich elaboration of the connection between gender relations and industrialization, see Young 1993. By highlighting the different configurations of "the material and the ideological in households" (18) she identifies divergent paths of women's incorporation into formal industrial employment or informal sector work.

22. Domestic work was the leading occupation for women in the United States from 1870 (52.3 percent) to 1940 (20.4 percent), especially for many African American and immigrant women. In 1979, the percentage was less than 3 percent of all female workers (Grossman 1980). Palmer 1989 states that "by 1920, 46 percent of black women workers were domestics and launderers, compared to 22 percent of employed foreign-born white women and eight percent of employed native-born white women, including Hispanics" (xiii).

23. David Katzman (1978b) provided the pioneering historical account of the shifts in domestic service in the United States, from live-in to live-out and day work, focusing on the period after 1870. His analysis reveals crucial differences in work relations of domestic servants arising from race and ethnicity differences. Faye Dudden (1983) studied the shift in domestic service from native-born "help" to the immigrant "domestic servant" of the nineteenth century, focusing only on nonsouthern states. She explains how domestic work became "demeaning" as changes in relations between home and work stemming from industrialization caused a rise in alternative employment opportunities. While some studies interpret the transition from the "servant" to the "employee" role as a consequence of domestic workers' own resistance rooted in support from church and family (Dill 1988; Clark-Lewis 1987), others (e.g., Palmer 1987) emphasize that the changes in the organization and relations of domestic service resulted from the activity of the charity associations of middle-class women on behalf of domestic workers.

24. According to the United Nations 1999 World Survey, "The main countries that have been sending out female migrant workers are Indonesia, the Philippines, Sri Lanka, and Thailand, and the main receiving countries are Brunei, Hong Kong SAR, Japan, Kuwait, Saudi Arabia, Singapore, and Taiwan Province of China" (United Nations 1999:34–35). In Latin America and the Caribbean, both the size of the domestic service and the percentage of women in the occupation are large. Elsa Chaney and Mary Garcia Castro estimate that employment in domestic service in these countries accounts for "one-fifth to one-third of the female labor force" (1989:3). Ximena Bunster and Elsa Chaney (1985) point out that the proportions of domestic workers in Latin America are much greater than those of comparable periods in western Europe.

25. Keleş and Danielson 1985 compares urban and rural birth rates: "Because of migration, urban population grew five times faster than rural population over the past thirty years, despite birth rates that were 40 percent higher in the country than in the cities" (29).

26. Granting women formal rights has also been regarded as Atatürk's tactic to disassociate himself and his single-party rule from the European fascist dictators of that era (Tekeli 1981).

27. The effects of the commodification of agriculture on women's labor and status depend on the nature of the crop produced, the specific labor process involved, and the type of land ownership (Kandiyoti, 1990). First, commodification of production and mechanization produced less need for female labor in the fields because of the mechanization of activities previously performed by women. Second, the extent and form of women's activities at home changed as a result of larger cash incomes available to households and infrastructural investments by the state. A decrease in the home production of foodstuffs and an increased availability of piped water and electricity reduced the work load of women. Third, it was found that the increasing connection of family farms with private and public credit and marketing institutions has had the effect of excluding women from production and distribution decisions (Sirman et al. 1989). Completely mechanized crops (such as wheat and barley) lead to women's withdrawal from the production process, whereas cash crops (cotton, tobacco, sugar beet), which involve labor-intensive processes, encourage continuation of female labor. In areas where production is completely mechanized and carried out by men, women's labor shifts from crop production to petty commodity production; otherwise, women are pushed from agricultural production. Findings of studies focusing on female carpet weavers in rural areas point to quite opposite conclusions about the effects of women's wage labor in rural areas. One study focusing on women in villages in central Anatolia shows that women's increasing participation in manufacturing in the form of carpet weaving, vital to the economic survival of village households, increases men's (i.e., fathers' and husbands') control over production and the marketing process and results in no control over women's earnings or enhanced power or less rigid sexual division of labor at home (Berik 1987). Yet another study of carpet makers conducted in western Anatolia arrives at the opposite conclusion that no gender distribution of labor takes place in carpet weaving workshops where both women and men participate equally in different phases of the production process. Furthermore, women's participation in carpet production changes the distribution of household work in such a way that men and women begin to share household tasks (Josephine Powell, quoted in Quataert 1991).

28. *Mantı* (dumplings with meat filling), a traditional dish requiring a good half-day's work and a lot of socializing among female relatives to prepare, are now sold in the take-out section ready to be cooked.

29. All these developments mark the end of traditional attitudes of middle-class parents to the schooling of children embodied in the Turkish saying "The flesh belongs to you, the bones to me" (*eti senin kemigi benim*), which expressed the complete trust given the teachers as the representative of the paternalistic Turkish state in molding and producing disciplined, productive citizens of the Turkish Republic.

30. Three research assistants, all sociology students, worked with me as interviewers to administer the survey to the doorkeeper group. In order to refine the survey questionnaire, a pilot study was conducted on ten domestic workers. The results of the pilot study indicated that no major changes were necessary on the

questionnaire, with the exception of the order of some questions and a few changes in language. The pilot study also served as training for the interviewers.

31. Although the refusal rate was quite low, it is useful to look at the reasons given for refusal. The refusal group falls into three categories: (1) Three women said their husbands were not home at the time of the visit and would not allow them to do it ("My husband isn't home; he wouldn't let me"); (2) One woman's husband did not permit the interview; and (3) Four women refused the interview on their own, without reference to their husbands.

32. The survey responses were examined as soon as possible to see whether there were any inconsistencies, confusions, or unanswered questions. In only two instances was it necessary to revisit a respondent to resolve such problems. Interviewers were asked to write an account of the interview immediately after they completed it. These observational notes covered such topics as the type of apartment, surrounding material possessions, reactions to the interview by the husband, the respondent's sense of self, demeanor, and appearance (dress, body language, kinds of words and expressions used), and who else was present during the interview, as well as the interviewer's opinion of how the interview went. These notes ranged in length from half a page to four or five pages for each interview and constituted another source of data in the form of field notes.

33. In another instance, it was not possible to complete an interview with an unhappily married woman who had been working without the knowledge her husband. She was engaged also in lace making with the consent of her husband. During the interview, the husband unexpectedly came home; I was introduced as a buyer who had come to see samples of her lace work. Although I made several attempts to complete the interview, I was unable to see the woman again, for I was told that she left home and was about to get a divorce.

34. I conducted two other related interviews. To obtain information about the number of doorkeepers in Ankara and the future prospects of this occupation in connection with the current citywide conversion of the heating system of apartment buildings into a natural gas system, I interviewed the president of the Doorkeeper's Association. Because survey data indicated that a large number of domestic workers recently had begun paying social security premiums to the mushrooming private insurance companies, I interviewed a representative of one of those insurance companies to learn more about their policies and whether they specifically target this vulnerable group of workers.

CHAPTER TWO

1. All respondents in this book are referred to by pseudonyms.

2. Doorkeeping is organized by the state. Labor legislation and condominium ownership laws passed in 1970 gave the doorkeepers formal worker status. Since then they have been included in a mandatory social insurance program under which they, like other workers in the formal sector, are covered and protected by the labor regulations of the state. These regulations entitle them to pension, paid holidays, and severance pay and offer them the protection of

health and safety regulations, the right to pension for disability and medical coverage, and automatic free health insurance for spouse and children. Doorkeepers are paid the official monthly minimum wage by the apartment house tenants.

3. Jenny White (1994:25) makes the observation that this territorial concentration by kin and compatriots from the same region has somewhat broken down in İstanbul because of high rents and the unavailability of housing.

4. This parallelism has its roots in Turkish marriage and kinship patterns, especially among peasants. Bride and groom are usually related (generally first or second cousins) or they come from the same village.

5. This conclusion is strengthened by the fact that doorkeeping, for a majority of the husbands (61 percent), is the first job held after migrating to Ankara.

6. Also, in a small number of cases (four), entry into domestic work was unrelated to doorkeeping. Two of the women moved to the city as children, one with her family and the other as an adopted daughter. Both of these women started their work lives in their early teens as childcare workers and continued to work after getting married. The third woman in this group came to the city as an adolescent and started cleaning houses when her father became a doorkeeper. The fourth case involves an unusual pattern of movement of migrants within the city. The woman began working immediately after arriving to Ankara; for three years she and her husband lived in a squatter settlement area, and later her husband took a doorkeeping post.

7. There was only one case where the husband's securing his job was dependent on his wife's agreeing to work as a domestic for the tenants, though the agreement was only in the form of an unwritten commitment.

8. In other studies of squatter settlement women, husbands' opposition, rather than the constraints of women's childcare and housework responsibilities, has been cited almost exclusively as the main hindrance to married women's participation in the formal labor force and domestic service and the explanation for their concentration in the urban informal sector, usually doing kinship-based organized piecework (Çınar 1991; White 1994).

9. In fact, during the middle of the interview, the husband unexpectedly came home; I was introduced as a buyer who came to see samples of her lace work.

10. But it is important to note that although all these jobs with which the women had been involved were of a "domestic" character, they are not feminized ones; on the contrary, in the Turkish case, they are male-dominated jobs, filled by men who are the social counterparts of these women.

11. This is not, of course, a new feminist question. Elson and Pearson (1989) revisit this question in their discussion of women workers in global factories. They argue that women's role in the family is socially constructed as a subordinated role that renders them unable fully to take on the classic attributes of free wage labor. "A woman is never 'free' in this way," they write. "She has obligations of domestic labor, difficulties in establishing control over her own body, and an inability to be a fully member of society in her own right" (28).

12. For example, when women are employed as wage laborers (seasonal workers to pick cotton, olives, or fruit) or in small-scale manufacturing, such as carpet weaving, their wages are negotiated by and paid to the head of the household, and, as a result, women control no cash.

13. Delaney (1991:172) explicates this notion of *izin* as "the source or cause of movement."

14. The idea that a woman is under the protection of a man and should be provided for by her husband is codified and sanctioned by the law. The civil code adopted in 1926 in the early years of the Republic includes many articles that sanction the gender inequality between men and women. For example, Article 152 states, "The husband is the head of the family. The choice of the family home and the nutrition and other requirements of the spouse and the children are his responsibility." Article 153 states, "The wife takes the husband's family name. The wife shall assist and advise the husband to the best of her ability in order to achieve the happiness of both. The home is taken care of by the wife" (Undersecretariat for Women's Affairs and Social Service 1993). Article 159 of the civil code, which was revoked by the constitutional court in 1992, denied women the right to pursue gainful employment without the consent of the husband.

15. Kandiyoti's concept of "bargaining with patriarchy" has been widely used, since the publication in 1988 of her article by the same name in *Gender & Society*, as a feminist conceptual tool in investigations of different forms of male dominance and women's responses to them, accommodating or subverting. In her later work (Kandiyoti 1995, 1997), she proposes the enlargement of feminist research agenda "to include the whole range of social institutions which are implicated structurally, relationally and symbolically in the reproduction of gender" (Kandiyoti 1995:307), in addition to studies of the mechanisms of male dominance in domestic patriarchy. See Bolak 1990 for a rich exploration of renegotiation of marital dynamics in urban working-class families in which the wife assumes the breadwinner role. Hale Bolak (1995) concludes that women's position as breadwinners ideologically challenges the traditional basis of male authority. She argues that the traditional justification of male authority is accepted by women as "a cultural script, without necessarily being internalized" (1996). Tahire Erman (1998) also employs Kandiyoti's "patriarchal bargains" framework in her ethnographic study of a group of squatter settlement women in Ankara. Her conclusions are similar to those of Bolak: most women continue to operate within the framework of "classical patriarchy" but the "normatively secured nature of gender roles and values" have been weakened, especially among what she calls "struggling young women" (mostly second-generation migrants). She asserts that the women in this group "are becoming active defenders of women's rights in the rural migrant community, representing a homegrown version of feminism" (Erman 1998:164). Jenny White (1994) recasts Kandiyoti's notion of bargain as a bargain not only between men and women in the family but as a bargain between the individual and group (larger family and community). She argues that women she studied claim "the protection and

support of the other members, including but not limited to their husbands and sons" by "adopting modest behavior and dress and by living up to the requirements of their role in the patriarchal compact" (White 1994:61). I discuss White's work in greater detail at the end of this chapter.

16. Establishing a definition of "dependent" children is inevitably problematic. The more frequently used definition of "dependent" children, children younger than 7 years old, or school age, is not appropriate here. During the course of this study, it was often observed that preschool children are also considered old enough to fend for themselves, especially in the squatter settlements, where home extends to the street, and that leaving children in front of the house on their own constitutes a viable childcare strategy because of an understanding that small children are watched by older children and adult members of the immediate community, even though no one is specifically designated as a minder of children.

17. The category of childcare provided by "other than husband" lumps together different strategies and agents of childcare. It includes childcare shared by the husband and older siblings (three cases); childcare provided by older siblings (two cases) and kin inside and outside the household (three cases); children who are on their own (three cases), and children who are taken to work (one case).

18. Beneria and Sen 1982 provides the most comprehensive analytical framework of this Marxist-feminist paradigm.

19. For a discussion of stratification in the South African informal sector by race and gender, see McKeever 1998. This study shows that nonwhites and women had the lowest income and occupational status, paralleling patterns of stratification in the formal economy. Carla Freeman's study (2000) of offshore informatics in Barbados demonstrates intimate linkages between women's employment in the formal informatics industry and their engagement in a variety of activities in the informal sector. To meet the demands of "professional" pink-collar identities and supplement their wages these Barbadian women engage in oversees "suitcase trade" and design and make clothes for themselves, their clients, and their fellow workers. For a rare illustration of the interactions among the internal divisions within the female urban informal sector, see Bunster and Chaney 1985. The authors demonstrate that Peruvian domestic workers who had live-in positions left domestic service after having children and entered street vending to accommodate their responsibilities as mothers.

CHAPTER THREE

1. Mary Romero (1992) describes the labor process of Chicana domestic workers in similar terms. She makes the analogy of the businesslike relationships established by domestic workers and by male workers employed in private households to shampoo carpets, paint, and do repairs. Romero defines this employee-employer relationship as the petit-bourgeois relation of customer-vendor (157).

2. It should be noted that in the calculation of mean hours for the squatter settlement group the adjusted work hours are used. In order to make an accurate estimation of work hours, rather than asking the respondents how many hours they spend on the job, they were asked to report the times they leave their own home and return. As expected, mean hours based on these unadjusted figures showed a considerable difference between the doorkeeper and the squatter settlement workers; the mean number of hours worked by doorkeeper workers was 7.60 a day, as compared with 8.59 for the squatter settlement workers, the greater figure for the squatter settlement group reflecting the time spend on commuting. But since this difference is due to the considerable amount of time that only squatter settlement workers spend commuting to and from work, this group's work hours are adjusted by deducting 2 hours—the time spent on commuting. After the adjustment, the difference is reversed.

3. According to local news reports, every year at least one or two domestic workers lose their lives on the job, usually by falling down while cleaning the windows.

CHAPTER FOUR

1. For exceptions, see Hansen 1989 and Lasser 1987. Karen Hansen, in her historical study of domestic service in Zambia, emphasizes the interactive nature of the relationships. Carol Lasser disputes the received interpretation of the shift in domestic service in the United States as a "decline" and argues that this shift in fact reflects the bargaining power of servants to initiate improvements in the conditions of their employments.

2. See White 1994 for the role of kinship in the organization of small-scale capitalist production in Turkey.

3. The importance of community networks for recruitment and internal occupational mobility from live-in to day work with multiple employers is also emphasized for Mexican immigrant women in the United States. Domestic workers without networks (newly arrived immigrant women) often find themselves laboring in severely underpaid live-in positions (Hondagneu-Sotelo 1994a:199–200).

4. V. Tellis-Nayak (1983) applies the concept of patronage to domestic service. He examines the nature of interaction between domestic workers and employers by using the concept of clientship in a South Indian community. He describes patronage as a dependency arrangement outside the formal caste tradition, since it involves rural and urban Christians. The structure of domestic service is organized in such a way that rural-born girls are placed in urban Hindu households by their parents as a way of ensuring economic relief and continuous economic and social support from urban classes with whom they share the same religion. In this arrangement the network of religious functionaries plays an important role as a mediator in recruiting rural daughters (and some sons) into elite, urban homes. Tellis-Nayak argues that an enduring vertical tie is established between domestic servants' rural family community and

those of employers through domestic service. Although this tie is between unequals, he describes it as a vertical solidarity because it involves a diffuse mutuality that includes honor, trust, generosity, and gift-giving through which the family of the servant receives help from the employer in times of illness and unemployment, as well as advice and protection in securing loans, for instance, or settling disputes. My analysis departs significantly from his. Although he defines the domestic worker as the client, it is her kin that becomes the client. Furthermore, as his critics have pointed out, the notion of paternalism is more useful to describe the relationship of servants and the households in which they live and are incorporated. For a critique of this and other points and Tellis-Nayak's reply, see the comments by Hansen, Shahani, and Walter following the article (Tellis-Nayak 1983).

5. The question asked whether they have ever received any *significant* help from employers either for themselves or for their family.

6. Situational relativity and differences in the perception of importance also explain why the majority of domestic workers in the doorkeeper group and about half of those in the squatter settlement group reported having received no patronage benefits, even thought they would have been subject to many different kinds of patronage. It is difficult to interpret the difference between the two study groups here. One plausible interpretation is that since doorkeeping also involves patron-client relationships, patronage received from the doorkeeping channel and from the domestic worker's own work get blurred, since in most cases the patron is the same person. Another interpretation is that squatter settlement domestic workers' greater participation in this clientship reflects their greater opportunity to pick good patrons.

7. In one ironic instance during the course of this study, I was offered the opportunity to become a patron. The husband of a domestic worker, a doorkeeper, told me that if I placed his 18-year-old daughter, a high school graduate with computer skills, in a modern job, he would send his wife to work for me.

8. Rina Cohen (1991) in her study of live-in domestic workers of Third World origin employed by middle-class Canadian families makes a similar point. According to her analysis, domestic workers' "extracting" gifts from employers is one of the "levelling mechanisms" to restore a more balanced exchange.

9. Although I did not systematically investigate this question, I had the opportunity to observe the existence of this practice because of the timing of my participant observation in squatter neighborhoods in the summer when domestic workers either visit their natal villages or send out other members of the household on such visits. On these occasions of preparation for the trip to the village and deciding what to purchase and take as gifts to friends and relatives, it became clear that household items, especially clothing given by employers, constituted an important pool of gift items, which includes a range of food and nonfood items.

10. This management of feelings resembles what Arlie Hochschild (1983) calls the "commercialization of human feeling" to explain the sense of falseness

and alienation from their own feelings that flight attendants report results from their emotional work.

CHAPTER FIVE

1. There is a vast literature in this area. In an overview Marion Tolbert Coleman (1991) delineates substantive and methodological questions that earlier empirical studies attempted to address and proposes new research questions informed by the gender stratification model she and Rae Lesser Blumberg (1984) developed; Sarah Fenstermaker Berk's meticulous time-budget study (1985) powerfully illustrates the shortcomings of Becker's New Household Economics model and Marxist-feminist approaches in understanding actual mechanisms of gendered division of labor; Heidi Hartmann (1981b) elaborates the Marxist-feminist approach, which links women's unpaid labor and gender subordination at home to the reproduction of the capitalist system; and Ruth Cowan's historical work (1983) focuses on the relation between changes in household technology and division of labor by gender.

2. A recent national survey of the division of labor by gender in Turkish families reveals that housework and childcare are territories of work occupied solely by women. The survey asked women to specify whether they have sole or shared or no responsibility for five general household tasks (cooking, cleaning, dishwashing, ironing, and shopping) and four areas of childcare (feeding, dressing, playing with children, and nursing sick children). The only area of work that men share with women is grocery shopping. Furthermore, contributions of the husbands of employed wives do not differ from those of unemployed wives, though employed wives do 10 percent less work than nonemployed wives. There is also no significant difference between urban and rural families' pattern of gendered division of labor (KSSGM 1998:50–57). For an ethnographic exploration of gender division of labor in rural families, see Delaney 1991. Carol Delaney argues that division of labor by gender in the village she studied parallels the perceived roles of men and women in the seed and soil theory of procreation. For other in-depth studies of Turkish families and gender division of labor within them, see Ayata and Ayata 1996; Bolak 1990; and Erkut 1982.

3. For a contrary argument see Ericksen, Yancey, and Ericksen 1979, which finds a positive correlation between spouses' relative resources and the sharing of housework. In an effort to identify the factors that lead to a lessening of gender division of labor among married couples, these authors, on the basis of an analysis of the gender division of labor among 1,212 couples in the Philadelphia area, suggest that the husband's success as an income provider is the best explanatory variable of his contribution to the housework. They find that lower-income husbands or unsuccessful husbands are more likely to do housework than their high-income counterparts. In both cases, however, wives end up doing more housework than their husbands do.

4. Translated by Jenny White (1994:51).

5. Note that this would never be framed as "repayment" or "bartering." Roger Lancaster (1992) and Carol Stack (1974) offer strikingly similar descriptions of redistributive mechanisms among the poor in Nicaraguan and black inner-city communities in the United States.

6. Analysis of other variables strongly corroborates what one of the respondents added to explain her response (and perhaps to bring forward the distinction that the interview question failed to do): "They [husbands] take care of children but do nothing related to the housework."

7. See Gültekin and Bülent (1978); Tüm Hukuk Sorunlariyla Kapıcılar, cited in Çulpan 1979.

8. This new "service worker" status also enabled doorkeepers to form a union, but without the right to collective bargaining, because their "workplaces" consist of single workers.

9. Labor legislation provides for one day off a week (Sundays) and an annual vacation (ranging from twelve to twenty-four workdays a year, depending on the length of service), İş Kanunu Tüzük ve Yönetmelikleri cited in Çulpan 1979:48.

10. Sarah C. Maza (1983) coined this phrase for a description of lackeys under the Old Regime in France. Despite vast differences between caretakers and servants in pre-industrial and industrializing Europe, the phrase can help us make some useful comparisons.

11. Note that the hours mentioned in the schedule are so meticulously specified because there is an eight-hour legal limit to the workday, the sum of the hours of work listed in the schedule.

12. A "board of managers" (yönetim kurulu) elected each year by the owners of the apartments manages the building's financial and other matters; one member of this body operates as the chief "manager" to handle all issues involving the maintenance of the building, and, as such, he is the highest person in command with regard to the doorkeeper. Yet, because of his absence from the workplace of the doorkeeper, he can rarely act as an immediate supervisor. Retired army officers who have plenty of time on their hands and the skills to discipline the doorkeeper are notorious managers.

13. Tenants address the doorkeeper by adding "Master" (efendi) after his given name. "Master" is here a device for giving him a sense of worthiness. This discursive inversion of the "master-servant" relationship is possible because, according to the slogan created by the elite of the Turkish Republic in an effort to incorporate the rural masses in the process of transforming a defunct empire into a modern nation state, "The peasant is the master of the nation."

14. Leonore Davidoff (1974:407) makes a similar analogy between servant and wife in Victorian and Edwardian England, although the basis of her analogy is different. Paternalistic domination, she argues, by definition structured the same kind of relationship between these two pairs, "master-servant" and "husband-wife." Thus, subordination to a master or a husband has similar meanings in circumstances where subordinate groups have "few other links to the wider society" and the right to be independent.

15. The family power/resource theory, first developed by Robert Blood and Donald M. Wolfe (1960), has many variants. For the Marxist-feminist perspective, which views gender-based unequal division of labor as the inevitable product of patriarchal structures of domination in the capitalist labor market and private sphere, see Bennholdt-Thomsen 1984 and Hartmann 1981a.

16. The expression "*Onunki de benimki de can*" is difficult to translate, since the word "*can*" has multiple meanings, including "soul" and "force." But in this context, "force" better conveys the meaning of the expression.

17. For excellent discussions of the relationships between women's identity, women's sexuality, and food preparation, see Goddard 1987 for the Italian case and Clark 1994 for the West African case.

CHAPTER SIX

1. For example, Blumberg (1991) suggests that gender-based inequalities in the division of household labor and decision making can change when wives earn more than their husbands. She writes, "For a further test of this hypothesis, however, we await research results from the frontier: American couples where the wife has long out earned the husband and makes enough to allocate surplus income as well as just subsistence" (21).

2. Eleanor Fapohunda (1988) argues that the practice of joint financial planning and each spouse's having knowledge of the other's income and where that income is spent are good measures of the existence of pooling. According to these criteria, households in my study are pooling households. First, the majority of women have full knowledge of their husbands' income (at least the stable part of it). In cases where they do not, the cause is more the unpredictability of the informal petty-cash earning activities than the separation of budgets or an imbalance in the intra-household power. Second, the women in the study have full knowledge of how their husbands spent their money. Third, they had an understanding that each spouse's income would go to particular items of spending and investment—regardless of who controlled the money and who had decision-making power.

3. I used three main variables to calculate the relative contribution of women's earnings to household economies: "women's total monthly earnings"; "husbands' total monthly earnings"; and "other household members' (including children's) total monthly earnings." The predominance of the nuclear family structure among these households made it relatively easy to compute an accurate estimate of the total household income. There were, however, other problems. Seventeen percent (N = 17) of husbands in the doorkeeper group and 11 percent (N = 7) of those in the squatter settlement group have other sources of income in addition to their primary jobs. In some cases, because of the informal nature of second jobs and the petty cash involved, women have some difficulty in reporting earnings from these informal sources of income. There were nine such cases. On the basis of field notes and comparison with other known cases, these nine cases were assigned to "major," "minor," and "equal" con-

tributor groups. Another problem was related to the "tips" in the doorkeeper group. The majority of doorkeeper wives know the amount and source of tips their husbands receive. In the total sample about one-third do not get tips at all and 53 percent of the husbands tell wives how much they receive and from whom; only 8 percent (N = 8) reported that their husbands do not tell them tip amounts. Given these complications, the amount of tips was not asked, and tips were not included in the total household income, perhaps resulting in the underestimation of some husbands' income. Women's earnings from income-generating activities other than domestic work are included in these computations. Few women engaged in other petty-cash earning activities, such as knitting and lace making (two in the squatter group and four in doorkeeper group.) Eight women in the doorkeeper group worked as doorkeepers themselves, four of whom earned less as doorkeepers than as domestic workers. Other household members' earnings that were reported as pooled are included in the calculation. Earnings that were reported as *partially* pooled were not included because of the changing and unpredictable nature of such "partial" pooling.

4. Such expensive ornamentation is worn not only at special occasions such as weddings. Gold may be primarily a form of savings, but its social function goes well beyond that in the day-to-day lives of the women in this study.

5. It may of course be held that the very existence of gender segregated spaces is a source of gender inequality. That argument, even if valid, does not entail that women's empowerment and modes of self-definition can be assessed according to masculine models.

6. Micaela di Leonardo 1987 also emphasizes the empowering effects of women's family and kinship work.

7. Most of the research on marital power in the past several decades has used resource theory originally developed by Robert Blood and Donald M. Wolfe (1960). Although the theory has been criticized widely for its conceptual and methodological weaknesses, it is still considered a primary source in generating hypotheses by researchers (Gillespie 1971; Goodwin and Scanzoni 1989; Lukes 1974; Safilios-Rothschild 1972, 1976; Scanzoni 1982, 1989; Scanzoni and Szinovacz 1980). The earlier critique of this theory developed around methodological concerns that later raised theoretical issues as well. The main concern involved the operationalization of the concept of power. The measurement of power with the outcome of decision making, it was argued, involves two problems: (1) a conception of marital power as a zero-sum game is invalid because family power is an ongoing and interactive process, and thus it is misleading to isolate specific decisions as representative of power; and (2) if power can be measured by decision making, hierarchy and frequency of decision making should be taken into account. Constantina Safilios-Rothschild (1976) elaborated on this by introducing a distinction between "orchestration" and "implementation of power." She also suggested that the range of resources be enlarged to include variables other than socioeconomic ones.

8. Decisions were defined as husband dominant when respondents answered 4 or 5, female dominant when respondents answered 1 and 2, and

equal when respondents answered 3. The ratio index involved the sum of all female-dominant decisions (1 + 2) plus one-half of the equal decisions divided by the sum of all male-dominant decisions (4 + 5) plus one-half of the equal decisions.

$$\text{Decision Influence Ratio} = \frac{1 + 2 + (\text{half of } 3)}{4 + 5 + (\text{half of } 3)}$$

The result is a ratio whose size shows the relative *aggregate* reported influence of the wife over that of the husband *within any specified group* in the sample. This ratio does not lend itself to a literal interpretation. Instead, it should be taken as a conceptually defensible measure of women's claimed influence in decision making. The justification for inclusion of the reported mid-point (i.e., "equal influence") in such a ratio is in the substantial social meaning of these women's reporting an "equal influence" with their men. Since the women in my sample belong to a culture that is thoroughly patriarchal, it would be highly misleading to underestimate the weight of the mid-point. Reporting to have an "equal say" in certain items may signal a claim to have very unpatriarchal powers in the family, and this measure is designed to capture that possibility. Furthermore, Joyce Elliott and William Moskoff (1983) found that the responses in their sample to similar family decision items clustered on the mid-point, decreasing the real variation they believe existed. My formula, by dispersing the mid-point toward the extremes, takes care of this problem—albeit with a considerable fiat of mathematical aesthetics.

9. The only national survey of Turkish family structure that obtained information on decision making was undertaken in 1968. Other small-scale studies do not easily lend themselves for comparison because of their divergent foci and methodologies. Serim Timur's (1972) national survey found that men make decisions on major issues in Turkish families. Only 1 percent of the husbands acknowledged that their wives could make important decisions. The proportion of the women who made such an acknowledgment was also very low (3 percent). This male-dominant decision-making profile did not differ significantly between rural and urban families. Oya Çifçi (1990) in her 1979 study of middle-class women working in the public sector reports the existence of a high level of joint decision making in the areas of food, clothing expenditures, birth control, and children's education. Yet, husbands made most of the decisions concerning women's professional life. The most recent findings on some aspects of decision making come from Ferhunde Özbay's survey (1990) of women in a small manufacturing town. Her analysis suggests that women make most of the routine household spending decisions, representing a shift from husbands to wives. However, this shift was less pronounced in decisions concerning major spending categories. In this area, she found that male-dominant and joint decision-making were equally represented. Among these previous studies the one that is most appropriate to use for comparison because of the similarity of sample characteristics is Nilüfer Kuyaş's study (1982) of sixty lower-class women

of peasant origin (composed of both employed women and housewives) and sixty middle-class women. Kuyaş found that among lower-class women perceptions of sharing in decision making were almost nonexistent. There was a male/female polarity: women made the decisions about childcare, education, and routine shopping and men had a monopoly over deciding how to bring up or discipline their children and how much and where to spend on major purchases. In contrast, joint decision-making was a pervasive feature of middle-class families, except for decisions on major issues, which were made by men unilaterally. But there was a striking resemblance between experiences of these women of different classes. In their families, decisions pertaining to women's physical mobility, women's employment, birth control, and sex belonged to men, regardless of women's social status as employed wives or housewives. My findings concerning decision making in the areas of women's social mobility, employment decisions, and sex do not run counter to the evidence presented in earlier studies of decision making but show interesting differences in other areas of decision making, especially when compared with the profiles of decision making of lower-class women by Kuyaş.

10. This finding is consistent with Safilios-Rothchild's observations (1990) in the cases of Greece, Honduras, and Kenya.

11. This finding contradicts with those of Kuyaş (1982). She found, among both lower- and middle-class wives, a "surprising correspondence or parallel between women's perception of their actual powerlessness and their normative preferences related to this powerlessness" (196). She also found no difference between employed wives and housewives.

12. To define "ideological discount rate," Blumberg 1984 and Blumberg and Coleman 1989 explain that because of "prevailing male/female gender ideologies," for every dollar a woman brings into the house she will get less economic power than her husband will get for every dollar he brings in.

13. The remaining (approximately) 20 percent of the respondents in each group said either that working makes no difference in their lives or that they began to work only recently and cannot yet form an opinion.

CHAPTER SEVEN

1. Some recent analyses that conceptualize the relation between the rise of Islam in Turkey and the modernity project in different ways are Bulaç 1992; Göle 1997; Gülalp 1997; and Saktanber 1994.

References

Abadan-Unat, Nermin. 1990. "The Legal Status of Turkish Women." In *Women, Family, and Social Change in Turkey*, ed. Ferhunde Özbay. Bangkok: UNESCO.
———. 1991. "The Impact of Legal and Educational Reforms on Turkish Women." In *Women in Middle Eastern History*, ed. Nikki R. Keddie and Beth Baron. New Haven: Yale University Press.
Abercrombie, Nicholas, and Stephen Hill. 1976. "Paternalism and Patronage." *British Journal of Sociology* 27, no. 4:413–29.
Abu-Lughod, Lila, ed. 1998. *Remaking Women: Feminism and Modernity in the Middle East*. Princeton: Princeton University Press.
Adam, Barbara. 1996. "Detraditionalization and the Certainty of Uncertain Futures." In *Detraditionalization: Critical Reflections on Authority and Identity*, ed. Paul Heelas, Scott Lash, and Paul Morris. Malden, Mass.: Blackwell.
Amin, Samir. 1974. *Accumulation on a World Scale*. New York: Monthly Review Press.
———. 1977. *Imperialism and Unequal Development*. New York: Monthly Review Press.
Appadurai, Arjun. 1996. *Modernity at Large: Cultural Dimensions of Globalization*. Minneapolis: University of Minnesota Press.
Arat, Yesim. 1997. "The Project of Modernity and Women in Turkey." In *Rethinking Modernity and National Identity in Turkey*, ed. Sibel Bozdoğan and Reşat Kasaba. Seattle: University of Washington Press.
Arizpe, Lourdes. 1975. "Women in the Informal Sector: The Case of Mexico City." *Signs* 3, no. 1:25—37.
Ayata, Ayşe. 1989. "Gecekondularda Kimlik Sorunu, Dayanışma Örüntüleri ve Hemşehrilik." Sosyal Bilimler Kongresine Sunulan Teblig. ODTÜ, Ankara.
Ayata, Sencer. 1988. "Statü Yarışması ve Salon Kullanımı." *Toplum ve Bilim* 42:5–25.
———. 1989. "Toplumsal Çevre Olarak Gecekondu ve Apartman" *Toplum ve Bilim* 42 Yaz.
Ayata, Sencer, and Ayse Ayata. 1996. "Konut, Komşuluk ve Kent Kültürü Housing, Neighborliness, and the Urban Culture." Housing Research Series 10. Ankara: Turkish Prime Ministry, Housing Development Administration.
Barkey, Henri. 1984. "The Political Economy of Industrialization: A Case Study of Turkey, 1960–80." Ph.D. dissertation, University of Pennslyvania.
Bawly, Dan. 1982. *The Subterranean Economy*. New York: McGraw Hill.
Beneria, Lourdes, and Martha Roldan. 1987. *The Crossroads of Class and Gender*. Chicago: University of Chicago Press.

Beneria, Lourdes, and Gita Sen. 1981. "Accumulation, Reproduction, and Women's Role in Economic Development: Boserup Revisited." *Signs* 7, no. 2:279–98.

———. 1982. "Class and Gender Inequalities and Women's Role in Economic Development: Theoretical and Practical Implications." *Feminist Studies* 8, no. 1:156–76.

Bennholdt-Thomsen, Veronika. 1984. "Towards a Theory of the Sexual Division of Labor." In *Households and the World Economy*, ed. Joan Smith, Immanuel Wallerstein, and Hans Dieter Evers. Beverly Hills: Sage.

Benson, Susan Porter. 1996. "Living on the Margin: Working-Class Marriages and Family Survival Strategies in the United States, 1919–1941." In *The Sex of Things*, ed. Victoria de Grazia and Ellen Furlough. Berkeley and Los Angeles: University of California Press.

Benton, Lauren A. 1990. *Invisible Factories: The Informal Economy and Industrial Development in Spain.* Albany: State University of New York Press.

Berik, Günseli. 1987. *Women Carpet Weavers in Turkey: Patterns of Employment, Earnings, and Status.* Geneva: International Labor Office.

Berk, Sarah Fenstermaker. 1985. *The Gender Factory.* New York: Plenum Press.

Berk, Sarah Fenstermaker, and Catherine White Berheide. 1977. "Going Backstage: Gaining Access to Observe Household Work." *Sociology of Work and Occupations* 4, no. 1:27–49.

Berkes, Niyazi. 1942. *Bazı Ankara Köyleri Üzerine Bir Araştırma.* Ankara: Uzluk Yayınevi.

Bhabha, Jacqueline, Francesca Klug, and Sue Shutter. 1985. *Worlds Apart: Women Under Immigration and Nationality Law.* London: Pluto Press.

Bickham Mendez, Jennifer. 1998. "Of Mops and Maids: Contradictions and Continuities in Bureaucratized Domestic Work." *Social Problems* 45, no. 1:114–35.

Bland, Lucy, Rachel Harrison, Frank Mort, and Christine Weedon. 1978. "Relations of Reproduction Approaches Through Anthropology. " In *Women Take Issue*, ed. Birmingham Women's Studies Group. London: Hutchinson.

Blood, Robert, and Donald M. Wolfe. 1960. *Husbands and Wives.* New York: Free Press.

Blumberg, Rae Lesser. 1984. "A General Theory of Gender Stratification." In *Sociological Theory*, ed. Randall Collins. San Francisco: Jossey-Bass.

———. 1991. "Income Under Female Versus Male Control: Hypotheses from a Theory of Gender Stratification and Data from the Third World." In *Gender, Family, and Economy: The Triple Overlap*, ed. Rae Lesser Blumberg. Newbury Park: Sage.

Blumberg, Rae Lesser, and Marion Tolbert Coleman. 1989. "A Theory-Guided Look at the Gender Balance of Power in the American Couple." *Journal of Family Issues* 10, no. 2:225–50.

Blumstein, Philip, and Pepper Schwartz. 1983. *American Couples: Money, Work, and Sex.* New York: William Morrow.

———. 1991. "Money and Ideology: Their Impact on Power and the Division of Household Labor." In *Gender, Family, and Economy: The Triple Overlap*, ed. Rae Lesser Blumberg. Newbury Park: Sage.

Bolak, Hale Cihan. 1990. "Women Breadwinners and the Construction of Gender: Urban Working-Class Households in Turkey." Ph.D. dissertation, University of California, Santa Cruz.

————. 1995. "Towards a Concepualization of Marital Power Dynamics: Women Breadwinners and Working-class Households in Turkey." In *Women in Modern Turkish Society*, ed. Şirin Tekeli. Atlantic Heights, N.J.: Zed.

Boran, Behice. 1945. *Toplumsal Yapı Araştırmaları İki köy çeşidinin mukayeseli tetkiki.* Ankara: Türk Tarih Kurumu.

Boratav, Korkut. 1988. *Türkiye İktisat Tarihi, 1908–1985.* İstanbul: Gerçek Yayınevi.

Boserup, Ester. 1970. *Woman's Role in Economic Development.* London: George Allen and Unwin.

Bozdoğan, Sibel. 1997. "The Predicament of Modernism in Turkish Architectural Culture: An Overview." In *Rethinking Modernity and National Identity in Turkey,* ed. Sibel Bozdoğan and Reşat Kasaba. Seattle: University of Washington Press.

Bozdoğan, Sibel, and Resat Kasaba. 1997. "Introduction." In *Rethinking Modernity and National Identity in Turkey,* ed. Sibel Bozdoğan and Reşat Kasaba. Seattle: University of Washington Press.

Bromley, Ray, and Chris Gerry, eds. 1979. *Casual Work and Poverty.* London: John Wiley and Sons.

Brydon, Lynne, and Sylvia Chant. 1989. *Women in the Third World.* London: Edward Elgar.

Bujra, Janet M. 1978. "Proletarianization and the 'Informal Economy': A Case Study from Nairobi." *African Urban Studies* 3:47–66.

Bulaç, Ali. 1992. *Din ve Modernizm.* İstanbul: Beyan.

Bunster, Ximena, and Chaney Elsa. 1985. *Sellers and Servants.* New York: Praeger.

Cardoso, Fernando Henrique, and Enzo Faletto. 1979. *Dependency and Development in Latin America.* Berkeley and Los Angeles: University of California Press.

Castells, Manuel, and Alejandro Portes. 1989. "World Underneath: The Origins, Dynamics, and Effects of the Informal Economy." In *The Informal Economy,* ed. Alejandro Portes, Manuel Castells, and Lauren A. Benton. Baltimore: Johns Hopkins University Press.

Castro, Mary G. 1989. "What Is Bought and Sold in Domestic Service? The Case of Bogota: A Critical Review." In *Muchachas No More,* ed. Elsa M. Chaney and Mary G. Castro. Philadelphia: Temple University Press.

Chaney, Elsa M., and Mary Garcia Castro, eds. 1989. *Muchachas No More.* Philadelphia: Temple University Press.

Chant, Syvia. 1991. *Women and Survival in Mexican Cities: Perspectives on Gender, Labour Markets, and Low-Income Households.* New York: Manchester University Press.

Chaplin, David. 1978. "Domestic Service and Industrialization." In *Comparative Studies in Sociology,* ed. Richard Thomasson. Greenwich, Conn.: Jai Press.

Charles, Nicola, and Marion Kerr. 1987. "Just the Way It Is: Gender and Age Differences in Family Food Consumption." In *Give and Take in Families: Studies* in *Resource Distribution*, ed. Julia Brannen and Gail Wilson. London: Allen and Unwin.

Çifçi, Oya. 1990. "Women in the Public Sector." In *Women, Family and Social Change in Turkey*, ed. Ferhunde Özbay. Bangkok: UNESCO.

Çınar, Mine. 1988. "Subcontracting at Home: Disguised Female Employment in Urban Turkey." Loyola University of Chicago School of Business Administration Working Paper no. 8810.

———. 1991. "Labor Opportunities for Adult Females and Home-Working Women in Istanbul, Turkey." Working Paper no. 2, G. E. von Grunebaum Center for Near Eastern Studies, University of California, Los Angeles.

Çınar, Mine, Günar Evcimen, and Mehmet Kaytaz. 1988. "The Present-Day Status of Small-Scale Industries (Sanatkar) in Bursa, Turkey." *International Journal of Middle East Studies* 20, no. 3:287–301.

Clark, Gracia. 1994. *Onions are My Husband: Survival and Accumulation by West African Market Women*. Chicago: University of Chicago Press.

Clark-Lewis, Elizabeth. 1987. "This Work Had an End: African Domestic Workers in Washington, D.C., 1910–1940." In *To Toil the Livelong Day*, ed. Carol Groneman and Mary B. Norton. Ithaca, N.Y.: Cornell University Press.

Cock, Jacklyn. 1980. *Maids and Madams: A Study in the Politics of Exploitation.* Johannesburg: Raven Press.

Cohen, Rina. 1991. "Women of Color in White Households: Coping Strategies of Live-in Domestic Workers." *Qualitative Sociology* 14, no. 2:197–215.

Coleman, Marion Tolbert. 1991. "The Division of Household Labor: Suggestions for Future Empirical Consideration and Theoretical Development." In *Gender, Family, and Economy: The Triple Overlap*, ed. Rae Lesser Blumberg. Newbury Park: Sage.

Colen, Shellee. 1986. " 'With Respect and Feelings': Voices of West Indian Child Care and Domestic Workers in New York City." In *All American Women: Lines That Divide, Ties That Bind*, ed. Johnetta Cole. New York: Free Press.

———. 1989. " 'Just a Little Respect': West Indian Domestic Workers in New York City." In *Muchachas No More*, ed. Elsa M. Chaney and Maria Garcia Castro. Philadelphia: Temple University Press.

Colen, Shellee, and Roger Sanjek. 1990. "At Work in Homes I: Orientations." In *At Work in Homes: Household Workers in World Perspective*, ed. Roger Sanjek and Shellee Colen. American Ethnological Society Monograph Series, no. 3. Washington, D.C.: American Anthropological Association.

Collins, Patricia Hill. 1991. "Learning from the Outsider Within: The Sociological Significance of Black Feminist Thought." In *Beyond Methodology*, ed. Mary Fonow and Judith A. Cook. Bloomington: Indiana University Press.

Connell, R. W. 1987. *Gender and Power*. Stanford: Stanford University Press.

Coser, Lewis. 1973. "Domestic Servants: The Obsolescence of a Social Role." *Social Forces* 52, no. 1:31—40.

Cowan, Ruth. 1983. *More Work for Mother*. New York: Basic Books.

Çulpan, Oya. 1979. *Kent Yaşamında Bir İşlev Türü: Kapıcılık*. Doçentlik Tezi. Ankara: T.C. Hacettepe Üniversitesi, Sosyal ve İdari Ilimler Fakültesi.

Davidoff, Leonore. 1974. "Mastered for Life: Servant and Wife in Victorian and Edwardian England." *Journal of Social History* 7, no. 4:406–28.

———. 1976. "The Rationalization of Housework." In *Dependence and Exploitation in Work and Marriage*, ed. Leonard Barker and Sheila Allen. London: Longman.

Davis, Kingsley. 1988. "Wives and Work: A Theory of the Sex-Role Revolution and Its Consequences." In *Feminism, Children, and the New Families*, ed. Sanford M. Dornbusch and Myra H. Strober. New York: Guilford Press.

Deere, D. Carmen. 1976. "Rural Women's Subsistence Production in the Capitalist Periphery." *Review of Radical Political Economics* 8, no. 1:9–17.

Delaney, Carol. 1991. *The Seed and the Soil*. Berkeley and Los Angeles: University of California Press.

Delphy, Christine. 1979. "Sharing the Same Table: Consumption and the Family." In *The Sociology of the Family: New Directions in Britain*, ed. C. C. Harris. Keele: University of Keele.

De Oliveria, Orlandina, and Bryan Roberts. 1994. "The Many Roles of the Informal Sector in Development: Evidence from Urban Labor Market Research, 1940–1989." In *The Informal Sector Debate in Latin America*, ed. Cathy Rakowski. Albany: State University of New York Press.

DIE State Institute of Statistics 1989. *1985 Census of Population: Social and Economic Characteristics*. Ankara: DIE.

di Leonardo, Micaela. 1987. "The Female World of Cards and Holidays: Women, Families, and the Work of Kinship." *Signs* 12, no. 3:440–53.

Dill, Thornton B. 1994. *Across the Boundaries of Race and Class: An Exploration of the Relationship Between Work and Family Among Black Female Domestic Servants*. New York: Garland.

———. 1988. "Making Your Job Good to Yourself: Domestic Service and the Construction of Personal Dignity." In *Women and the Politics of Empowerment*, ed. Ann Bookman and Sandra Morgen. Philadelphia: Temple University Press.

Douglas, Mary. 1989. *Purity and Danger: An Analysis of the Concepts of Pollution and Taboo*. London and New York: Ark Paperbacks.

DPT (State Planning Office). 1992. "Türk Aile Yapısı Araştırması." *DPT Yayinları*, no. 2313.

Duarte, Isis. 1989. "A Question for the Feminist Movement: Household Workers in the Dominican Republic." In *Muchachas No More*, ed. Elsa M. Chaney and Mary Garcia Castro. Philadelphia: Temple University Press.

Duben, Alan. 1982. "The significance of family and kinship in urban Turkey." In *Sex Roles, Family and Community in Turkey*, ed. Çiğdem Kağıtcibaşı. Bloomington, Indiana: Indiana University Press.

Duben, Alan, and Cem Behar. 1991. *Istanbul Households: Marriage, Family, and Fertility, 1880–1940*. Cambridge: Cambridge University Press.

Dudden, Faye. 1983. *Serving Women: Household Service in Nineteenth-Century America*. Middleton: Wesleyan University Press.

Dwyer, Daisy, and Judith Bruce, eds. 1988. *A Home Divided: Women and Income in the Third World*. Stanford: Stanford University Press.

Ehrenreich, Barbara. 1989. *Fear of Falling: The Inner Life of the Middle Class.* New York: Pantheon Books.

Elliott, Joyce, and William Moskoff. 1983. "Decision-Making Power in Romanian Families." *Journal of Comparative Family Studies* 14, no. 1:38–51.

Elson, Diane, and Ruth Pearson. 1988. "The Subordination of Women and the Internationalisation of Factory Production." In *Of Marriage and the Market: Women's Subordination in International Perspective*, ed. Kate Young, Carol Wolkowitz, and Roslyn McCullagh. London: Routledge.

Eralp, Atilla. 1990. "The Politics of Turkish Development Strategies." In *Turkish State, Turkish Society*, ed. Andrew Finkel and Nükhet Sirman. London: Routledge.

Ericksen, Julia, William Yancey, and Eugene Ericksen. 1979. "The Division of Family Roles." *Journal of Marriage and Family* 41:301–13.

Erkut, Sumru. 1982. "Dualism in Values Toward Education of Turkish Women." In *Sex Roles, Family, and Community in Turkey*, ed. Çiğdem Kağitçibaşi. Bloomington: Indiana University Press.

Erman, Tahire. 1998. "The Impact of Migration on Turkish Rural Women: Four Emergent Patterns." *Gender & Society* 12:146–68.

Esmer, Yılmaz, Hamit Fişek, and Ersin Kalaycıoğlu. 1986. *Türkiye'de Sosyo-Ekonomik Öncelikler, Hane Gelirleri, Harcamaları ve Sosyo-ekonomik ihtiyaçlar üzerine bir araştırma dizisi.* Vol 1. İstanbul: TUSIAD.

Espinal, Rosario, and Sherri Grasmuck. 1993 "Gender, Households, and Informal Entrepreneurship in the Dominican Republic." Paper presented at the 18th Annual Convention of the Caribbean Studies Association, May 24—29, at Kingston and Ocho Rios, Jamaica.

Fairchilds, Cissie. 1984 *Domestic Enemies: Servants and Their Masters in Old Regime France.* Baltimore: Johns Hopkins University Press.

Fapohunda, Eleanor. 1988. "The Nonpooling Household: A Challenge to Theory." In *A Home Divided: Women and Income in the Third World*, ed. Daisy Dwyer and Judith Bruce. Stanford: Stanford University Press.

Featherstone, Mike, ed. 1990. *Global Culture, Nationalism, Globalization, and Modernity.* London: Sage.

Fenstermaker, Sarah, Candace West, and Don H. Zimmerman. 1991. "Gender Inequality: New Conceptual Terrain." In *Gender, Family, and Economy: The Triple Overlap*, ed. Rae Lesser Blumberg. Newbury Park: Sage.

Fernandez-Kelly, Maria Patricia. 1983. *For We Are Sold, I and My People: Women and Industry in Mexico's Frontier.* Albany: State University of New York Press.

Fernandez-Kelly, Maria Patricia, and Anna M. Garcia. 1989. "Informalization at the Core: Hispanic Women, Homework, and the Advanced Capitalist State." In *The Informal Economy*, ed. Alejandro Portes, Manuel Castells, and Lauren A. Benton. Baltimore: Johns Hopkins University Press.

Finkel, Andrew, and Nükhet Sirman, eds. 1990. *Turkish State, Turkish Society.* London: Routledge.

Folbre, Nancy. 1988. "The Black Four of Hearts: Toward a New Paradigm of Household Economics." In *A Home Divided: Women and Income in the Third*

World, ed. Daisy Dwyer and Judith Bruce. Stanford: Stanford University Press.

Frank, Andre Gundar. 1972. "The Development of Underdevelopment." In *Dependence and Underdevelopment: Latin America's Political Economy,* ed. James D. Cockcroft, Andre Gundar Frank, and Dale L. Johnson. New York: Monthly Review Press.

———. 1979. *Dependent Accumulation and Underdevelopment.* New York: Monthly Review Press.

Freeman, Carla. 2000. *High Tech and High Heels in the Global Economy: Women, Work, and Pink-Collar Identities in the Caribbean.* Durham: Duke University Press.

Frobel, Folker, Otto Kreye, and Jurgen Heinrichs. 1979. *The New International Division of Labor.* Cambridge: Cambridge University Press.

Gerry, Chris, and Chris Birkbeck. 1981. "The Petty Commodity Producer in Third World Cities: Petit Bourgeois or 'Disquised Proletarian'?" In *The Petite Bourgeoisie: Comparative Studies of the Uneasy Status,* ed. Frank Bechofer and Brian Elliot London: Macmillan.

Gillespie, Dair L. 1971. "Who Has the Power? The Marital Struggle." *Journal of Marriage and the Family* 33, no. 3:445–58.

Glenn, Evelyn Nakano. 1986. *Issei, Nissei, Warbride: Three Generations of Japanese American Women in Domestic Service.* Philadelphia: Temple University Press.

———. 1988. "A Belated Industry Revised: Domestic Service Among Japanese-American Women." In *The Worth of Women's Work: A Qualitative Synthesis,* ed. Anne Statham, Eleanor M. Miller, and Hans O. Mauksch. Albany: State University of New York Press.

Goddard, Victoria. 1987. "Honour and Shame: The Control of Women's Sexuality and Group Identity in Naples." In *The Cultural Construction of Sexuality,* ed. Pat Caplan. New York: Routledge.

Godwin, Deborah D., and John Scanzoni. 1989. "Couple Consensus during Marital Joint Decision-Making: A Context, Process, Outcome Model." *Journal of Marriage and the Family* 51, no. 4:943–56.

Goffman, Erwing. 1959. *The Presentation of Self in Everyday Life.* New York: Doubleday Anchor Books.

———. 1963. *Stigma: Notes on the Management of Spoiled Identity.* Englewood Cliffs, N.J.: Prentice-Hall.

Gold, Ray. 1952. "Janitors vs. Tenants: A Status-Income Dilemma." *American Journal of Sociology* 57:487–93.

Göle, Nilüfer. 1997. *The Forbidden Modern: Civilization and Veiling.* Ann Arbor: University of Michigan Press.

Grasmuck, Sherri. 1991. "Bringing the Family Back In: Towards an Expanded Understanding of Women's Subordination in Latin America." Paper presented at the meetings of the Latin American Studies Association, 16th International Congress, Washington, D.C.

Gregson, Nicky, and Michelle Lowe. 1994. *Servicing the Middle Classes.* New York: Routledge.

Grossman, Allyson. 1980. "Women in Domestic Work: Yesterday and Today." *Monthly Labor Review*, August, 17–21.

Gülalp, Haldun. 1997. "Modernization Policies and Islamist Politics in Turkey." In *Rethinking Modernity and National Identity in Turkey*, ed. Sibel Bozdoğan and Reşat Kasaba. Seattle: University of Washington Press.

Gültekin, Şener, and Bülent Gürel. 1978. *Tüm Hukuk Sorunlarıyla Kapıcılar*. İstanbul: Üçer Matbaacılık.

Gutmann, Matthew C. 1996. *The Meanings of Macho: Being a Man in Mexico City*. Berkeley and Los Angeles: University of California Press.

Hansen, Karen Tranberg. 1989. *Distant Companions*. Ithaca: Cornell University Press.

Hanson, Susan, and Geraldine Pratt. 1995. *Gender, Work, and Space*. London. Routledge.

Harris, Olivia. 1981. "Households as Natural Units." In *Of Marriage and the Market: Women's Subordination Internationally and Its Lessons*, ed. Kate Young, Carol Wolkowitz, and Roslyn McCullagh. London: Routledge and Kegan Paul.

Harris, Olivia, and Kate Young. 1981. "Engendered Structures: Some Problems in the Analysis of Reproduction." In *The Anthropology of Pre-Capitalist Societies*, ed. Joel S. Kahn and Joseph R. Llobera. Atlantic Highlands, N.J.: Humanities Press.

Harrison, Faye V. 1991. "Women in Jamaica's Urban Informal Economy: Insights from a Kingston Slum." In *Third World Women and the Politics of Feminism*, ed. Chandra Talpade Mohanty, Ann Russo, and Lourdes Torres. Bloomington: Indiana University Press.

Hartmann, Heidi. 1976. "The Historical Roots of Occupational Segregation: Capitalism, Patriarchy, and Job Segregation by Sex." In *Women and the Workplace*, ed. Martha Blaxall and Barbara Reagen. Chicago: University of Chicago Press.

———. 1981a. "The Family as the Locus of Gender, Class, and Political Struggle: The Example of Housework." *Signs* 6, no. 3:366–94.

———. 1981b. "The Unhappy Marriage of Marxism and Feminism: Towards a More Progressive Union." In *Women and Revolution*, ed. Lydia Sargent. London: Pluto Press.

Harvey, David. 1989. *The Conditions of Postmodernity*. Oxford: Blackwell.

Heper, Metin. 1983. *Turkiyede Kent Göçmenleri ve Bürokratik Örgütler*. İstanbul: Üc Dal.

HIPS (Hacettepe Institute of Policy Studies). 1989. *1988 Turkish Population and Health Survey*. Ankara: Hacettepe University.

Hochschild, Arlie R. 1983. *The Managed Heart*. Berkeley and Los Angeles: University of California Press.

———. 1989. *The Second Shift*. New York: Viking.

Holmstrom, Engin Inel. 1973. "Changing Sex Roles in a Developing Country." *Journal of Marriage and the Family*, August, 546–53.

Hondagneu-Sotelo, Pierrette. 1994a. *Gendered Transitions: Mexican Experiences of Immigration*. Berkeley and Los Angeles: University of California Press.

———. 1994b. "Regulating the Unregulated? Domestic Workers' Social Networks." *Social Problems* 41:50–64.

Hondagneu-Sotelo, Pierrette, and Ernestine Avila. 1997. " 'I am here, but I'm there': The Meanings of Latina Transnational Motherhood." *Gender & Society* 11, no. 5:548–71.

Hondagneu-Sotelo, Pierrette, and Cristina Riegos. 1997. "Sin Organizacion, No Hay Solucion: Latina Domestic Workers and Non-Traditional Labor Organizing." *Latino Studies Journal* 8, no. 3:1–28.

Hood, Jane C. 1988. "The Caretakers: Keeping the Area Up and the Family Together." In *The Worth of Women's Work: A Qualitative Synthesis*, ed. Anne Statham, Eleanor M. Miller, and Hans O. Mauksch. Albany: State University of New York Press.

Hoodfar, Homa. 1988. "Household Budgeting and Financial Management in a Lower-Income Cairo Neighborhood." In *A Home Divided: Women and Income in the Third World*, ed. Daisy Dwyer and Judith Bruce. Stanford: Stanford University Press.

Hughes, Everett. 1958. *Men and Their Work*. Glencoe, Ill.: The Free Press of Glencoe.

Huntington, Samuel P. 1968. *Political Order in Changing Societies*. New Haven: Yale University Press.

Illich, Ivan. 1981. *Shadow Work*. Boston: Marion Boyars.

Inkeles, Alex, and David H. Smith. 1974. *Becoming Modern: Individual Change in Six Developing Countries*. Cambridge, Mass.: Harvard University Press.

Jayawardena, Kumari. 1986. *Feminism and Nationalism in the Third World*. London: Zed.

Jelin, Elizabeth. 1977. "Migration and Labor Force Participation of Latin American Women: The Domestic Servants in the Cities." *Signs* 3, no. 1:129–41.

———, ed. 1991. *Family, Household, and Gender Relations in Latin America*. London: Kegan Paul International.

Kandiyoti, Deniz. 1982. "Urban Change and Women's Roles in Turkey: An Overview and Evaluation." In *Sex Roles, Family, and Community in Turkey*, ed. Çiğdem Kağıtçıbaşı. Bloomington: Indiana University Press.

———. 1988. "Bargaining with Patriarchy." *Gender & Society* 12, no. 3:274—90.

———. 1989. "Women and the Turkish State: Political Actors or Symbolic Pawns?" In *Woman-Nation-State*, ed. Nira Yuval-Davis and Floya Anthias. London: Macmillan.

———. 1990. "Rural Transformation in Turkey and Its Implications for Women's Status. In *Women, Family, and Social Change in Turkey*, ed. Ferhunde Özbay. Bangkok: UNESCO.

———. 1995. "Patterns of Patriarchy: Notes for an Analysis of Male Dominance in Turkish Society." In *Women in Modern Turkish Society*, ed. Şirin Tekeli. London: Zed.

———. 1997. "Gendering the Modern: On Missing Dimensions in the Study of Turkish Modernity." In *Rethinking Modernity and National Identity in Turkey*, ed. Sibel Bozdoğan and Reşat Kasaba. Seattle: University of Washington Press.

Karpat, Kemal. 1976. *The Gecekondu: Rural Migration and Urbanization*. Cambridge: Cambridge University Press.

Kartal, S. K. 1978. *Kentleşme ve İnsan*. Ankara: Türkiye ve Orta Doğu Amme İdaresi Enstitüsü.

———. 1983. *Ekonomik ve Sosyal Yönleriyle Türkiye'de Kentleşme*. Ankara: Yurt Yayinevi.

Katzman, David. 1978a. "Domestic Service: Woman's Work." In *Women Working*, ed. Ann H. Stromberg and Shirley Harkess. Palo Alto: Mayfield.

———. 1978b. *Seven Days a Week: Women and Domestic Service in Industrializing America*. New York: Oxford University Press.

Kazgan, Gülten. 1981. "Labor Force Participation, Occupational Distribution, Educational Attainment, and the Socio-Economic Status of Women in the Turkish Economy." In *Women in Turkish Society*, ed. Nermin Abadan-Unat. Leiden: E. J. Brill.

Keleş, Ruşen. 2000. *Kentlesme Politikası*. Ankara: İmge.

Keleş, Ruşen, and Michael N. Danielson. 1985. *The Politics of Rapid Urbanization: Government and Growth in Modern Turkey*. New York: Holmes and Meier.

Keyder, Çaglar. 1979. "The Political Economy of Turkish Democracy." *New Left Review*, no. 115:3—44. .

———. 1987. *State and Class in Turkey: A Study in Capitalist Development*. London: Verso.

Khoo, Siew-Ean, Peter C. Smith, and James T. Fawcett. 1984. "Female Rural to Urban Migration in the Third World: Comparative Perspectives and Research Notes." *IMR* [*International Migration Review*] 18, no. 4:1247—63.

Kıray, Mübeccel. 1964. *Ereğli: Agir Sanayiden Önce Bir Sahil Kasabası*. Ankara: Devlet Planlama Dairesi.

———. 1985. "Metropolitan City and the Changing Family." In *Family in Turkish Society*. Ankara: The Turkish Social Science Association.

———. 1991. "Introduction: A Perspective." In *Structural Change in Turkish Society*, ed. Mübeccel Kıray. Bloomington: Indiana University Press.

Köker, Eser. 1988. *Women in Turkey, Education and Politics: An Investigation on the Position of Women in Institutions of Higher Education*. University of Ankara, Unpublished Ph.D. dissertation in Turkish.

Komarovsky, Mirra. 1967. *Blue-Collar Marriage*. New York: Vintage Books.

Kongar, Emre. 1972. *İzmir'de Kentsel Aile*. Ankara: Türk Sosyal Bilimler Derneği.

KSSGM (Republic of Turkey State Ministry of Directorate General on the Status and Problems of Women). 1995. *Women in Statistics*. Ankara: UNICEF.

———. 1998. *Türkiye'de Kadının Durumu*. Ankara: Takav.

Kuyaş, Nilüfer. 1982. "Female Labor Power Relations in the Urban Turkish Family." In *Sex Roles, Family, and Community in Turkey*, ed. Çiğdem Kağıtçıbaşı. Bloomington: Indiana University Press.

Kuznesof, Elizabeth. 1989. "A History of Domestic Service in Spanish America, 1492–1980." In *Muchachas No More*, ed. Elsa M. Chaney and Mary Garcia Castro. Philadelphia: Temple University Press.

Lancaster, Roger N. 1992. *Life Is Hard: Machismo, Danger, and the Intimacy of Power in Nicaragua*. Berkeley and Los Angeles: University of California Press.

Lasser, Carol. 1987. "The Domestic Balance of Power: Relations Between Mistress and Maid in Nineteenth- Century New England." *Labor History* 28:5–22.

Lerner, Daniel. 1958. *The Passing of Traditional Society*. New York: Free Press.

Levine, Ned. 1973a. "Old Culture-New Culture: A Study of Migrants in Ankara, Turkey." *Social Forces* 51, no. 4:355–68.

———. 1973b. "Value orientation among Migrants in Ankara, Turkey: A Case Study." *Journal of Asian and African Studies* 8:50–68.

———. 1982. "Social Change and Family Crisis: The Nature of Turkish Divorce." In *Sex Roles, Family, and Community in Turkey*, ed. Çiğdem Kağıtçıbaşı. Bloomington: Indiana University Press.

Lewis, Bernard. 1961. *The Emergence of Modern Turkey*. New York: Oxford University Press.

Lim, Linda. 1983. "Capitalism, Imperialism, and Patriarchy: The Dilemmas of Third World Women Workers in Multinational Factories." In *Women, Men, and the International Division of Labor*, ed. June Nash and Maria Patricia Fernandez-Kelly. Albany: State University of New York Press.

Luke, Timothy W. 1996. "Identity, Meaning and Globalization: Detraditionalization in Postmodern Space-time Compression." In *Detraditionalization: Critical Reflections on Authority and Identity*, ed. Paul Heelas, Scott Lash, and Paul Morris. Malden, Mass.: Blackwell.

Lukes, Steven. 1974. *Power: A Radical View*. London: Macmillan.

Maanen van, John. 1988. *Tales of the Field: On Writing Ethnography*. Chicago: University of Chicago Press.

Magnerella, Paul J. 1972. "Conjugal Role Relationships in a Modernizing Turkish Town." *International Journal of Sociology of Family* 2:179–92.

Maher, Vanessa. 1988. "Work, Consumption, and Authority Within the Household: A Moroccan Case." In *Of Marriage and the Market: Women's Subordination in International Perspective*, ed. Kate Young, Carol Wolkowitz, and Roslyn McCullagh. London: Routledge.

Mardin, Şerif. 1997. "Projects as Methodology: Some Thoughts on Modern Turkish Social Science." In *Rethinking Modernity and National Identity in Turkey*, ed. Sibel Bozdoğan and Reşat Kasaba. Seattle: University of Washington Press.

Marx, Karl. 1976. *Capital*. Vol. 1. Harmondsworth: Penguin.

Mauss, Marcel. 1954. *The Gift: The Form and Reason for Exchange in Archaic Societies*. Translated by W. D. Halls. New York: W. W. Norton.

Maza, Sarah C. 1983. *Servants and Masters in Eighteenth-Century France: The Uses of Loyalty*. Princeton: Princeton University Press.

McBride, Theresa Marie. 1974. "Social Mobility for the Lower Classes: Domestic Servants in France." *Journal of Social History* 8:63–78.

McClelland, David C. 1976. *The Achieving Society*. Reprint. New York: Irvington.

McKeever, Matthew. 1998. "Reproduced Inequality: Participation and Success in the South African Informal Economy." *Social Forces* 76, no. 4:1209–43.

Meara, Hannah. 1974. "Honor in Dirty Work." *Sociology of Work and Occupations* 1, no. 3:259–83.

Mencher, Joan. 1988. "Women's Work and Poverty: Women's Contribution to Household Maintenance in South India." In *A Home Divided: Women and Income in the Third World*, ed. Daisy Dwyer and Judith Bruce. Stanford: Stanford University Press.

Mies, Maria. 1982. *The Lace Makers of Narsapur*. London: Zed.

———. 1986. *Patriarchy and Accumulation on a World Scale: Women in the International Division of Labour*. London: Zed.

Migdal, Joel S. 1997. "Finding the Meeting Ground of Fact and Fiction: Some Reflections on Turkish Modernization." In *Rethinking Modernity and National Identity in Turkey*, ed. Sibel Bozdoğan and Reşat Kasaba. Seattle: University of Washington Press.

Mills, Mary B. 1997. "Contesting the Margins of Modernity: Women, Migration, and Consumption in Thailand." *American Ethnologists* 24, no. 1:37–61.

Mohanty, Chandra Talpade. 1991a. "Cartographies of Struggle: Third World Women and the Politics of Feminism." In *Third World Women and the Politics of Feminism*, ed. Chandra Talpade Mohanty, Ann Russo, and Lourdes Torres. Bloomington: Indiana University Press.

———. 1991b. "Under Western Eyes: Feminist Scholarship and Colonial Discourses." In *Third World Women and the Politics of Feminism*, ed. Chandra Talpade Mohanty, Ann Russo, and Lourdes Torres. Bloomington: Indiana University Press.

———. 1997. "Women Workers and Capitalist Scripts: Ideologies of Domination, Common Interests, and the Politics of Solidarity." In *Feminist Genealogies, Colonial Legacies, Democratic Futures*, ed. M. Jacqui Alexander, and Chandra Talpade Mohanty. New York: Routledge.

Moser, Caroline. 1978. "Informal Sector or Petty Commodity Production? Dualism or Dependence in Urban Development?" *World Development* 6, no. 9/10:1041–64.

———. 1981. "Surviving in the Suburbs." In *Women and the Informal Sector: Institute of Developmental Studies Bulletin* 12, no. 3 (July): 19–29.

Moser, Caroline, and Kate Young. 1981. "Women of the Working Poor." *IDS Bulletin* 12, no. 3:54–62.

Nalbantoğlu, Gülsüm Baydar. 1997. "Silent Interruptions: Urban Encounters with Rural Turkey." In *Rethinking Modernity and National Identity in Turkey*, ed. Sibel Bozdoğan and Reşat Kasaba. Seattle: University of Washington Press.

Nash, June, and Maria Patricia Fernandez-Kelly, eds. 1983. *Women, Men, and the International Division of Labor*. Albany: State University of New York Press.

Nash, June, and Helen Safa, eds. 1985. *Women and Change in Latin America*. South Hadley, Mass.: Bergin and Garvey.

Oakley, Ann. 1974. *The Sociology of Housework*. New York: Pantheon Books.

Oliveria, Anazir Maria de, and Odete Maria da Conceicao. 1989. "Domestic Workers in Rio de Janeiro." In *Muchachas No More*, ed. Elsa M. Chaney and Mary Garcia Castro. Philadelphia: Temple University Press.

Olson, Emily. 1982. "Duo Focal Family Structure and an Alternative Model of Husband-Wife Relationship." In *Sex Roles, Family and Community in Turkey*, ed. Çiğdem Kağıtçıbaşı. Bloomington: Indiana University Press.

Öncü, Ayşe. 1981. "Turkish Women in the Professions: Why So Many?" In *Women in Turkish Society*, ed. Nermin Abadan Unat. Leiden: E. J. Brill.

Ong, Aihwa. 1987. *Spirits of Resistance and Capitalist Discipline: Factory Women in Malaysia*. Albany: State University of New York Press.

———. 1988. "Colonialism and Modernity: Feminist Representations of Women in Non-Western Societies." *Inscriptions*, no. 3/4:79—93.

Özbay, Ferhunde. 1989. "Family and Household Structure in Turkey: Past, Present, and Future." Paper presented at conference, Changing Family in the Middle East, December 16—18, at Amman, Jordan.

———. 1995. "Changes in Women's Activities both Inside and Outside the Home." In *Women in Modern Turkish Society*, ed. Şirin Tekeli. Atlantic Heights, N.J.: Zed.

Özbek, Meral. 1997. "Arabesk Culture: A Case of Modernization and Popular Identity." In *Rethinking Modernity and National Identity in Turkey*, ed. Sibel Bozdoğan and Reşat Kasaba. Seattle: University of Washington Press.

Özbudun, Ergun. 1976. *Social Change and Political Participation in Turkey*. Princeton: Princeton University Press.

Pahl, Jan. 1980. "Patterns of Money Management within Marriage." *Journal of Social Policy* 3, no. 9:313–35.

———. 1983. "The Allocation of Money and the Structuring of Inequality within Marriage." *The Sociological Review*, May 31, 237–62.

Palmer, Phyllis. 1987. "Housewife and the Household Worker: Employer-Employee Relationship in the Home, 1928–1941." In *To Toil the Livelong Day*, ed. Carol Groneman and Mary B. Norton. Ithaca: Cornell University Press.

———. 1989. *Domesticity and Dirt: Housewives and Domestic Servants in the United States, 1920–1945*. Philadelphia: Temple University Press.

Papanek, Hanna, and Laurel Schwede. 1988. "Women Are Good with Money: Earning and Managing in an Indonesian City." In *A Home Divided: Women and Income in the Third World*, eds. Daisy Dwyer and Judith Bruce. Stanford: Stanford University Press.

Parsons, Talcott. 1970. *Social Structure and Personality*. New York: Free Press.

Portes, Alejandro. 1994. "The Informal Economy and Its Paradoxes." In *Handbook of Economic Sociology*, ed. Neil J. Smelser and Richard Swedberg. Princeton: Princeton University Press.

Portes, Alejandro, and Lauren A. Benton. 1984. "Industrial Development and Labor Absorption: A Reinterpretation." *Population Development Review* 10, no. 4:589–611.

Portes, Alejandro, and Saskia Sassen-Koob. 1987. "Making It Underground: Comparative Material on the Informal Sector in Western Market Economies." *American Journal of Sociology* 93, no. 1:30–61.

Portes, Alejandro, and Richard Schauffler. 1993. "Changing erspectives on the Latin American Informal Sector." *Population and Development Review*. 19, no. 1 (March): 33–60.

Portes, Alejandro, and John. Walton. 1981. *Labor, Class, and the International System*. New York: Academic Press.

Portes, Alejandro, Manuel Castells, and Lauren A. Benton, eds. 1989. *The Informal Economy: Studies in Advanced and Less Developed Countries*. Baltimore: Johns Hopkins University Press.

Pyle, Jean L. 1990. "Export-Led Development and the Underemployment of Women: The Impact of Discriminatory Development Policy in the Republic of Ireland." In *Women Workers and Global Restructuring*, ed. Kathryn Ward. Ithaca, N.Y.: ILR Press.

Quataert, Donald. 1991. "Ottoman Women, Households, and Textile Manufacturing." In *Women in Middle Eastern History*, ed. Nikki R. Keddie and Beth Baron. New Haven: Yale University Press.

Redclift, Nanneke, and Enzo Mingione, eds. 1985. *Beyond Employment: Household, Gender, and Subsistence*. Oxford: Basil Blackwell.

Roberts, Bryan. 1994. "Informal Economy and Family Strategies." *International Journal of Urban and Regional Research* 18:6–23.

Roldan, Martha. 1985. "Industrial Outworking, Struggles for the Reproduction of Working-Class Families and Gender Subordination." In *Beyond Employment: Household, Gender, and Subsistence*, ed. Nanneke Redclift and Enzo Mingione. Oxford: Basil Blackwell.

Rollins, Judith. 1985. *Between Women: Domestics and Their Employers*. Philadelphia: Temple University Press.

Romero, Mary. 1988. "Day Work in the Suburbs: The Work Experience of Chicana Private Housekeepers." In *The Worth of Women's Work: A Qualitative Synthesis*, ed. Anne Statham, Eleanor M. Miller, and Hans O. Mauksch. Albany: State University of New York Press.

———. 1992. *Maid in the USA*. New York: Routledge.

Rostow, W. W. 1960. *The Stages of Economic Growth: A Non-Communist Manifesto*. Cambridge: Cambridge University Press.

Ruiz, Vicki L. 1987. "By the Day or Week: Mexicana Domestic Workers in El Paso." In *To Toil the Livelong Day*, ed. Carol Groneman and Mary B. Norton. Ithaca: Cornell University Press.

Safa, Helen. 1986. "Urbanization: The Informal Economy and State Policy in Latin America." *Urban Anthropology* 15, no. 1–2:135–63.

———. 1990. "Women and Industrialization in the Caribbean." In *Women, Employment, and the Family in the International Division of Labor*, ed. Sharon Stichter and Jane L. Parpart. Philadelphia: Temple University Press.

Safa, Helen, and June Nash, eds. 1976. *Sex and Class in Latin America*. New York: Praeger.

Safilios-Rothschild, Constantina. 1970. "Study of Family Power Structure: 1960–69." *Journal of Marriage and the Family* 32 (November): 539–52.

———. 1976. "A Macro and Micro-Examination of Family Power and Love: An Exchange Model." *Journal of Marriage and the Family* 38:355–62.

———. 1984. "The Role of the Family in Development." In *Women in Third World Development*, ed. Sue Ellen M. Charlton. Boulder: Westview Press.

———. 1990. "Socio-Economic Determinants of the Outcomes of Women's Income-Generation in Developing Countries." In *Women, Employment, and the*

Family in the International Division of Labor, ed. Sharon Stichter and Jane L. Parpart. Philadelphia: Temple University Press.

Saktanber, Ayşe. 1994. "Becoming the 'Other' as a Muslim in Turkey: Turkish Women vs. Islamist Women." *New Perspectives on Turkey* 11:99–134.

Salzinger, Leslie. 1991. "A Maid by Any Other Name: The Transformation of 'Dirty Work' by Central American Immigrants." In *Ethnography Unbound: Power and Resistance in the Modern Metropolis,* ed. Michael Burowoy. Berkeley and Los Angeles: University of California Press.

Sanjek, Roger, and Shellee Colen, eds. 1990. *At Work in Homes: Household Workers in World Perspective.* American Ethnological Society Monograph Series no. 3. Washington, D.C.: American Anthropological Society.

Sassen, Saskia. 1988. *The Mobility of Labor and Capital: A Study of International Investment and Labor Flow.* Cambridge: Cambridge University Press.

———. 1996. "Toward a Feminist Analysis of the Global Economy." *Indiana Journal of Global Legal Studies* 4, no. 1:7–41.

Sassen-Koob, Saskia. 1981. "Exporting Capital and Importing Labor: The Role of Caribbean Migration to New York City." Occasional Paper no. 28. Center for Latin American and Caribbean Studies, New York University.

———. 1984. "The New Labor Demand in Global Cities." In *Cities in Transformation,* ed. Michael P. Smith. Beverly Hills: Sage.

Scanzoni, John. 1982. *Sexual Bargaining: Power Politics in the American Marriage.* Chicago: University of Chicago Press.

Scanzoni, John, and Maximiliane Szinovacz. 1980. *Family Decision-Making: A Developmental Sex Role Model.* London: Sage.

Scott, Catherine V. 1995. *Gender and Development: Rethinking Modernization and Dependency Theory.* Boulder: L. Rienner.

Scott, James. 1985. *Weapons of the Weak: Everyday Forms of Peasant Resistance.* New Haven: Yale University Press.

Scott, Joan. 1988. *Gender and the Politics of History.* New York: Cambridge University Press.

Segal, Lynne. 1990. *Slow Motion: Changing Masculinities, Changing Men.* London: Virago.

Sen, Gita, and Caren Grown. 1987. *Development, Crises, and Alternative Visions.* New York: New Feminist Library.

Sennett, Richard, and Jonathan Cobb. 1972. *The Hidden Injuries of Class.* New York: Knopf.

Şenyapılı, Tansı. 1981a. *Ankara Kentinde Gecekondu Gelişimi.* Ankara: Kent Koop Yayinları.

———. 1981b. "A New Component in Metropolitan Areas: Gecekondu Women." In *Women in Turkish Society,* ed. Nermin Abadan Unat. Leiden: E. J. Brill.

———. 1982. "Economic Change and the Gecekondu Family." In *Sex Roles, Family, and Community in Turkey,* ed. Çiğdem Kağıtçıbaşı. Bloomington: Indiana University Press.

Sirman, Nukhet. 1988. "Peasants and Family Farms: The Position of Households in Cotton Production in a Village of Western Turkey." Ph.D. dissertation, University of London.

———. 1989. "Feminism in Turkey: A Short History." *New Perspectives on Turkey* 3:1–34

———. 1995. "Friend and Foe? Forging Alliances with Other Woman in a Village of Western Turkey." In *Women in Modern Turkish Society*, ed. Şirin Tekeli. London: Zed.

Sirman, Nükhet, Haluk Kasnakoğlu, Mehmet Ecevit, and Nazım Ekinci. 1989. "The Social and Economic Aspects of Decision-Making Related to Labour Utilisation and Choice of Technology: A Case Study of a Turkish Village-Kinik." In *Agricultural Labor and Technological Change*, ed. Dennis Tully. Boulder: Westview Press.

Stack, Carol B. 1974. *All Our Kin: Strategies for Survival in a Black Community.* New York: Harper and Row.

Standing, Hilary. 1985. "Resources, Wages, and Power: The Impact of Women's Employment on the Urban Bengali Household." In *Women, Work, and Ideology in the Third World*, ed. Haleh Afshar. London: Tavistock.

Statham, Anne, Eleanor M. Miller, and Hans O. Mauksch, eds. *The Worth of Women's Work: A Qualitative Synthesis.* Albany: State University of New York Press.

Steinberg Ronnie, and Lois Haignere. 1991. "Separate But Equivalent: Equal Pay for Comparable Worth." In *Beyond Methodology*, ed. Mary Margaret Fonow and Judith A. Cook. Bloomington: Indiana University Press.

Tekeli, İlhan. 1984. "Ankara'nın Başkentlik Kararının Ülkesel Mekan Organizasyonu ve Toplumsal Yapıya Etkileri Bakımından Genel bir Değerlendirmesi." *Tarih İçinde Ankara.* Ankara: Mimarlik Fakültesi, ODTÜ.

Tekeli, Şirin. 1981. "Women in Turkish Politics." In *Women in Turkish Society*, ed. Nermin Abadan Unat. Leiden: E. J. Brill.

———. 1990. "The Meaning and Limits of Feminist Ideology in Turkey." In *Women, Family, and Social Change in Turkey*, ed. Ferhunde Özbay. Bangkok: UNESCO.

Tellis-Nayak, V. 1983. "Power and Solidarity: Clientage in Domestic Service." *Current Anthropology* 24, no. 1 (February): 67–74.

Thompson, John B. 1996. "Tradition and Self in a Mediated World." In *Detraditionalization: Critical Reflections on Authority and Identity*, ed. Paul Heelas, Scott Lash, and Paul Morris. Malden, Mass.: Blackwell.

Thorne, Barrie, and Marilyn Yalom, eds. 1982. *Rethinking the Family: Some Feminist Questions.* New York: Longman.

Tilly, Louise A., and Joan Scott. 1978. *Women, Work, and Family.* New York: Holt, Rinehart, and Winston.

Timur, Serim. 1972. *Türkiye'de Aile Yapısı.* Ankara: Hacettepe University.

———. 1981. "Determinants of Family Structure in Turkey." In *Women in Turkish Society*, ed. Nermin Abadan Unat. Leiden: E. J. Brill.

Türel, Ali. 1987. "Ankara Kent Formunda Konut Alanlarının Gelir Gruplarına Göre Farklılaşması." *Ankara 1985'den 2015'e.* ODTÜ Şehir ve Bölge Planlama Bölümü Çalışma Grubu. Ankara: Ajans İletim.

Undersecretariat for Women's Affairs and Social Services, Prime Ministry of the Turkish Republic. 1993. *The Report Prepared in Accordance with Article 18 of the Convention of the Elimination of All Forms of Discrimination Against Women.*

UNICEF 1991. *The Situation Analysis of Mothers and Children in Turkey.* UNICEF Country Program 1991–1995 series, no. 2. Ankara.

United Nations. 1999. *1999 World Survey on the Role of Women in Development: Globalization, Gender, and Work.* New York: United Nations.

Wallerstein, Immanuel. 1974. *The Modern World System.* New York: Academic Press.

Ward, Kathryn. 1984. *Women in the World System: Its Impact on Status and Fertility.* New York: Praeger.

West, Candace, and Don H. Zimmerman. 1987. "Doing Gender." *Gender & Society* 12:125–51.

White, Jenny. 1991. "Women and Work in Istanbul: Linking the Urban Poor to the World Market." *Middle East Report,* November–December, 18–22

———. 1994. *Money Makes Us Relatives.* Austin: University of Texas Press.

Whitehead, Ann. 1988. "'I'm Hungry, Mum': The Politics of Domestic Budgeting." In *Of Marriage and the Market: Women's Subordination Internationally and Its lessons,"* ed. Kate Young, Carol Wolkowitz, and Roslyn McCullagh. London: Routledge.

Wilson, Gail. 1987. "Money: Patterns of Responsibility and Irresponsibility in Marriage." In *Give and Take in Families: Studies in Resource Distribution,* ed. Julia Brannen and Gail Wilson. London: Allen and Unwin.

Wolf, Lauren Diane. 1992. *Factory Daughters: Gender, Household Dynamics, and Rural Industrialization in Java.* Berkeley and Los Angeles: University of California Press.

Yasa, İbrahim. 1953. *Hasanoğlan Köyünün İçtimai-İktisadi Yapısı.* Ankara: Doğuş.

Young, Gay. 1993. "Gender Inequality and Industrial Development: The Household Connection." *Journal of Comparative Family Studies* 24:1–20.

Index

Page numbers followed by letters *f* and *t* refer to figures and tables, respectively.